D1423031

1

NEAR-DEATH
EXPERIENCE
The Illustrated Dossier

NEAR-DEATH EXPERIENCE

The Illustrated Dossier

Marisa St Clair

BLANDFORD

Dedication

For my father.
I hope you liked the garden.

Guide to abbreviations

The following abbreviations have been used throughout the book:

ASC – Altered state of consciousness
NDE – Near-death experience
OBE – Out-of-body experience
PFF – Personal flash forward
RV – Remote viewing

630248
MORAY COUNCIL
Department of Technical
& Leisure Services
133.9013

First published in the UK in 1998 by Blandford,
an imprint of Cassell plc
Wellington House
125 Strand
London WC2R 0BB

Copyright © 1997 Brown Packaging Books Ltd

All rights reserved. No part of this book may be reproduced or transmitted in
any form or by any means, electronic or mechanical, including photocopying,
recording or any information storage and retrieval system, without permission
in writing from the copyright holder and publisher.

British Library Cataloguing-in-Publication Data
A catalogue entry for this publication is available from the British Library

ISBN: 0-7137-2726-8

Conceived and produced by
Brown Packaging Books Ltd
Bradley's Close
74–77 White Lion Street
London N1 9PF

Project Editor: Nina Hathway
Design: Robert Mathias
Picture Research: Adrian Bentley
Front Cover Design: Colin Hawes

Printed in Italy

Contents

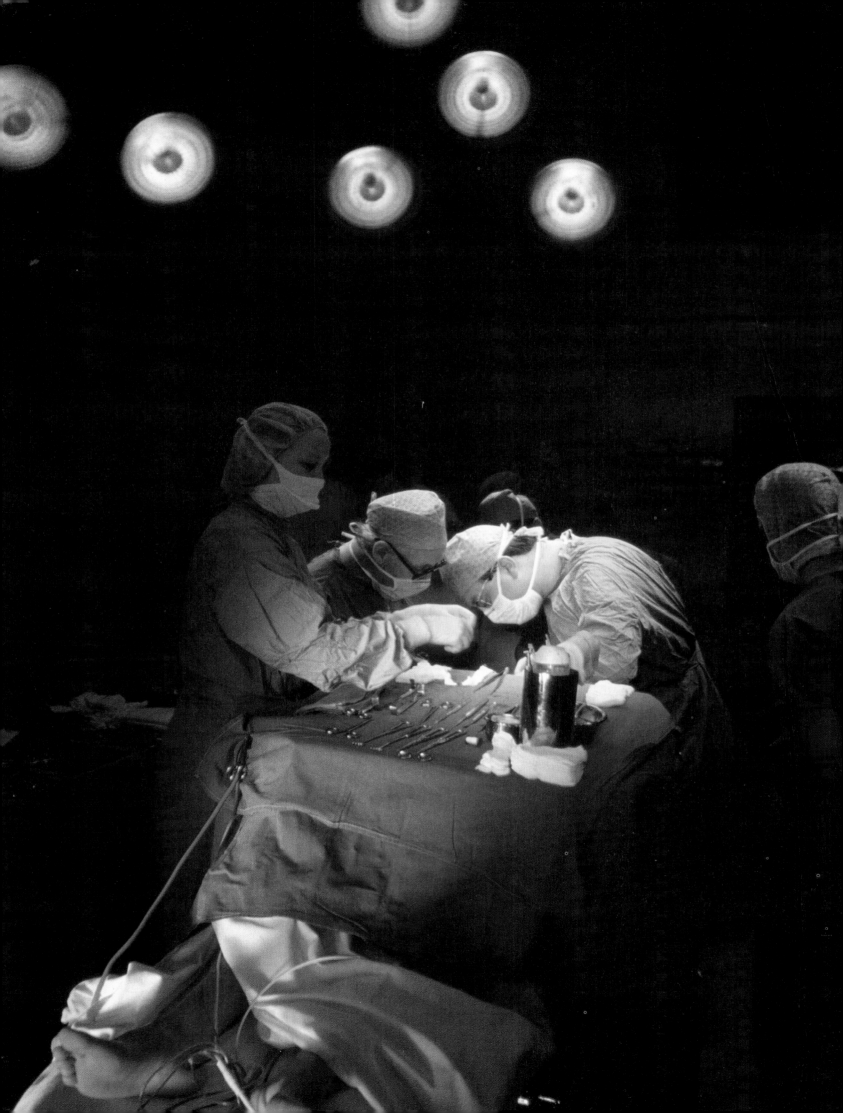

'An Awfully Big Adventure'

William Shakespeare's Hamlet mused that death was the 'undiscover'd country ... from whose bourne no traveller returns'. Death has always been the one unique mystery to which there was no solution other than the pious hope of faith – the great unknown that was the most pervasive source of all our fears.

The very thought of death raises the most terrifying questions, which are all the more disturbing because there appear to be no answers. Is death the end of us, the total cessation of everything that makes us unique? Is it oblivion, or a dream – perhaps a nightmare that never ends? Do we each have a spiritual essence, a soul, that must journey into the unknown, naked, afraid and alone once the body has outgrown its usefulness? But what happens then? Are we seized by demons eager to gobble our souls and condemn us to fiery torments for all eternity? Or are we met by angels, entering into a life of joy for ever?

Throughout human existence on earth there have been no answers, only the suggestions and clues of mysticism, religion or the seance room. However, since the 1970s there have been thousands of cases of people who have died and who have

◀ **Many NDEs happen during surgery, when induced unconsciousness seems to release the soul. NDEs are common today, largely owing to efficient resuscitation techniques.**

returned to tell us what it is like. The phenomenon of the near-death experience (NDE) came to the public's attention because increasingly sophisticated resuscitation techniques enabled more people than ever before to be brought back from apparent death. Gradually, as we will see, certain courageous doctors took note that these NDEs were remarkably consistent, despite the wide variations of social status, race, age and religious beliefs of the individuals concerned. Clearly, the NDE was of unique significance, not only to those who experienced it, but also to science, and to all who are mortal.

The NDE is very much an experience – often those who have had one claim it was the most vivid and influential experience of their lives, but it must be remembered that it has happened to people who were clinically dead. Their brains showed not even a flicker of activity, yet they were somehow capable of hearing, seeing and even smelling in a much more vivid way than usual. But how? What possible process could enable a brain-dead person to have such an experience?

More significantly, how could a dead person travel to another room or even another building and observe what is going on there, and later report overhearing private conversations in minute and accurate detail?

The NDE has happened to people in many different circumstances: to those undergoing the slow process of dying from diseases such as cancer or AIDS, to heart-attack victims, and to healthy individuals who have sudden accidents. It is reported by people of different religions, those with no beliefs, and even by die-hard sceptics and atheists who had previously dismissed the idea of an afterlife, and who scorned the concept of a separate, non-physical soul as pathetic nonsense. It has even happened to tiny children, who have never heard of the NDE.

Since the ground-breaking work of NDE pioneer doctors Elisabeth Kubler-Ross and Raymond Moody in the 1970s, the NDE has received a huge amount of media attention; a number of television programmes and magazine articles have been devoted to the subject, and as a result of the ensuing publicity, more people have come forward to tell their stories. Where once they were afraid to be ridiculed, now they feel reassured that they were not mad, nor were they alone in having the experience.

And as medics and hospice workers begin to shake off the threat of professional derision, and share the stories of their patients who have reported NDEs, it is beginning to look as if this is not an isolated nor even a relatively uncommon experience. Although no one knows precisely how many people have had NDEs, it is safe to say that the documented cases are merely the tip of a very large iceberg.

Clearly, the NDE is enormously significant, perhaps never more so as this tormented materialist society hurtles uncertainly towards a new millennium, fearful of the future and dismissive of the past. Yet the NDE is not the sole prerogative of the late twentieth century, nor – as we shall see – does the phenomenon stand alone in providing strong evidence for the existence of the soul.

What is an NDE?

First, let us decide what we mean by an NDE. Despite the large number of reported NDEs, meticulous analysis has shown that it is possible to break the experience down into several distinct stages, although there are many variations; not everyone experiences all the stages, or goes through them in exactly the same order. However, in general these are the characteristic stages of an NDE:

- A sudden sense of peace and serenity, and a cessation of pain.
- Separating from the physical body in an out-of-the-body experience (OBE), and viewing it from a new perspective, usually from above. Feeling emotionally detached.

- Floating elsewhere, perhaps to another room or building, and observing the scene there.
- Being drawn into a black tunnel, often at incredible speed, towards a bright light, with growing feelings of joy and love.
- Meeting a figure at the end of the tunnel, usually a relative or friend who is already dead, but sometimes a religious figure or simply a 'being of light'.
- The figure shows the individual a beautiful garden where they may hear celestial music, or meet deceased relatives, even God. Some report being shown a city of golden light.
- There may follow a life review, which some have described as a 'film show' where they are shown the whole of their lives. They see what they have done wrong and learn their purpose on earth. This is non-judgmental; a feeling of being unconditionally loved and totally understood pervades.
- Being told to return to earth, often because it is not yet their time to die, or because their work is unfinished. Usually they plead to be allowed to stay, but their request is refused and they find themselves back in their body, alive and conscious.

The vast majority of those who have had NDEs claim that their lives have been changed for the better as a result. They realize that there really is such a thing as a soul, that the body is simply not very important, and that there is no death. Often people become much less materialistic and take up a life of greater spirituality, although, interestingly, very few become more religious in a dogmatic sense. Some develop psychic gifts such as precognition and even the ability to heal simply through the laying on of hands.

◀ In the West, death is treated as the great enemy, but many other cultures still see it as a solemn rite of passage, in which families and friends can all play a part.

As J.M. Barrie's Peter Pan said: 'Dying must be an awfully big adventure'. The NDE reveals that no other experience comes close as the most intensely personal epic anyone can even hope to experience – this side of death's door.

Fourteen million people die every day, yet how many of them can honestly say that they have given the idea of their own death much thought? In the West there is a tendency to consider such matters morbid, and although many of the 'forbidden' topics of the past – such as sex – are now common conversational currency, death is the last taboo, and a subject that can still cause grave embarrassment. Death is bad taste if mentioned at almost any social gathering. Yet the last 20 years have brought about a subtle change in this resistance to facing up to the inevitable fact of death. We have discovered the NDE.

Through the sophisticated resuscitation techniques now routinely used

DEATH AT THE MOVIES

Although there are countless films that have a vaguely supernatural theme, very few of them deal directly with the subject of being dead. Even the hugely successful Dracula movies are not about death but about the undead.

Among earlier films that did tackle this difficult subject was *A Matter of Life and Death* (1946), starring David Niven, and directed, to great professional acclaim, by Emeric Pressberger. In it a World War II RAF officer, played by Niven, hovers between life and death while a great trial is held in heaven to decide his fate. (There are hundreds of representatives of all the then Allied nations and the Commonwealth at the trial, but of course none of the enemy Axis powers are there. Presumably the censor would have considered such an element treasonable.) Impassioned pleading by a great friend – newly promoted to the throng due to a motorcycle accident – means that Niven remains, for the time being, in the land of the living (and gets the girl). In most respects, the airman's experience seems closest to an NDE than a dream or fantasy.

Another film of the 1940s was the comedy *Blithe Spirit*, written by Noel Coward. Rex Harrison and his new bride were harassed by the ghost of his former wife whose poltergeist-like antics were hilariously investigated by the eccentric Madame Arcati, played to perfection by Margaret Rutherford. By the end of the film both bride and Harrison himself joined the dead woman, leaving the distinct impression that they would spend their afterlives indulging in childish pranks. By modern standards the story was perhaps over frivolous and two-dimensional, without any contrasting dark moments or serious points to consider. Ironically, only Madame Arcarti's understanding of poltergeists, played for cheap laughs, revealed any real research into the paranormal.

The 1989 film *Always*, starring Richard Dreyfus, told a slight story of

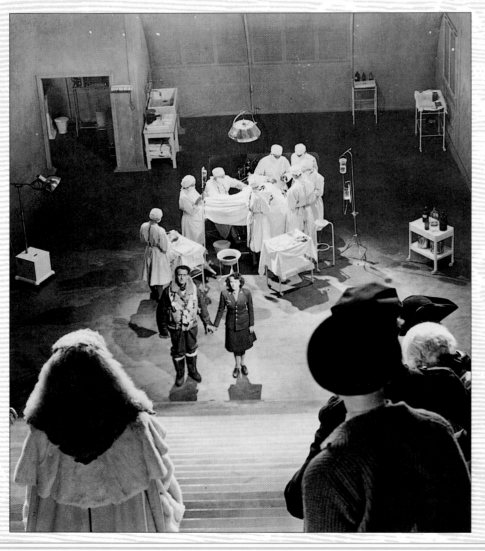

▶ In the hit film *A Matter of Life and Death*, a disembodied airman pleads – successfully – with the heavenly court for more earthly time with his fiancée.

in hospital emergency departments, many who would once have been immediately and irrevocably committed to the morgue are now returned to life. In many cases even those whose hearts have stopped and brain activity has ceased, perhaps for several minutes, have been brought back to normal functioning. But many who return from beyond the brink of physical death have a story to tell: as the crash team frantically tried to revive their apparently lifeless body, they entered into a great adventure.

The NDE has changed thousands of lives, almost always for the better. Those who experience it usually report leaving their poor, stricken body and being able to float free, eventually arriving in a world of light and being received by beings who emanated pure love. As Joe, a British man who had an NDE, said:

"I believe I died and went to heaven, but it wasn't my time, so I was sent back. There are no words to do

a firefighting airman who returned after his death to intervene in the subsequent love affair of his widow. The afterlife that greeted him immediately after his death was a beautiful landscape similar to those described by many who have had NDEs. Chillingly, the angel who came to welcome him was played by Audrey Hepburn, who was herself to die just months after the movie was completed.

However, by far the most successful film ever to deal with the subject of death was *Ghost* (1990), in which Patrick Swayze is murdered and has to learn how to make his presence felt in the material world in order to protect his widow, played by Demi Moore, against his murderer who has designs on her. Finding it hard to adjust to the postmortem life, the hero learns how to manipulate physical objects with the power of his mind from the ghost of an earthbound psychopath who haunts subway trains. But one of the joys of the film is his encounter with a fake medium played by Whoopi Goldberg, who is profoundly shocked to discover she is genuinely in communication with a dead man!

In the end, the dead Swayze manages to kill off his murderer, who is immediately carried off screaming by shadowy gibbering demons. And Demi Moore, thanks to the by now genuine mediumship of Whoopi Goldberg, finally gets to see the spirit of her dead husband and kiss him goodbye, before he 'goes towards the light' and disappears, saying 'I'll see you'. Although an unashamed

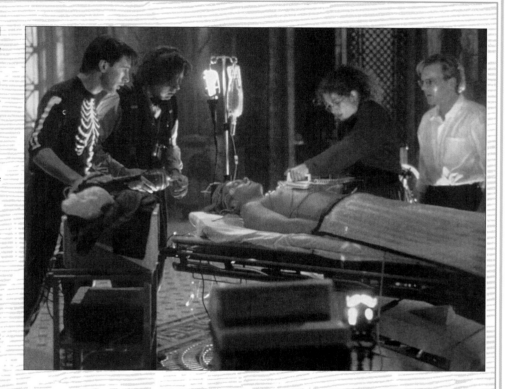

tear-jerker, the film is nicely balanced by the Goldberg comedy and also achieves the near-impossible with such a storyline. It makes the ghost-world seem entirely plausible.

The NDE itself has appeared in a few modern films, especially *Flatliners* (1991), starring Julia Roberts and Keifer Sutherland as medical students who deliberately induce NDEs as a cold-blooded scientific experiment, in order to discover what is on the other side. With a small group they persist with their highly dangerous experiments – literally dicing with death – and on their resuscitation each has a story to tell. At first they report 'flying' over beautiful countryside, or returning to the place where they grew up, but gradually a darker element intrudes,

▲ The group of young medics in *Flatliners* induced NDEs in order to further scientific knowledge, but their experiments rapidly turned their lives into a nightmare.

and they begin to suffer from the effects of the life review. Trying to put right the wrongs that, thanks to the NDE, they realize they have committed, leads to nightmarish situations in both the spirit and material worlds.

Perhaps now the whole subject of being dead has successfully been given big-screen treatment there will be a whole influx of such films which dare to develop this controversial theme. However, it seems that the topic of death is still regarded with some caution by film makers to whom the box office remains the ultimate sanction.

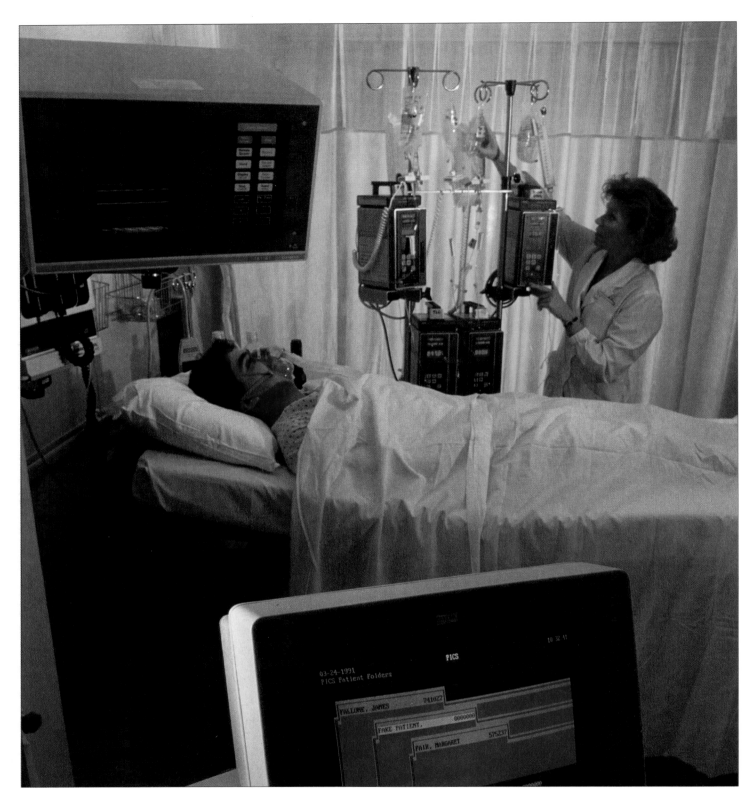

▲ NDEs often happen to people who register as being clinically dead on the most sophisticated medical monitoring equipment. But how can they experience anything?

justice to what happened to me. It was a hundred times more exciting than even waiting for Christmas when you're a tiny child, more exhilarating than driving the fastest car or having the best sex. I had entered into a world that had a sort of flavour of ecstasy. All the colours were brighter than anything you can imagine, all the sights and sounds somehow geared to being blissful. It was like being in love a million times over. I met a being who could have been God and I was content just to be around him, but that wasn't to be. I remember actually sobbing my heart out when he told me I had to go back. I begged like I'd never

► According to many reports, once through death's door adults and children are greeted by beings of light – religious figures, deceasd loved ones, or simply welcoming guides.

begged before to be allowed to stay, but suddenly, with a sort of loud click, I was back in my body feeling awful. I was utterly miserable for days, because I was back in this dreadful heavy, grey and dull world when I could have been dead! That's a joke, isn't it - the idea that being dead is terrifying. If I had a choice right now, I'd choose death over life any time. "

Joe is one of many whose everyday lives have been radically changed for ever by their brush with death. Their stories have reached out and touched the hearts and minds of others, as the NDE is increasingly featured by the media. The beauty, comfort and reassurance of the experience is such a far cry from the grimness surrounding a corpse that it is beginning, at last, to remove the stigma from the topic of death. Perhaps it is ironic that the medical profession has, inadvertently, succeeded where countless generations of priests have failed – they have produced evidence for the existence of the human soul. The paraphernalia of modern technology, which was designed to keep the body alive at all costs, has revealed that we are not just bodies – we have nonphysical, invisible selves that can separate and fly free.

Research into the NDE has escalated and now involves thousands of people the world over, including health professionals, psychical researchers, clergy and those who have had NDEs. It is arguably the most exciting and important research of any kind, for what can be more significant to anyone than information about our one shared, and inevitable, experience?

This book seeks to present the latest research into the NDE, and includes many hitherto unpublished stories, some of which had to be coaxed out of very reticent subjects with promises of anonymity. While these uncheckable anecdotes will not serve as evidence for the more rigid parapsychologists, it is hoped that their inherent sincerity and sense of wonder communicates to the reader.

I have also included other exciting evidence, gleaned from a variety of sources – some very surprising – for the existence of the soul. Combined with the material for the NDE, I believe the case for survival after death is very persuasive. Whether you believe it or not is a matter of personal choice; however, what is certain is that one day we will all have a chance to discover the truth of the matter for ourselves.

Marisa St Clair
London 1997

13

CHAPTER ONE

A History of Heaven

The late twentieth century has seen the NDE becoming one of the best-known paranormal phenomena: nowadays magazines and newspapers often carry stories about NDEs, and celebrities, such as Elizabeth Taylor, can admit to having had such an experience without fear of ridicule or scorn.

As researchers continue to collect more cases, it appears that NDEs are relatively common, due to ever-improving resuscitation techniques. Whereas once the cessation of breathing and the end of brain activity meant unequivocally that death had claimed another victim, today even those pronounced clinically dead can make a comeback, thanks to the miracles of modern medicine. Yet it would be a mistake to consider the NDE exclusive to our own era. There are many reports of pseudo-deaths that go back centuries, although they tend to be obscured by inaccurate reporting and personal interpretation.

The ancient Egyptian Pyramid Texts, which are the oldest known writings in the world, hint that NDEs were known in at least 3000 BC, but the first recognizable case is that of a soldier called Er, whose story was told by the philosopher Plato

◀ **The great Greek philosopher Plato, whose story of Er may have provided one of the rare reports of an historical NDE. Many early accounts may have been misinterpreted.**

(427–347 BC) in his *Republic*. According to this tale, Er was apparently killed by the enemy, and lay among the corpses on the battlefield. Together with the souls of his dead compatriots, he journeyed to another realm, where he was judged. All around him men were choosing their next incarnations, then wiping out the memories of their previous life by drinking from the River of Forgetfulness. But Er was commanded not to drink like the others, and returned to consciousness, not a moment too soon, on his funeral pyre.

In many respects, Er's story is similar to what we have come to think of as the classic NDE: he leaves his body and enters a realm of spirits where a judgment takes place; he is told to return and is revived, in his case spontaneously. But there are several significant differences, particularly the element of reincarnation (although some modern NDE cases report something startlingly similar), which was then a belief held by sophisticated Greeks, especially initiates of the secret Mystery Schools, perhaps like Plato himself. And the

River of Forgetfulness is certainly simply another name for the River Lethe of Greek mythology, the waters of which obliterate all earthly memories in preparation for the next life. But do these Greek elements imply that the entire story was just invented by Plato?

Given the striking resemblance to what we now recognize as an NDE, it seems unlikely that Er's story was a total fabrication, although Plato may have embellished it to make it more palatable for his audience. Or perhaps he told the story much as Er recounted it, without any significant changes – but the experience itself may have been geared to the cultural understanding of his fellow Greeks. As we will see, some aspects of today's NDEs appear to be customized by the powers that be – whoever or whatever they are – presumably for optimum emotional and spiritual impact.

It has been suggested that Plato was simply telling an allegorical story as a morality tale to encourage people to live better lives. But although he is known to have been fond of symbolism, it is much more likely to be the other way around; he may have used a real NDE as the basis of a cautionary tale, and did not have to invent one. Death, judgment and rebirth were also standard elements of the initiation ceremonies of, among others, the Greek Mystery Schools, where the seeker of wisdom had to undergo a ritual death before receiving enlightenment. Perhaps these ceremonies were based on the actual experiences of people such as Er.

Caught up in paradise

The term 'near-death experience' was coined only in the 1970s, and so it is sometimes difficult to tease out genuine NDEs from the records of history. Even the previous catch-all term 'deathbed visions' was often haphazardly applied to a whole host of similar phenomena. However, journeys to other realms of existence have been an essential part of many spiritual beliefs, and never more so than at the time of Christ when many religions shared a myth about their gods 'harrowing hell' and undergoing otherworldly quests. The Egyptian god Osiris was believed to enter into the underworld every winter, where he was sought by his consort, the goddess Isis, and was duly restored to the upper realm in spring, in time to release the life-giving flood water of the River Nile.

Similar myths depicted other 'dying-and-rising' gods, including the Greek Orpheus and his 'other half' Eurydice. By association of ideas these gods became rulers of the dead, who were believed to live in the underworld. In the same way Jesus entered hell to release the souls imprisoned there: in an early Gnostic Christian story, he even has a goddess to help him, in the form of Mary Magdalene.

Although the history of Christianity is liberally sprinkled with examples of mystics and saints who had intensely personal experiences of heaven, there are few stories that really seem to describe what we would call an NDE. One that seems to pass the test may have belonged to St Paul. The account, in his 'Second Epistle to the Corinthians', Chapter 12, is given in the third person. He says:

DIFFERENT VIEWS OF HEAVEN

Most religions have taught the concept of heaven as a place of surpassing splendour in which there is no pain or suffering and no more death. It was the home of the gods, and was traditionally thought of as being in the sky, out of reach of mere mortals: the ancient Egyptians even believed that their god-kings actually became stars after death, so they could continue to look down on their people.

Ideas about heaven have always been coloured by the expectations and delights of each particular society: the Native Americans' ancestors lived in the celestial Happy Hunting Ground, while the old Norse warriors found themselves in Valhalla where they could enjoy slaughtering as many enemies as they liked without fear of permanent hurt or damage. Each day's killing ended with a celebration on a scale fit for heroes; hearty horns of mead and haunches of roast pig, all prepared for them by those lusty female warriors, the Valkyries.

In the Greek concept of heaven a disturbing note of doubt creeps in: at first they believed that everyone ended up in the Elysian Fields, where it was always spring and nobody was unhappy, but this idea was later refined so that the place was reserved only for the righteous.

Several cultures, such as the Romans, believed that paradise was in the West, where the sun sets, and the somewhat dated slang phrase 'to go west' (meaning to die) comes directly from the ancient Egyptians. Both the Greeks and the Romans cherished the idea of the mythical 'Isles of the Blest', which was an earthly paradise 'without grief, without sorrow, without death', located somewhere in the West. Some early adventurers mistook the British Isles for this heaven on earth, although they soon realized their mistake.

The early Christians had a confused view of heaven, for on the one hand it was where Jesus and his saints lived (entry being strictly at St Peter's discretion), and on the other there was a prevalent belief that the soul slept until Judgment Day when the righteous would be physically resurrected. Curiously, although the Church was to define the afterlife much more clearly over the centuries that followed – dividing it up into heaven, hell, purgatory and limbo – this essential confusion has never been completely resolved.

However, most of the main religions agree that heaven is a series of levels through which a good person may ascend, becoming increasingly ecstatic as he draws closer to God. These heavenly worlds are peopled with angels, a word that comes from the Latin *angelus* meaning messenger. In Christianity and Judaism, angels belong to a complex hierarchy somewhat akin to a medieval court, with the chief prince of the angelic host being in both cases Michael, who is also revered in Islam. Muslim angels are very much involved in day to day life, protecting people against the *djinn*, or evil spirits, who lay in wait to steal their soul.

The concept of a multilayered paradise is shared by the spiritualists, who believe that there are at least three heavens (although some say there are seven) each of which is progressively more spiritual and rarified, and from which contact with the living is increasingly unlikely.

"I knew a man in Christ above 14 years ago, (whether in the body, I cannot tell; or whether out of the body, I cannot tell: God knoweth;) such an one caught up to the third heaven ... How that he was caught up into paradise, and heard unspeakable words, which it is not lawful for a man to utter ... Of such a one will I glory; yet of myself I will not glory ..."

Whoever actually had this experience returned from paradise and at least lived to tell the tale, which is, after all, a basic requirement of any NDE. But was the mysterious voyager into another realm actually St Paul himself? All we can do at this point in history is read between the lines, but it certainly seems to be a possibility. His reticence in admitting to this experience may be simply – as he hints rather strongly – due his modesty. In saying '... of myself I will not glory', he is clearly not wishing to be set apart and feted by his fellow Christians as one who was specially chosen.

Tantalizingly, he does not give any further details of the experience, but perhaps during his visit to paradise he was also given some information about the future, either personal or

▲ The apostle Paul preaches at Ephesus. Was his third-person description of a man who went to heaven and returned a description of his own NDE?

global in nature, just as those who have had NDEs in more modern times are sometimes given prophecies while in heaven.

St Paul's reticence about speaking of his NDE is by no means unique: many people who have had any kind of paranormal experience often find it impossible to share, sometimes for decades, out of a mixture of fear of ridicule and a suspicion that sharing such a private and wonderful event

17

THE BODY AFTER DEATH

Death may not always be the clearly defined state science would have us believe. For example, certain pathological conditions such as catalepsy have induced death-like morbidity in individuals who then spontaneously revived. (The contorted position of many exhumed bodies has revealed that they had been buried alive, finally meeting their death in the airless confines of their coffin, without food, water or hope. It is thought that such terrible sights gave rise to many allegations of vampirism.)

Many Victorians feared premature burial so much that they had breathing tubes and bells fitted in their coffins, while others simply requested that their corpses should remain unburied until they showed irrefutable signs of decomposition. Yet some dead bodies have triumphed over even the process of putrefaction: these are the 'incorruptibles'.

Not embalmed or otherwise preserved, and often buried in the kind of ground that should, if anything, have hastened decomposition, these corpses simply do not rot. For years after death, they continue to look lifelike, sometimes with a natural colour and flexible limbs. And far from giving off the expected stench of death, they are often reported to produce a heady scent of flowers or even incense.

This phenomenon has come to be exclusively associated with Catholic saints, but this may be misleading. It is true that much of the evidence for incorruptibility does come from the Church's records – Bernadette of Lourdes is one of many saints whose body remains uncorrupted by death – but as this phenomenon used to be taken as one of the signs of sainthood, many candidates for beatification have been routinely exhumed, whereas of course most corpses are not. Significantly, other examples of incorruptibility have come from outside the ranks of saints, including 1000-year-old Chinese corpses, and a young woman who died in Chicago in the 1920s. Who can say how many incorruptibles lie in their graves as fresh and lifelike as the day they died?

It is strange that scientists have totally ignored this phenomenon, for surely the very existence of such bodies is an affront to the laws of nature, and challenges the most basic of our certainties. Could it be that death itself is something that we do not understand?

would somehow sully it irrevocably. Perhaps St Paul felt the same way, and could only bring himself to hint about it. However, those who came after him more than made up for his reticence, and did not hesitate to put words in his mouth. Within 300 years there were several versions circulating of what St Paul had seen.

Dr Carol Zaleski, a lecturer in religion at Harvard University, has made an extensive study of the NDE in Christian literature. In her book, *Otherworld Journeys* (1987), she writes of this attempt to turn St Paul's half-told story into dogma:

"*For medieval readers, however, much of the vision's glamour derived from its vivid depiction of the experiences that are in store for individuals at death and in the period before the final judgment.*

◄ **Devout pilgrims pray at St Patrick's Cross, Lough Derg, Ireland, where Mystery school techniques may have once been used to induce the visions of NDEs.**

Although Paul himself does not die, he observes the departure of three souls from their bodies and witnesses their journeys after death; the soul of a just man exits his body in the company of shining angels who defend him against the hostile powers of the air and escort him to the heavenly court to be vindicated and welcomed by God; a wicked man is dragged roughly from his body by 'angels without mercy', harassed by his animating spirit, claimed as a fellow traveller by the hostile powers, and consigned to torment in the outer darkness; a second wicked man, after spending seven days before his trial on a forced tour of the cosmos, faces conviction when his own guardian angel turns state's evidence, producing a manuscript record of his sins and bringing forward the souls of those he had murdered or betrayed. "

As Europe entered the Dark Ages, the Church increasingly emphasized the terrors and reality of hell to its illiterate and largely credulous congregations; the idea of a place of bliss and reward was not a favourite topic for sermons.

Successive waves of plague, famine and the witch hysteria meant that evil and torment were everywhere, but to thousands of poor wretches this atrocious life was only a curtain-raiser to the even worse conditions to come – the fires of eternal hell. There must have been a few who had NDEs, especially when the cry of 'bring out your dead' often resulted in the collection of both corpses and coma victims. At least they would know that the terrors promised them from the pulpit on Sunday were not inescapable, and that there was such a place as heaven.

Interestingly, the thirteenth-century heretical Christian sect, the Cathars of southwestern France, believed that this earthly life was hell, and that the afterlife was a world of light and joy, which could be reached once and for all through dying 'a good

THE SOUL'S GLIMPSE OF HEAVEN

Most people who have an NDE describe their journey into a world of indescribable beauty, full of light and celestial music, where unconditional love reigns supreme. Not surprisingly they are reluctant to return to their bodies and all the problems and suffering of earthly life. But had they really glimpsed heaven?

Spiritualists believe that the spirit passes into what is known as 'Summerland', a realm of happiness and wish fulfilment. It operates by mind-power, so that an individual's environment is produced to his or her own specifications, simply by imagining it. This 'ideoplastic' dimension, however much it may seem at first to be the postmortem equivalent of winning a fortune in the Lottery, is not without its more serious side.

In fact, the souls in Summerland are said to receive a rude awakening from their hedonistic existence in the form of 'The Judgment', which comes unbidden. There is no stern God or avenging angel: the individual is shown a replay of his or her own life in minute detail, with the full knowledge of the effect their every word, thought and action had on others.

According to British spiritualist Paul Beard in his book *Living On: A Study of Continuing Consciousness After Death* (1980), spirit communications received by many talented and ethical mediums agree about the nature of the afterlife, but stress that Summerland is merely the first of a series of heavens, which become progressively less sybaritic and more spiritual. However, we have less information about the higher realms, as the journey of the soul moves one further and further away from contact with the earthly plane.

death' – preferably martyrdom through burning. (Curiously, this was a belief that was shared by the sinister modern cult known as the Solar Temple, which also had connections with the Languedoc area of France.)

The Cathars were known to train themselves against the inevitable torments of the Inquisition, using a Buddhist-like, meditative practice by means of which they could leave their bodies even during torture, and therefore feel no pain. We will never know how effective this was. Some of them must have been less proficient at it than others, and presumably they suffered horribly. But the Cathars were also rumoured to know the secret of glimpsing heaven. Was this a reference to a secret practice that somehow enabled them to induce NDEs, rather like the medical students in the film *Flatliners*? Is this how the Cathars had learned of a heaven of light and joy at a time when most Christians believed only too strongly in a guaranteed postmortem trip to the fiery pit?

When the cell shook

One medieval account that closely resembles a classic NDE, was that of a holy man of sixth-century Gaul (modern France). The hermit Salvius, who was later to become a bishop, was stricken with an unspecified illness. He was believed to be dead, and was set on his funeral bier as night fell. However, by the next morning he had regained consciousness, and had an amazing story to tell:

"Four days ago, when the cell shook [unfortunately we do not know what this refers to], and you saw me lifeless, I was taken up by two angels and carried up to the height of heaven, and it was just as though I had beneath my feet not only this squalid earth, but also the sun and moon, the clouds and the stars. Then I was brought through a gate that was brighter than our light, into a dwelling-place where the entire floor shone like gold and silver; there was an ineffable light and it was indescribably vast."

This heavenly place was suffused with beautiful perfumes – no doubt particularly exquisite to a former hermit – and Salvius loved it. But then a voice came, saying: 'Send this man back to the world, since he is necessary to our church'. Of course this is strikingly similar to more modern examples of NDEs when individuals have described voices telling them to return to life because their work is not yet completed. Salvius, like many others in his position, fought back, saying:

"Alas, alas, Lord, why have you shown me these things, if I was to be cheated of them? Behold! Today you are casting me out from your face, to return to the perishable world, so that in the end I won't have the power to come back here."

Poor Salvius seems to think that if he returns to the material world he will get too old and weak ever to make it back to heaven! It is to be hoped that he discovered in the course of time that youth and athletic ability were not essential requirements for entry to the afterlife. His story has come down through the ages without alteration, perhaps simply because he was a literate man largely writing for others such as priests who, like himself, could read and write. Undoubtedly many other NDEs from the Middle Ages were lost to posterity because they were never written down, or were never even confided to anyone beyond the immediate circle of the family. And some stories of NDEs were buried in myth and legend, open to misinterpretation and probably completely ignored.

Into the magic cave

The problems of interpreting the messages hidden in old texts is illustrated by the twelfth-century *Treatise on the Purgatory of St Patrick*, which was written by a monk of the Cistercian order. It tells of the spiritual adventures of one Knight Owen, a soldier returning to Ireland from foreign campaigns, who seeks forgiveness for his sins by entering the sacred cave near Lough [Lake] Derg in County Donegal. As we will see, this is a magic place, which St Patrick had converted into a place of pilgrimage, and where visions were virtually guaranteed.

The Knight Owen is barricaded into the cave at night, and enters a deep tunnel that leads towards a bright light. Some monks try to persuade him to turn back, but he does not heed them and immediately experiences a terrifying earthquake before passing into the underworld. He witnesses the damned frying in hell, then travels along a sulphurous river to a bridge that leads to an enchanting world of brilliant light. There, two clerics bar his further progress, telling him that God's true kingdom lies beyond that realm. They urge him to observe the Church's rites on his return, and send him back, despite his reluctance to leave that taste of heaven. On his return the king advises him that he can best fulfil his new religious ardour by serving the Cistercian order, specifically by building them a new Abbey in Ireland.

Clearly the Cistercian scribes had made the Knight Owen's story very much their own, and for obvious self-seeking reasons. Indeed, as Dr Zaleski points out, the treatise was actually used as propaganda by the Order. However, she believes that there was an underlying element of real spirituality in this tale – the 'pilgrimage discourse', or the dramatization of the idea that life is a pilgrimage. She believes that this and similar stories from that time, even those that appear to be classic NDEs, merely reflect a tradition of present-

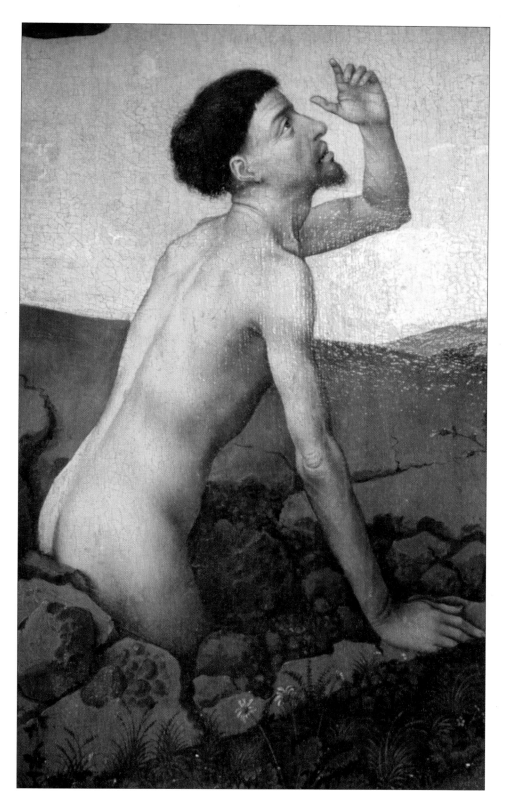

ing 'the otherworld journey as a spiritual pilgrimage'. She does not believe that the NDE has ever been a real, objective experience.

Cistercian trappings may have obscured the issue even more than Dr Zaleski realizes, for the important part of the story is its location. The

▲ A soul awaits the Last Judgement: in medieval times the emphasis was on hell and damnation, but modern NDEs reveal that the afterlife is often pure bliss.

cave, destroyed in the eighteenth century, originally was a site held sacred by the old pagans who

▲ Body snatchers at their grim task: sometimes they discovered that people had been
buried alive, only to die in their own graves.
Bloody corpses gave rise to vampire myths.

believed it was a portal to the otherworld. St Patrick cannily converted it
into a place of Christian pilgrimage,
but the old customs were hardly
changed: pilgrims were locked in the
cave in order to induce visions that
would bestow enlightenment, as were
those of the Greek Mystery School of
Plato's day.

Caves were once the preferred
places of initiation all over the world,
perhaps because they were continu-
ally dark. Seekers had to find their
way around tortuous labyrinths that
contained real dangers, such as wild
beasts. But more often than not it
was the person's own imagination
that produced the menace, going into
nightmarish freefall in the mind-
altering dark.

Artificially induced visions

Sometimes the would-be initiate
was given drugs to induce hallucinations in which the gods would speak
to him directly, and perhaps (as in
Flatliners – see page 11) there were
experiments in pushing the initiate
further and further into the twilight
world of the NDE in a deliberate
attempt to gain more knowledge of
the otherworld.

It is said that certain snake cults,
which possibly included the ancient
Minoans of Knossos on Crete, encouraged their members to be bitten by
snakes or drink their venom in order
to see visions before being taken up
into the otherworld. There was
always a danger that they would not
return from their artificially induced
NDEs, but that was deemed to be, as
it were, an occupational hazard.

No doubt the various secret societies that took over from the Mystery Schools of the ancient world continued to play dangerous games with induced altered states of consciousness. But for the ordinary Christian, what we now call NDEs became lumped together with other phenomena under the general heading of 'deathbed visions'.

Encounters with angels

In his book *The Return from Silence: A Study of Near-Death-Experiences* (1989), the late American parapsychologist D. Scott Rogo discusses the true deathbed vision, which he defines as: 'Those unusual perceptions sometimes reported by the dying that explicitly point to survival.' Usually these visions take the form of the dying person apparently seeing and hearing dead relations and friends who have come to accompany them into the afterlife. Scott Rogo goes on to compare these visions to the NDE as it is defined today. He writes:

1. The dying patient is usually lucid when making the observation and doesn't make the report upon recovering from pseudo-death.

2. The vision takes place while the witness's consciousness remains 'inside' the body.

Deathbed visions are similar to classic NDEs, however, since they share some of its characteristics:

1. The patients often see their dead friends, relatives, or spiritual guides coming to greet them.

2. The patient may glimpse the realm of the afterlife. While not experiencing a literal otherworld journey, sometimes the dying see panoramic scenes of great beauty.

Although there was a tendency among sentimental Victorians to describe deathbed visions as vague

encounters with angels (these therefore tended to be dismissed out of hand by objective researchers), some cases did manage to find their way into print. One was the superficially grim story of little Daisy Irene Dryden, who died in 1854 at the age of 10. It was published by her mother in a pamphlet entitled *Daisy Dryden - A Memoire by Mrs S.H. Dryden*, and dealt with the child's deathbed visions.

Desperately ill with virulent enteritis, Daisy began to see visions of Jesus, who told her of her imminent death when she would go to join him. Despite her great physical suffering, the child had several lucid phases when she actually seemed gleeful at the prospect.

When the superintendent of her Sunday School paid her a visit and uttered the astoundingly insensitive words: 'Well, Daisy, you will soon be over the dark river,' the child retorted:

"*There is no river, there is no curtain, there is not even a line that separates this life from the other life ... it is here and it is there: I know it is so, for I can see you all, and see them there at the same time.***"**

Daisy began to hear beautiful music, and gave a neighbour a message from her dead son. He was not the only otherworldly figure who came to her bedside. She saw angels, who confused her because they had no wings as she had been led to believe, and then came her own brother, who had died six months before of scarlet fever. Mrs Dryden writes:

"*I was sitting beside her bed, her hand clasped in mine. Looking up so wistfully at me, she said, 'Dear Momma, I do wish you could see Allie: he's standing beside you.' Involuntarily I looked around, but Daisy thereupon continued, 'He says you cannot see him because your spirit eyes are closed, but that I can, because my body only*

*holds my spirit, as it were, by a thread of life.' Then I enquired, 'Does he say that now?' 'Yes, just now,' she answered. Then wondering how she could be conversing with her brother when I saw not the least sign of conversation, I said, 'Daisy, how do you speak to Allie? I do not hear you or see your lips move'. She smilingly replied, 'We just talk with our think'. I then asked her further, 'Daisy, how does Allie appear to you? Does he wear clothes?' She answered, 'Oh no, not clothes such as we wear. There seems to be about him a white, beautiful something, so fine and thin and glistening, and oh, so white, and yet there is not a fold or sign of a thread in it, so it cannot be cloth. But it makes him look so lovely.' Her father then quoted from the Psalmist: 'He is clothed with light as a garment.' 'Oh yes, that's it,' she replied.***"**

Little Daisy died while cuddling up to her father, waiting for Allie to come and take her away. Because she was totally certain of her continued existence – of her imminent entry into a wonderful new world – she died peacefully and without pain. (Modern researchers have noted the connection between deathbed visions and peaceful death, see Chapter 2.) Mrs Dryden ended her account with the simple but heartfelt remark, 'There was a solemn stillness in the room. We would not weep, and why should we?'

Although we are not told that Daisy had what would be termed an NDE today, at times she seemed half in this world and half in the next. As she herself said, the spirit world became visible to her because her life hung by the slenderest thread. The child of a Methodist missionary, Daisy inadvertently reinforced the belief of the then fledgling Spiritualist Movement when she described the 'veil' between the two realms that normally prevents the living seeing the dead and vice versa, but which is

EARLY MORMON REPORTS OF THE NDE

Not far from the New York State hamlet where spiritualism was to be born, farmboy Joseph Smith had the visions that led to the founding of the Church of Jesus Christ of Latter Day Saints, otherwise known as the Mormons (although the church members themselves prefer 'Saints'). Recent research into the nineteenth-century Mormon archives has revealed that experiences similar to the NDE were well known to the pioneers.

Mormon leader Heber C. Kimball reported the case of one Saint, Jedediah M. Grant:

"He said to me, Brother Heber, I have been into the spirit world two nights in succession, and of all the dreads that ever came across me, the worst was to have to return to my body, though I had to do it.**"**

▼ Nineteenth-century Mormon leaders. Mormon archives apparently contain several valuable reports of historical NDEs which give the phenomenon a background.

During his sojourn to the world of light, Grant met many deceased relatives, but it was his encounter with his late wife that was the most poignant. As Kimball records:

"He saw his wife, she was the first person that came to him. He saw many that he knew, but did not have conversation with any but his wife Caroline. She came to him, and he said that she looked beautiful and had their little child, that died on the plains, in her arms, and said, 'Mr Grant [this formal mode of address was common between wives and husbands at that time], here is little Margaret: you know that the wolves ate her up; but it did not hurt her, here she is all right.**"**

Like many other religions and sects, the Mormons use the NDE as evidence of the truth of their beliefs, but wider and more objective studies of the phenomenon reveal that entrance to the world of light is open to those of any religion – or of none. Heaven is the ultimate experience open to all human beings.

apparently moved aside for the dying.

Daisy's story is also remarkable for its similarities to the classic NDE: hearing celestial music, meeting her deceased brother Allie and Jesus, and discovering that the realm of the dead appears to interpenetrate our own. Finally, she meets her death with quiet joy, welcoming it whole-heartedly because of the comfort she had received from her deathbed visions. As we will see, the testimony of children is of crucial importance to a true assessment of the NDE as an objective experience, and – largely due to the pioneering and compassionate work of Dr Elisabeth Kubler-Ross – hospice and hospital workers are now incorporating lessons learned from them into the care of terminally ill youngsters.

Heavenly music for all

In his unfinished book *Death-bed Visions*, the eminent British psychical researcher Sir William Barrett (who died in 1925) set out a fascinating collection of true stories about the paranormal experiences of the dying. He records that sometimes celestial music was heard by the dying person's visitors, just as those who have had NDEs in more recent years often describe hearing the sweetest music imaginable.

For example, when Mrs L died in 1881, all her friends except one heard some strange music, as the main witness explains:

"Just after dear Mrs L's death between 2 and 3 a.m., I heard a most sweet and singular strain of singing outside the windows; it died away after passing the house. All in the room [except Mrs L's son] heard it, and the medical attendant, who was still with us, went to the window, as I did, and looked out, but there was nobody. It was a bright and beautiful night. It was as if several voices were singing in perfect unison a most sweet melody which died away in the distance. Two persons had gone from the room to fetch something and were coming upstairs at the back of the house and heard the singing and stopped, saying, 'What is that singing?' They could not, naturally, have heard any sound from outside the windows in the front of the house from where they were at the back."

The doctor also heard unexplained music, although, perhaps significantly, it took a different form for him:

"I remember the circumstances perfectly. I was sent for about midnight, and remained with Mrs L until her death about 2.30 a.m.. Shortly after we heard a few bars of lovely music, not unlike that from an aeolian harp - and it filled the air for a few seconds. I went to the window and looked out, thinking there must be someone outside, but could see no one though it was quite light and clear. Strangely enough, those outside the room heard the same sounds, as they were coming upstairs quite at the other side of the door [house]."

Yet there are two discrepancies in this story: one is that the doctor heard instrumental music, whereas the others heard singing, and the other is that Mrs L's son heard nothing at all. This argues in favour of the music being a paranormal event, and therefore open to all the vagaries of perception and interpretation. However, all except one were agreed that there was an unexplained phenomenon, and that it was musical in nature.

'A way of the world'

Most people regard the NDE as a single, dramatic and life-changing event, yet occasionally some of its characteristic phenomena may occur individually and over a much longer period of time to the same person.

For example, Maud Grimshaw was a working-class woman from the slums of Leeds, in the industrial northeast of England, who died in 1975 aged 98. Hers had been a tough existence – married to a tubercular drunkard who was usually unemployed, she would often face the day with no food for her large family. By the time she died only three of the 11 original children survived: childhood illness had carried off Alice, Billy and May; epilepsy brought about Claude's early demise; Molly was burnt to death in a home fire; Hilda died of a heart attack in her 60s; and Elsie succumbed to the ravages of cancer aged 72. Lizzie, 75, was found by neighbours with her head in the gas oven. She had been dead for four days.

This catalogue of tragedy was not uncommon for a woman of Maud's era and social background, but as she grew older she began to experience psychic phenomena that proved to be a great comfort to her, and which sometimes included the all-important checkable, or 'veridical' elements. Shortly before she died she described them to her granddaughter, Lisa M, who recorded her words. Maud said:

"I'd always had very vivid dreams about my children. Not about anything else, mind you. I was always too exhausted to dream much. I remember the first odd dream I had although it happened during the Great War [1914-18]. Our Claude took [had epileptic] fits, so they put him in the asylum because he was a danger to himself. I went to see him as often as I could but I had a young family and was mostly tied to the house. One afternoon I sat in the chair for a cup of tea and must have dozed off because I saw Claude as clear as anything standing in front of me, smiling and looking wonderful, real healthy. I rubbed my eyes but he was still there. 'Mam,' he said, 'Don't cry. I'm well and happy but I've got to go now. We'll meet up again.' Then

he was gone. I don't remember waking up, but I must have. About an hour later a policeman knocked to tell me Claude had died, but I already knew. **"**

As the years passed, Maud became an invalid, and spent a lot of time dozing in her favourite chair. In 1970 she began to have recurring dreams of 'our little Alice' coming to visit her.

"*It was that grand to see our pretty little Alice again, bless her. I missed her so bad when she died, it was so sudden and I was too young. I thought I wouldn't be able to bear the grief, but I had to get on*

▼ Religion gives great comfort to many, but those who have an NDE often return to life more spiritual and less rigidly dogmatic. It seems that no one religion has exclusive entry to heaven.

and bring up the family. But there she was, just yesterday - after all this time - looking just as she used to, so real. She came and sat on my bed and kissed my face, just here. I could feel her breath. She laughed at me, 'Oh Mam,' she said just as she used to all those years ago, 'you've got so old and so tired. Soon you're coming with me and the others and you'll get young and strong again. But not yet. I'll come again. **"**

Alice kept her word, returning approximately once a month to her increasingly elderly and frail mother. Usually she was alone, but twice she brought Billy and May, who had also died as children. Their visits delighted Maud, but one night Alice brought an unexpected companion.

"*Alice came right up to me and stared, ever so serious, into my*

face. 'Mam,' she said, 'Please try not to be too upset. Look who I've got with me now.' A sort of grey mist came up and then out of it stepped our Lizzie, looking pale and confused. Alice went up and put her little arm round her, then Lizzie seemed to light up from inside. She started to smile and turned to wave at me. They both sort of moved backwards until they disappeared into a cloud of light. I woke up and cried, it was so beautiful. I was worried though, so I tried ringing our Lizzie but she didn't answer. I knew then that Alice had come for her and that she was dead, but when they found her she had been gone, poor thing, for a few days. She'd had a terrible time towards the end, and took her own life. **"**

As Maud herself approached death,

her dead children appeared to her with increasing frequency, sometimes when she was awake. Although she remained mentally alert, she came to accept their presence and expected her visitors to do the same. 'Don't stand in front of our Alice,' she told one sharply. 'She looks so lovely in her new frock.' And as she slipped peacefully into her transition from this world to the next she is said to have beamed with such delight that she looked like a young woman again. 'It's marvellous. They're all here now,' she sighed happily. 'They've all come for me.' But then her eyes seemed to catch sight of something of even greater interest in the corner of the room. 'It's my Mam and Dad! They've come for me! They're so young … And just listen to that music …' And with a radiant smile Maud ended her long life of tragedy, which had nevertheless been made more bearable because of its repeated episodes of strange comfort from the spirit world.

Maud's many paranormal experiences fall into several categories, including crisis apparitions (of Claude and later Lizzie), typical deathbed visions spread out over a period of years, which progressed to their inevitable climax at her own death, and the hearing of celestial music. Significantly, Maud was rarely surprised by the phenomena, and claimed that such things were common among members of her family and her neighbours in the Leeds slums. She said:

"We thought nowt [nothing] about it much. You always knew something was wrong when a child that's passed on or someone else who'd gone came to see you. Either it was your turn or somebody else close to you. It must have happened 10 times in our street alone when I was a young woman. I used to hand out cups of tea to them who had a story about one of them dreams, so I knew all about them. I used to tell them it was just the

---

CELEBRITY EXPERIENCES

Many celebrities have had a dramatic brush with death, including film star Elizabeth Taylor and singer Marie Osmond.

In the 1980s, Elizabeth Taylor was rushed into the Wellington Hospital in north London with a severe respiratory infection that required drastic surgery. While she was under the anaesthetic she found herself in a black tunnel looking up towards a great light in which she saw her late husband, Michael Wilding, who had been killed in a plane crash.

Feeling great love and comfort, she started to move towards him, but he told her she had to return because it was not yet her time to die. When she came round and told the doctors, they thought she had been hallucinating.

More recently, the singer Marie Osmond was on tour in the United States, when she fell asleep with her children at the back of the hire bus. Suddenly she felt a strong presence urging her to get up and go to the front of the bus immediately. She did so – and discovered the driver had collapsed at the wheel. Acting quickly, she managed to pull the bus safely off the road.

A devout Mormon, she ascribes this miraculous escape to angelic intervention. 'Without God's help we would have all died,' she says.

---

way of the world. When it was your time, they came for you."

Sceptics would say that a combination of lack of education, exhaustion from trying to bring up a family in such grim circumstances, wish fulfilment, and superstition no doubt helped to fuel Maud's imagination, creating these vivid dreams of her lost children. Yet in every other respect she was a down-to-earth practical woman, who never had any time for what she called 'idle fancies'. Besides, her stories exactly mirror many classic phenomena of which she could have had no knowledge. And even if she had, it is doubtful she would have been interested in the academic research of those such as Sir William Barrett, whom she would have regarded as the idle rich.

Accepting the spirits

Such anecdotal evidence as Maud's is usually deemed of little interest by today's sceptical breed of parapsychologists, to whom scientifically repeatable experiments are everything. But there are thousands of families the world over where similar phenomena were just as common and

where they are totally accepted as 'the way of the world'. Maud and her like never wrote their memoirs or replied to an Society for Psychical Research (SPR) survey, never sought publicity or even kept a diary. Yet a historical overview of the NDE and its allied phenomena would not be complete without including the evidence of those such as Maud, with her uncomplicated acceptance of the reality of the spirit world. Maud would have pitied the sceptics.

Those who have worked with the dying have always had stories to tell about deathbed visions of deceased loved ones, angels of light, and what we now call NDEs, but such subjects were frowned upon by the medical profession. Maud's doctor, for example, brushed aside her stories as reactions to drugs, or to her 'mind wandering', despite the fact that she was completely lucid in every other respect, right to the end. Millions of people have had to keep their most precious and sublime experiences to themselves for fear of ridicule, or even of being diagnosed as insane. But all this was to change, with the work of two doctors – Elisabeth Kubler-Ross and Raymond Moody.

CHAPTER TWO

First Steps into the Light

Doctors are busy people whose profession demands a practical and clinical approach and a certain emotional detachment from their patients. They are unlikely to be given to flights of fancy or whimsy, so when evidence for a spiritual afterlife comes from their ranks, it is particularly impressive and thought provoking.

In the immediate aftermath of World War II, the Allies entered the Nazi death camps, and the sights that greeted them gave lasting nightmares even to battle-hardened soldiers. One of the medical helpers they had with them was the young Elisabeth Kubler, from Switzerland, who was never to forget the horrors of the Polish concentration camps where she was stationed. But that baptism of fire was to prove of great value to many people, for it effectively removed once and for all from her any fear or revulsion about death and the dying. She had seen it all, there was nothing left to fear, and therefore nothing to deny or avoid.

Elisabeth Kubler married an American doctor and moved to the USA where she became assistant professor of psychiatry at Chicago's Billings Hospital. She realized that there was one area in modern medical care that was ignored, especially

◀ **The sufferings of Polish concentration camp victims were witnessed by Elizabeth Kubler, the pioneering NDE researcher. This experience helped her better understand the needs of the dying.**

in the most sophisticated hospitals – the care of the dying. While medical advances mean that terminally ill patients can be kept relatively pain free, and that much of the humiliation and discomfort of their last days has been ameliorated, the fact remains that the medical profession regard death as the enemy. Devoted to saving lives at all costs, they tend to avoid the fact of death to such an extent that they fail to acknowledge that people who are dying have requirements that cannot be provided by extensive funding: they need human compassion. All too often modern deathbeds are surrounded by impersonal medical equipment in noisy hospitals: many deaths are lonely. There is nothing to celebrate a life or acknowledge that death is a major rite of passage for each individual. Dr Kubler-Ross, as she had become, was not afraid to confront death, nor to spend time with the dying as their friend.

When she began her seminars on Death and Dying at the Billings Hospital in Chicago her approach was so new that a word had to be

coined for her work. The term was thanatology, from the Greek *thanos* (death). But, as Dr Kubler-Ross admits, her work as thanatologist was to be a very humbling and life-changing experience. She began as an agnostic, without any belief in a hereafter, or any perception of a spiritual dimension to life – something apparently borne out by her graphic experience of people's inhumanity to each other, when there appeared to be nothing to save millions from appalling torture and death except a merciful extinction. But as she devoted more time to observing the dying, she began to change her opinion.

The moment of death

In the course of her work with terminally ill patients, many of whom took months to die of cancer, Dr Kubler-Ross realized that there are distinct stages in the drawn-out process of dying. Many patients go into denial ('it can't happen to me'), become angry that their life has been cut short, or try to bargain with the doctors, their families or with God in order to be cured or have their life

CASE STUDY: DEATH OF AN OLD SOLDIER

Cecil P had spent most of his adult life in the British Army, but since retiring in 1968 he became very ill. His daughter Margaret explains that he had never 'given in to illness':

"It was totally in character for him to suffer in silence and keep well away from doctors. But we nagged him so much – and anyway he was weakening by the day and in terrible pain – that he went for a checkup. They found he was riddled with cancer, having left it far too long to do anything about it. He was sent home to die, although what now appears to me to be the most dreadful decision was taken by our GP not to tell him the truth about his condition. So my mum and I were confronted daily by this skeletal man in pain and still talking in terms of getting better. So many times we had to leave his room hurriedly, so he couldn't see us crying.

Then one Thursday evening when I took him a cup of tea he said, 'Sorry it will be on a Sunday, but I can't keep them waiting.' Suddenly I felt chilled to the bone, even though it was a hot day. I knew he was talking about his death, though I pretended not to. But he smiled at me,

and he hadn't had the strength or the will to smile for weeks. 'Sorry, Pet. The light will come back for me then, you see. It came last night and it was lovely.'

I asked him what he meant. He said: 'They've sent the light to do a recce [army slang for reconnoitre], but next time I have to go away with it.' He sighed. 'I can't wait,' he said. Afterwards I realized that he stopped asking for painkillers after that, and when mum took him some he refused them and smiled at her in a knowing kind of way. Funny, it was almost lighthearted, sort of roguish. 'I'm all right, now.' was all he would say then.

On the Saturday night he actually had some pink in his cheeks, but when I pointed this out, he took my hand and whispered (he could hardly speak by then): 'Not getting better, Pet. But glad you like it. I go away tomorrow.'

The next day he died with a boyish smile on his face. It was, as he had predicted, the Sunday.**"**

---

extended. These reactions are now accepted by psychologists, sociologists and doctors worldwide. But Dr Kubler-Ross had the courage to note other, less accepted (or acceptable) reactions in the dying: they knew when death was imminent. As she writes:

"*Even the angriest and most difficult patients very shortly before death began to deeply relax, have a sense of serenity around them, and were pain free in spite of perhaps a cancer-ridden body full of metastases.***"**

(These were not necessarily people with a belief in God or an afterlife.) Dr Kubler-Ross goes on:

"*Also, the moment after death occurred their facial features expressed an incredible sense of peace and equanimity and serenity which I could not comprehend since it was often a death that occurred in a state of anger, bargaining or depression.***"**

Of course, over the centuries this phenomenon has often been noted by

those caring for the dying: many nurses tell tales of how someone who had put up a real fight against death suddenly refused food, 'turned their face to the wall', and died peacefully, with a smile on their face. Or people who have announced the day – even the time – of their coming deaths, although they were in perfect health at the time (see box above).

However, modern doctors have little sympathy for anything that smacks of the spirit, so medical textbooks never even mentioned this phenomenon until Dr Kubler-Ross came along. She began to listen seriously to everything else that the dying said, and it opened up a whole new world for her.

She noticed that terminally ill patients frequently reported seeing and hearing deceased friends and relatives that remained invisible and inaudible to others present. These spirit visitors were there for a purpose: to welcome and escort the dying person into the next world. Routinely ignored by Dr Kubler-Ross's fellow doctors – or at best, dismissed as wish fulfilment – she took them seriously enough to remember what was

said. And she discovered an amazing fact: many of these deathbed visions included people who were newly dead, and whose death had actually been deliberately kept from the patient. Even tiny children excitedly talked of a family member coming for them who, in their minds, should have been firmly in the land of the living, but who were actually dead – sometimes just by minutes, as in the case of a family car crash. (This phenomenon is dealt with in more detail in Chapter 7.)

But sometimes the descriptions of meetings with 'beings of light' did not come from deathbeds, but from patients who had had an NDE, and who had lived perhaps for some time afterwards.

A long-lost brother

One special story that Dr Kubler-Ross tells in her book *On Life After Death* (1991), is that of a 12-year-old girl who had died and been resuscitated. She felt that she could not share her experience with her mother, because she had visited a place of blissful light and love from which she had no wish to return – not even to go home – and felt her mother might be hurt by her desire to stay dead. But after agonizing about this for some time, the girl finally told her father about it.

She described the wonderful realm she had entered, and how she had met her brother, who had embraced her lovingly. But the young girl was puzzled, saying, 'But the only problem is I don't have a brother.'

Her father burst into tears. He confessed that she had once had a brother but he had died three months before she was born, and whose existence had been rigorously kept from her. Yet here he was, welcoming her into his world.

There are many similar cases on record, which will be discussed more

fully in Chapter 7. They argue forcibly against the criticism that the beings of light are created by the unconscious mind as a sort of wish fulfilment. How could a little girl wish to be met by a brother she didn't know she had?

The return of Mrs Schwartz

As soon as she began to listen to her dying patients with a very un-doctor-like humility, Dr Kubler-Ross began to realize that what is now known as the NDE was a very common phenomenon but one that was totally inexplicable in strictly agnostic or scientific terms. However, very soon she was to have some very unusual experiences of her own.

Recognizing that the process of

death encompasses many unexpected and unscientific elements, Dr Kubler-Ross encouraged her patients to share their OBEs and NDEs with other members of her profession in seminars on death and dying. One of her star OBE subjects was a certain Mrs Schwartz, who described to an enthralled audience how it feels to leave the physical body for an unimaginable freedom, just like a butterfly shedding its cocoon. However, Mrs Schwartz had a highly significant, if very bizarre role to play in Dr Kubler-Ross's own spiritual

▼ A corpse is prepared for a Hindu cremation. Rituals surrounding death ensure that the dying can accept the inevitable and the bereaved can find a natural outlet for their grief.

▲ The Greek god Orpheus celebrates his annual emergence from the Underworld of death, as did all the dying-and-rising gods of the ancient world, which coincides with Spring.

development and awareness later on. As Dr Kubler-Ross puts it matter of factly:

"*[Mrs Schwartz] died two weeks after her son was of age. She was buried ... and I'm sure I would have forgotten her if she had not visited me again.*"

About 10 months after that lady was dead and buried, Dr Kubler-Ross found herself wondering how to break it to her new seminar partner that she could no longer work with him. As she escorted him to the lift

(before returning to her office, which was on the same floor) she became desperate to explain the situation to him and grabbed him, saying, 'You're gonna listen'.

But he did not listen and this made her even more desperate. Then something distracted her attention; she saw a woman near the lift who she vaguely recognized, although there was something odd about her. As Dr Kubler-Ross says:

"*She was very transparent, but not transparent enough that you could see very much behind her...*"

The moment her partner entered the lift and was whisked away, the woman said, 'Dr Kubler-Ross, I had to come back. Do you mind if I walk

you to your office? It will only take two minutes.' And still Dr Kubler-Ross did not remember the woman's name! As she allowed herself to be escorted to her office by a semi-transparent woman, Dr Kubler-Ross was thinking of how she had often said to her schizophrenic patients that she knew they could see things that she couldn't. Now she said to herself, 'Elisabeth, I know you see this woman, but that can't be.'

It was the longest walk imaginable: all the while Dr Kubler-Ross was thinking 'I am both an observing psychiatrist and a patient.' She realized later that she had repressed the thought that her unusual companion was actually Mrs Schwartz come back from the dead.

Once in the office, the ghost told

her that she had come back to thank her (and a colleague) for what they had done for her, but also to urge her not to give up her work with the dying yet. But Dr Kubler-Ross was busy on a 'reality check', touching objects in the room to ensure she wasn't dreaming. They were all real, solid things, but the woman was still there, and now she was saying:

"Dr Ross, do you hear me? Your work is not finished. We will help you, and you will know when the time is right, but do not stop now. Promise?"

Thinking swiftly, Dr Kubler-Ross told her 'impossible' guest that the colleague she had mentioned had moved away, but would love to get a note from her. And then surely what must be one of the most remarkable things ever to happen in a doctor's office took place – the ghost wrote a note to be sent to this man, and it was signed 'Mrs Schwartz'. Once she had made Dr Kubler-Ross promise not to give up her work with the dying just yet, Mrs Schwartz vanished. Dr Kubler-Ross still has the note.

This was just the beginning of Dr Kubler-Ross's long quest for spiritual truth. She was a practising doctor who had begun as a sceptic and disbeliever. Over the years she was to have many paranormal and other experiences that were evidence for an afterlife, in which she now totally believes. She was to receive great enlightenment, but only at the cost of enormous personal suffering, as we will see, as if being tested to the utmost, and in the course of time she was even to have her own NDE, which proved to her that her patients had been telling the truth.

A far-reaching death

In 1943, George Ritchie, a 20-year-old private soldier in the US Army, fell desperately ill with double pneumonia and died. But as he was about to be taken to the morgue a sharp-eyed orderly noticed that the dead man's

---

NDE RESEARCHERS

In just three decades of investigative NDE research, our understanding of the phenomenon has come a long way, and the change in attitudes over the years is reflected in the titles of the books written about it. At first there were doctors, albeit with enormous compassion, such as Elisabeth Kubler-Ross and Raymond Moody. The titles of their ground-breaking works revealed a difference in emphasis. For Dr Kubler-Ross, whose everyday professional life was bound up with terminally ill patients, her lectures and seminars (from which she was to draw the material for her books) were given the unvarnished title *On Death and Dying*. But Raymond Moody, who was a philosopher by training, chose to stress the regenerative aspects of the NDE in his first book: *Life After Life*.

The titles of many of the first books on the subject reflect a new confidence in discussing the old taboo of death, and include Dr Grey's *Return from Death*, Ian Wilson's *The After Death Experience*, and Dr Maurice Rawlings's *Beyond Death's Door*.

But the new generation of NDE books are even more positive in tone, stressing the transformative power of the main element in most NDEs: encountering the light. These books include: Betty J. Eadie's *Embraced by the Light*; Dannion Brinkley's *Saved by the Light*; Cherie Sutherland's *Children of the Light*; Melvin Morse's *Closer to the Light* and his major study, *Transformed by the Light*. Significantly, many of the newer books have been written by those who have actually had an NDE and whose lives have been radically changed as a result.

---

arm twitched. At first it seemed as if he had been imagining things – the medical officer initially found no signs of life – but after the corpse had been given an injection of adrenaline straight into the heart, Ritchie came round. He made a complete recovery and qualified as a doctor, becoming a well respected psychiatrist with a practice in Virginia.

However, as far as his peers were concerned, there was a somewhat embarrassing problem with Dr Ritchie. He would not keep quiet about what he had experienced while dead. He talked of going towards a glorious light, and feeling indescribably peaceful and elated. Of course his fellow doctors preferred to ignore his story, and if they had to comment, they would always put the experience down to hallucination (despite the fact that it was a clinically dead man who was doing the alleged hallucinating!). Although Dr Ritchie gave many talks about his NDE, few in his own profession took him seriously, except one, who was to have a

profound influence on the way NDEs came to be understood by people the world over.

This was Raymond Moody, a young medical student. He was so impressed by Dr Ritchie's unwavering conviction about what had happened to him when he was dead that he set about investigating the topic of the NDE for himself. He soon discovered that, far from being some form of individual hallucination or one-off phenomenon, the NDE was extremely common among those who had been in life-threatening situations, but who had managed to return from the brink of death.

Raymond Moody's collection of NDEs was published in 1975 as *Life After Life*. The work contained a foreword by Dr Kubler-Ross, who in recommending the book to anyone 'with an open mind', wrote that, 'It is research such as Dr Moody presents in this book that will enlighten many and will confirm what we have been taught for 2000 years – that there is life after death ...'

Core experiences

All of Raymond Moody's respondents told a strikingly similar story, even though their personal brush with death may have come about in a variety of ways. Moody analyzed hundreds of NDEs and realized that the essential phenomenon, which was to become known as the 'core' experience, can easily be divided up into 15 'separate elements that recur again and again …'

In order to make his point, he presents the reader with a 'brief, theoretically "ideal" or "complete" experience, in the order in which it is typical for the stages to occur'. This is his 'ideal' NDE:

"A man is dying and, as he reaches the point of greatest physical distress, he hears himself pronounced dead by his doctor. He begins to hear an uncomfortable noise, a loud ringing or buzzing, and at the same time feels himself moving very rapidly through a long dark tunnel."

However, these are only the preliminary stages of the NDE. The reconstruction continues:

"After this, he suddenly finds himself outside of his own physical body, but still in the immediate environment, and he sees his own body from a distance, as though he is a spectator. He watches the resuscitation attempt from this unusual vantage point and is in a state of emotional upheaval.

After a while, he … becomes more accustomed to his odd condition … he still has a 'body', but one of a very different nature and with very different powers from the physical body he has left behind."

Once out of his body, other things begin to happen to the subject:

"Others come to meet and help him. He glimpses the spirits of relatives and friends who have already died, and a loving, warm spirit of a kind he has never encountered before - a being of light - appears before him. This being asks him a question, nonverbally, to make him evaluate his life and helps him along by showing him a panoramic, instantaneous playback of the major events in his life."

The panoramic life review may contain reminders of shameful or traumatic episodes, but it is shown to the person in a spirit of unconditional love and understanding. The being of light is not judging the person, rather encouraging him or her to judge him or herself. But then comes a shock:

"…[the man] finds himself approaching some sort of barrier or border, apparently representing the limit between earthly life and the next life. Yet, he finds that he must go back to the earth, that the time for his death has not yet come. At this point he resists, for by now he is taken up with his experiences in the afterlife and does not want to return. He is overwhelmed by intense feelings of joy, love and peace. Despite his attitude, though, he somehow reunites with his physical body and lives."

After returning to the physical body, those who have had an NDE find they wish to share their experiences with others, but have difficulty, not only because they cannot find the words to describe such an unparalleled experience, but also because they learn the hard way that others greet their stories with ridicule. Even so, their life from that time onwards is radically changed by the experience, especially concerning their views about death and the afterlife.

The stages

Raymond Moody discerned 15 stages characteristic of a classic NDE, although he was careful to point out that not one of his hundred or so respondents experienced all of them – the most anyone had was 12 stages . Neither did they always happen in the same order, although 'wide variations are unusual'. The main stages he listed are:

1. **Ineffability:** The impossibility of describing the experience, and the inadequacy of mere words. As one respondent said:

"Now, there's a real problem for me as I'm trying to tell you this, because all the words I know are three-dimensional … of course our world … is three-dimensional, but the next one definitely isn't …"

2. **Hearing the news:** Many people report hearing someone, often a doctor or nurse, saying that they are dead. One man (from a more recent British investigation) explains:

"I heard a horrible rusty sound coming out of my throat as if it belonged to someone else, and suddenly doctors and nurses came running from all directions and started work on me. One of them stood back and murmured 'He's gone. It's no use.' It took me a couple of seconds to realize what he meant and I wanted to get up and walk about to show him that I wasn't dead. But I couldn't move so much as an eyelid. Then they put the sheet over my face and went away."

3. **Feelings of peace and quiet:** Even though an individual may have died in extremely traumatic circumstances and suffered greatly, the moment of transition is typically pain free and peaceful (although, once again, respondents are at a loss to find the right words to describe the experience). A woman who was knocked down by a car, says:

"I felt a tremendous blow as the car hit me, but no actual pain. It

was more of a terrible shock. I was thrown high in the air, but never experienced coming back down to earth - although of course I did, and was pronounced dead as a result. It was as if I carried on going up into the sky, feeling lighter and lighter as I went. All shock left me. Instead there was a complete feeling of peace and wholeness, and a sense of it being right somehow."

4. **The noise:** A variety of inexplicable sounds have been reported by people who have had NDEs. Some of the sounds were not pleasant, although others were ineffably beautiful. Among the unpleasant noises are insistent buzzing or ringing sounds, clickings and bangings and wind like roaring. Since Dr Moody's early work, many have described experiencing a sound like 'Velcro being torn apart, or fabric being ripped' during an NDE, which may or may not be perceived as unpleasant. Similarly 'neutral' are sounds of bells ringing. At the other end of the scale, celestial music (perhaps the legendary 'music of the spheres') has been much reported, although it tends to come later in the experience. A young man who collapsed and died of a rare blood disorder said:

"*I immediately heard a loud click inside my head, which made me think something momentous was going to happen. It reminds me (thinking of it now) of someone flicking a switch. Maybe it was switching off my life, or switching on my death.*"

One of Dr Moody's respondents said:

"*I began to hear music of some sort, a majestic, really beautiful sort of music.*"

5. **The dark tunnel:** Sometimes simultaneously with the noise, during a NDE the person is drawn rapidly into a dark space, usually (but by no means exclusively) described as a 'tunnel'. Occasionally

▼ According to many reports the unseen drama of an NDE regularly takes place in ambulances on the way to hospital.

CASE STUDY: A LIFE OR DEATH DECISION

Betty Jo was rushed into hospital due to a miscarriage. Dangerously weak from loss of blood
and complications, she drifted into:

"*A misty world in which I floated very peacefully, without pain, fear or anxiety. The mist seemed to keep me afloat and caress me as if I was a baby again, and I loved it ... I seemed to float on to an island, which was covered in wonderful flowers of every possible hue, shape and size. I found myself on my feet and wandered around happily looking at the flowers and enjoying the tranquillity of it all. Then I sensed a presence, a very familiar entity whose name I couldn't quite recall, but who just poured love over me, into me, all around me. I could feel it healing all the hurt and fear that goes with being an ordinary human being. The presence drifted invisibly in front of me, show-ing me scenes from my life that sort of flashed before my eyes. I instantly understood what had gone wrong and how I could put it right, and something in me stirred. I wanted so much to stay on the island, but now I knew how to change my life for the better. As I thought that, I found myself confronted by a low stone wall. I knew I could easily climb over it, but that if I did I would die. The presence hovered, allowing me to make my own decision. I looked at the wall and thought of my husband and my two children, and all the people I'd wronged and wanted to make it up to. I shook my head and turned back, and that was when I found myself in my body.*"

it is called a 'funnel', a 'cave', a 'tube' – even a 'sewer'! Perhaps strangely in a society that tends to be frightened of complete darkness (city-dwellers often become unexpectedly terrified of their first encounter with the natural pitch blackness of a rural night), most who have NDEs recall this darkness as 'welcoming', 'utter bliss', 'like being stroked with velvet', although there are a few who were disorientated or even upset by it. As ever the experience is intensely subjective.

One American woman could only describe her experience in terms of a famous television series:

"*There was a feeling of utter peace and quiet, no fear at all, and I found myself in a tunnel - a tunnel of concentric circles. Shortly after that I saw a TV programme called* The Time Tunnel, *where people go back in time through this spiralling tunnel. Well, that's the closest thing to it that I can think of.*"

A British woman says:

"*It was, like, whoosh into blackness, which sounds somehow threatening. Well, believe me, it wasn't - quite the reverse! This darkness was like a long corridor* or tunnel through which I was being tugged at enormous speed. I could hear a roaring sound, maybe the wind, as I flew down this space ... I was very, very happy.*"

One of Dr Moody's respondents used a particularly evocative turn of phrase:

"*Suddenly, I was in a very dark, very deep valley. It was as though there was a pathway, almost a road, through the valley, and I was going down the path ... Later, after I was well, the thought came to me, 'Well, now I know what the Bible means by "the valley of the shadow of death", because I've been there.'*"

6. **Out of the body:** The crucial part of any NDE, when the individual realizes that this is no ordinary experience, is when they are separated from the body. The conscious, thinking part, the personality, is suddenly revealed as being quite different from the body. To the vast majority of people who have NDEs, this is an enormous, totally surprising revelation, for most people consider that they *are* their bodies. As Raymond Moody says, 'For many people it is an impossible task even to conceive of what it would be like to exist in any other way than in the physical body to which they are accustomed.' Unimaginably shocked to discover themselves very much alive but disembodied, the person can never be the same again, can never look at the material world as before, and can never view death with the same mixture of avoidance and fear as they did prior to the NDE. Yet despite the astonishing implicit drama of separating from the body, most who experience it describe it similarly to one woman, who said it was: 'perfectly natural, more so than being in my body ...' (As we will see in the next chapter, OBEs are surprisingly common, and can even be deliberately induced, with startling results.)

The dying person may observe the attempts to resuscitate their body, or may accompany it to hospital in the ambulance, often from a novel vantage point above it! But rarely is there any sense of panic, or even great involvement in the scene. As one of Dr Moody's female respondents said:

"*As I saw them [the medical staff]*

▶ Many who experience an NDE describe meeting beings of light, who some believe to be angels. However, very few report that they have the expected wings!

beating on my chest and rubbing my arms and legs, I thought, 'Why are they going to so much trouble? I'm just fine now.'

The person may feel as if he or she is 'watching a movie', or as if they are not meant to be there. As one young man said:

"I hung about my body, which looked ashen and forlorn with a sort of pity, as if it belonged to someone else. But that feeling soon passed and I began to feel as if I was a sort of voyeur. It was an uneasy sensation, which only disappeared as I got swallowed up in a gigantic feeling of comfort and bliss. But I will never forget becoming detached from my body and starting to feel as if it was wrong to be there with it at that stage."

An eight-year-old boy had an OBE which he later described in the following words:

"I felt like the inner part of me was ... up like a ghost and I felt like my inner body was going out ... of me and I felt like ... a dummy almost, that my body was a dummy and I was outside it."

Often the unaccustomed sight of one's own body is surprising:

"Boy, I sure didn't realize that I looked like that! You know, I'm only used to seeing myself in pictures or from the front in a mirror, and both of those look flat. But all of a sudden there I - or my body - was and I could see it. I could definitely see it, full view, from about five feet away. It took me a few moments to recognize myself."

During an OBE people characteristically feel 'light, free and happy' and find themselves 'hovering', 'bobbing along', 'floating' or 'flying'. Some are aware of being in a lighter version of their earthly body, whereas others are 'just thought, all mind'. Solid objects are soon discovered to present no barrier, and they can glide through them, like a ghost, which is precisely what they are! (Just like the Patrick Swayze character in the film *Ghost*, one individual admits to 'going through a wall a few times, just for the hell of it.') A little further experimentation reveals that he can go anywhere, more or less instantaneously, at more or less the speed of thought, and observe any scene accurately, as his later report reveals. It is

as if, with the shedding of the physical body, a sense of time disappears, too, so that the person is now free of both time and space.

7. **Meeting others:** According to the evidence of the NDE, nobody dies alone; the spirits of deceased relatives and friends come to protect and guide the newly dead, as described in Chapter 1, and in the story told above about the little girl who encountered her 'nonexistent' brother. These spirits bring with them feelings of complete peace and joy (although sometimes they later pass on the bad news that the person must return to life).

These 'welcoming parties' are occasionally sensed rather than seen, although they are usually so real that the dead person wonders why other people are oblivious to them. A radiant glow comes from these guiding souls, enveloping the deceased in love and light.

One 20-year-old woman said:

"I was standing by the hospital bed, already bored with my pasty-faced body, when I sensed someone new in the frame. I didn't have to turn round to look for them; as

---

CASE STUDY: 'THE DAY I DIED'

Ted was electrocuted one day in 1961 when he accidentally severed a water pipe with an electric drill.
He was amazed to discover he was 'dead'. He describes the event as follows:

"I think of it as 'the day I died', which amuses some people because they think you can't live to tell the tale. Well, I'm living proof that you can. It started off with a flash and a bang, and with me being thrown violently across the kitchen where I was doing some repairs to the plumbing. I hit the wall and from then on that thing lying on the floor wasn't me any more.

I was looking at it, my body, without much interest, really. Then I found I could float upwards and as I did so the ceiling sort of dissolved and I flew up through it. By then I'd started to have a holiday feeling – excited and happy and carefree, only much more so than you can imagine. The thought occurred to me that I must be dead, but to me that was nonsense because death is grim and

nasty and the end of everything. This was none of those things – it certainly wasn't the end!

Then I was pulled into a thick black darkness. No, not terrifying at all. Like some giant cuddly blanket all around me, comforting. I found myself flying fast through this black space towards a brilliant white light. Oh, and the feeling that went with it! I can't describe it. All the best things you've ever felt multiplied by a million. I looked at the light and the light looked at me, and we were the best of friends.

When I got there, I sort of floated on to a platform where there was a tall man in a white robe who I thought must be Jesus. I asked him if he was, and he just grinned and said, 'Whoever. What matters is you...'"

soon as I thought of them, there they were. It was my godfather, Ben, who had died 10 years before. We'd been very close - closer, if I'm honest, than my parents - and I had gone to pieces when he died. I'd never got over it. But there he was, shining with a sort of inner light. He was smiling his head off, not a trace of the terrible pain he'd suffered from at the end ... Funny, I say 'the end', but obviously it had only just been the beginning for him! ... Ben didn't say anything, but he didn't have to.

I knew he was here for me, to look after me, teach me about this new life. I knew with Ben there nothing could go wrong or harm me. I've never been so happy as I was at that moment. "

8. **The being of light:** Dr Moody describes how of all his respondents who described encountering a brilliant light, not one 'expressed any doubt whatsoever that it was a being, a being of light'. Although subsequent research has revealed a tendency to personify the light, in fact, there have been many more recent cases where it is simply described as the light. (The discrepancies between Dr Moody's findings and those of later research will be discussed in detail below.)

Dr Moody notes that this being of light is interpreted according to the 'religious background, training or beliefs of the person involved'. This is an important point, as later commen-

▲ **Jesus descends into Hell to help the damned. Does this describe a personification of the unconditional feeling of love that is reported by most people who have an NDE?**

tators, and a few who have actually had NDEs, have attempted to hijack this phase of the phenomenon to further their own missionary zeal. For example, one prominent British writer who makes no secret of the fact that he is a Catholic convert, gives the NDE a completely Christian gloss and uses it to prove the exclusive validity of his religion, even though there is ample evidence that the message of the NDE is that denominations and dogma are unwelcome in 'heaven'. What matters, as we will see, is unconditional love.

But clearly each person interprets

the being of light as the quintessence of love, goodness and justice. Obviously for a Christian this will be Jesus, but Jews have reported meeting an angel, and one modern pagan (see page 71) described the light as being the great god of light of the ancient Egyptians. And all of these people experienced the same intensity of unconditional love, no matter what their beliefs.

Whoever this entity is perceived as being, it addresses the individual in a nonverbal, telepathic form, which is again an experience that defeats most people when they try to describe it. One girl said:

"The being sort of flowed into my soul and I felt consumed with love and perfect understanding. Because that never happens when you've got a body - it can't because it's a barrier between you and true reality - I can't describe it. Imagine being a tiny child lost in a giant super-market then suddenly the crowds part and you see your mom with her arms held out and this big smile on her face. That gets some-where near what I'm trying to describe, but still stops quite a long way short. "

The being may ask if the person is ready to die and stay there, and often adds, 'What have you done with your life that is sufficient?' But it is stressed that this question is not asked in an intimidating or judgmental way; the point of the question appears to be to make the individual consider his or her life in terms of usefulness or service to others, or as a specific mission to be accomplished. One of Dr Moody's respondents described this encounter as follows:

" ... Yet, from the moment the light spoke to me, I felt really good - secure and loved. The love which came from it is just unimaginable, indescribable. It was a fun person to be with! And it had a sense of humour, too - definitely! "

9. **The review:** This encounter is only a preliminary stage, for the real purpose of this meeting with the being of light is to be shown a life review, a panoramic rewind of one's whole life so its failures and triumphs are understood; and one's effect on other people is illuminated, often for the first time. One man described his life review as 'a series of pictures: like slides. It was just like someone clicking off slides in front of me, very quickly.'

Dr Moody points out that although the review can only be described in terms of memory, it has 'characteristics which set it apart from any normal type of remembering'. It is at the same time extremely vivid and swift, encompassing a unique kind of clarity and emphasis. Some people describe it as being seen and comprehended holistically, so the entire chronology and its message is taken in at one glance. Every scene that presents itself is immediately and completely remembered and understood, and the emotions associated with the events are recalled in depth.

One woman remembers apparently insignificant events leaping out at her during her life review:

"Funny, I cringe now at the memory. But in the company of the being of light I took it all in without feeling embarrassed. Things I wouldn't have thought at all worth remembering ... how I interrupted someone at a certain dinner party and because of that they never got to pass on a piece of information that another guest needed to hear at that moment. Or how I often told lies about having flu or having a bad back to stay off work when in fact I had a hangover ... all the grubby little things that add up to making you less than you are supposed to be. Yet the being never once passed judgment on me either directly or indirectly. I got the impression he loved me no matter

what I'd done, but wanted me to see me as I really am. "

10. **The border or limit:** Of course all these cases are NDEs: the only reason that we know about them is that the person concerned did not remain dead, but came back and described the experience. And many of them tell of encountering a border, limit or barrier during their NDE that marked the moment when their fate was sealed, and they knew they must indeed return.

This may take many forms: a mist, a fence or wall, a line (visible or merely sensed), a body of water and so on, although once again it may be a matter of personal interpretation rather than an objective, shared reality. Perhaps the image that presents itself is intended to be symbolic.

One woman told Dr Moody how she was in a small ship, sailing for a far shore on which stood all her relatives who had died, beckoning her to join them. She was saying, 'No, no, I'm not ready to join you. I don't want to die. I'm not ready to go.' Although the ship nearly reached the shore, it turned round at the last minute, and the woman returned to the land of the living.

(Something very similar took place in an episode of the cult television series *The X Files*, when Agent Dana Scully nearly died in an intensive care unit: during her NDE she was seated in a boat that drifted, at the end of a mooring rope, towards a far shore. At one point the rope actually snaps, leaving the boat adrift and the viewers agog – does this mean she is dead? But her guardian angel in the form of a nurse calls her back from the near shore, and she is revived.)

11. **Coming back:** Dr Moody discusses two main reasons for a return to life: a decision on the part of the individual (based on the need to look after children or to

finish some work), or being sent back by God/the being of light for similar reasons. The deeper an individual goes into the experience, the less likely they are to want to come back! In fact, many report that they pleaded to be allowed to stay. One man said:

"The angel said, 'You must go back' and I couldn't believe it. I begged and pleaded to be allowed to stay. The thought of being clogged up with a body again was infinitely depressing, appalling ... But already the angel seemed to be fading away, saying: 'Sharon needs you'. Then in an instant I realized that I had a responsibility. Sharon is my wife, who's crippled with multiple sclerosis. As soon as I realized that, I was back in my body, fighting for life."

Others are told to return in order to finish their mission, which frequently involves a certain amount of learning. Some have it spelt out to them that they must acquire specific knowledge, and as we shall see they often become zealous students on recovery from their experience.

Dr Moody also noted, almost in passing, that the grief-stricken prayers of family and friends can apparently call the dying back to life. One dying woman, who had already experienced the other side in an NDE, told her niece to stop praying for her recovery, as 'your prayers are holding me over here'. The family stopped praying, and their aunt died peacefully.

Of course there are problems with this consideration: what happens when even the most heartfelt prayers of untold numbers of people fail to bring their loved one back? For example, in 1952 the spiritual leader of Argentina, Eva Perón (on whom the musical movie *Evita* is based), was known to be dying of cancer at the age of 32. Hundreds of thousands of Argentinians, who all adored her, stood in the pouring rain for days to

pray that she might be restored to health. But she died, and shortly afterwards the country was plunged into chaos as a result.

If prayers can heal and keep loved ones on the earth, even against their will, what went wrong in the case of Eva Perón? Perhaps this is an example of how difficult it is to extract 'rules' from the mass of material about NDEs.

▲ If heartfelt prayers can, as some people who have had NDEs claim, prevent loved ones from dying, why did the Argentinian first lady, Eva Perón, die of cancer?

13. **Telling others:** Telling others today is less of a problem than it was when Raymond Moody and Elisabeth Kubler-Ross began their work in the late 1960s. Thanks to the publicity surrounding the publication of *Life*

After Life (although it was a mixed blessing, as we will see), those who have an NDE today are more likely to encounter a sympathetic and understanding ear. But even today the majority of medical workers tend to dismiss NDEs as 'hallucinations', either drug induced or the result of oxygen starvation, so there is little wonder that those who have had them have soon learnt the hard way not to confide their experiences to too many people in white coats. Besides the obvious fear of ridicule, many are wary of sharing their experience with others because they see it as too intensely personal and precious to do so. As one woman put it:

"What I'd seen was for my eyes only. It was all about my life and my death and my relationship with God. It's impossible to put into words and anything I managed to say about it would have been less than perfect. I didn't want to sully my memory of it by putting it into words."

14. **Effects on lives:** When Raymond Moody published his findings he noted that no one was likely to get on a podium and preach about an NDE, due to the extreme reticence described above. However, since then several people who have had the experience have written and publicized books that do proselytize about the subject without any fear of ridicule. Indeed, in some circles, such as the New Age community, NDEs are now common conversational currency, which is something that was literally unthinkable when *Life After Life* was first published.

Other researchers were to concentrate on the effects on lives, or aftermath aspect of the NDE, notably Dr Melvin Morse of Seattle, whose work is discussed in depth later. His discovery of the lasting power of NDEs is explicit in the title of his 1992 book (co-written with Paul Perry)

Transformed by the Light.

But even in the early days, no one who knew someone well who had died and come back to life could ever say they were the same. Remember, these people could personally verify the existence of the human soul and the unimportance of the body. They had walked with angels (in some cases with God himself), had seen their past and sometimes into the future. They had passed beyond the fearsome final frontier and discovered there never had been anything to be afraid of. They had also, they believe, discovered the great secret, which is simply to love and respect all life no matter what outward form it takes. All that changes a person.

15. **Corroboration:** Raymond Moody discusses the objective evidence for the NDE, including reported conversations overheard while out of the body that later were checked and discovered to be accurate. This aspect of the NDE is discussed in Chapter 7.

His book was an unexpected, massive bestseller on both sides of the Atlantic, and suddenly the NDE became a hot issue, from the lurid pages of the tabloid press to sophisticated dinner parties. This did not mean that Dr Moody's work was greeted with acclaim by his scientific peers. Dr Kubler-Ross had warned in her Foreword that he must prepare himself for ridicule and hardship and in some ways this fame was a mixed blessing. Dr Moody was worried that:

"Some of the sensational claims which were made ... might have the effect of frightening off legitimate investigators from an area which I continue to believe has a profound significance for clinical medicine and human psychology."

However, as events soon showed, his anxiety was, on the whole, unjustified.

'I don't believe it'

NDE research has been dependent on an extraordinary chain of synchronistic events that brought together a handful of key people. Another young doctor who was drawn into this field was the initially very sceptical Michael Sabom, a cardiologist whose reaction to a talk about Raymond Moody's book, given by psychiatric social worker Sarah Kreutzinger, was 'I don't believe it'. But urged by the speaker to conduct his own informal survey, he began to ask newly resuscitated patients if they had any strange experiences to share with him. Imagine his utter amazement when just the third person he asked described an NDE that matched those in *Life After Life* almost perfectly! As Dr Sabom says:

"At the conclusion of the interview I had the distinct feeling that what this woman had shared with me that night was a deep personal glimpse into an aspect of medicine of which I knew nothing."

Impressed as much as anything else by the patient's unequivocal sincerity, Dr Sabom was determined to look further into this mysterious human experience. He began a distinguished second career as an NDE researcher, which led to the publication in 1982 of his *Recollection of Death: A Medical Investigation.*

Another cardiologist who became interested in the NDE as a result of talking to a newly resuscitated patient was Dr Maurice Rawlings of Chattanooga Diagnostic Center, Tennessee.. But his work, published as *Beyond Death's Door* in 1978, was to prove so controversial among NDE researchers that many still refuse to accept it. As we will see in Chapter 6, if the classic NDE can be seen as a visit to heaven, Rawlings uncovered evidence of OBEs in which people went to hell and back.

Another American medical man who was to become prominent among NDE researchers was Dr Kenneth

Ring, Professor of Psychology in Storrs, Connecticut. He interviewed over a hundred patients who had been near death, the results of which appeared in his major work, *Life at Death: A Scientific Investigation of the Near-Death Experience* (1980). He in turn was to provide inspiration for one of the emerging non-American researchers in this field, the British psychologist Dr Margot Grey, whose initial interest in the subject, however, came about as a result of her own NDE. Her book, *Return from Death*, was published in 1985.

Other prominent British researchers include David Lorimer, whose sterling work has helped to establish the highly influential International Association for Near Death Studies (IANDS), and Dr Peter Fenwick of the London Institute of Psychiatry, whose exciting experiments with potential NDE cases are discussed in Chapter 9.

From its early beginnings as a mainly Anglo-Saxon preoccupation, near-death studies have now spread throughout most of the world, and new insights into the phenomenon continue to be added. For example, in Zambia Dr Nsama Mumbwe – inspired by Dr Melvin Morse's book *Closer to the Light* (1992) – began her research with 15 local people who had had NDEs, none of whom could have invented their stories, and all of whom described experiences that were remarkably similar to those of the West. However, what was fascinating was the very different interpretation the Africans put on their NDEs, as we will see. Other major studies have been undertaken in many countries, including Japan, China and Australia.

Dr Moody muses

In his *Life After Life*, Dr Moody had mused about the reality of the OBE, and the corroborative evidence it often produced in the form of accurate and very detailed information about distant people and places. In a semi-serious aside he says:

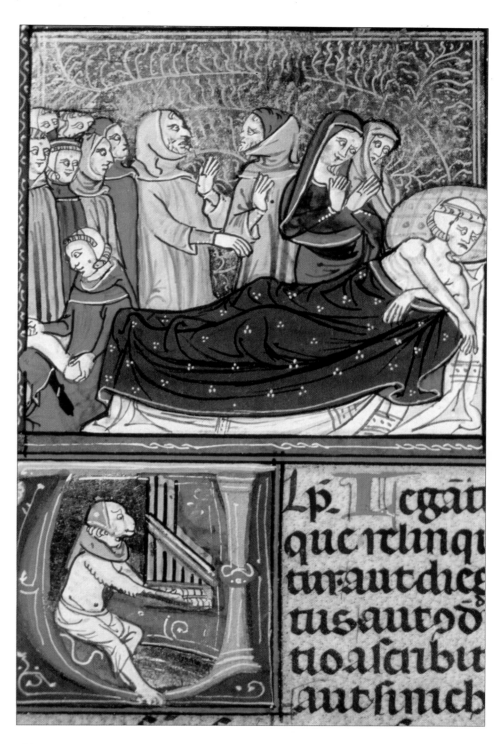

"A person in the spiritual body is in a privileged position in relation to the other persons around him. He can see and hear them, but they can't see or hear him. (Many a spy would consider this an enviable condition ...)"

Little did he realize that, more or less at the same time as he was conducting his survey of NDEs, some hard-headed groups were making use of

▲ A dying medieval man dictates his will. In today's society, few people accept their imminent death, and therefore fail to prepare financially, emotionally and spiritually, for it.

this 'enviable condition' – induced OBEs *were* being used in espionage! This was no science fiction, but deeply disturbing fact. At least a side effect of this sinister use of the ability to leave the body was the best proof yet that these things really happen.

CHAPTER THREE

The Living Ghost

The evidence suggests that during the NDE and at death itself the spirit separates from the body and enters another dimension of reality that is normally invisible and unknown. This OBE can also happen under other circumstances – in dreams, hypnosis, during surgery or other periods of unconsciousness.

Some OBEs can even occur spontaneously for no apparent reason. They can also be deliberately induced through the taking of drugs (although those experiences may be significantly different from OBEs that arise in other ways).

OBEs are what happens when the consciousness or awareness – the 'soul' – separates from the body and views it from an unusual perspective, often from above. The person will continue to hear and see in the normal way, but without physical ears or eyes, and may experience both normal reality and that of another spirit realm.

Alan Gauld, in his *Mediumship and Survival* (1983), which was published on behalf of the Society for Psychical Research (SPR), writes:

"OBEs are surprisingly common: different surveys have yielded somewhat differing results, but all in all I think that one would not be too far wrong if one said that somewhere between one person in

◀ **The ancient Egyptian goddess Isis was a central figure in a religion that celebrated and prepared for eternal life. Its followers believed the afterlife consisted of a series of exciting adventures.**

10 and one person in 20 is likely to have had such an experience at least once ... "

The very term 'out-of-the-body' implies that something other than the body exists in order to leave it. This spirit body has always been recognized by mystics and others of many religions and cultures: to the ancient Egyptians it was the 'Ka' or 'Ba', while to the Christian or Jew it was simply the soul. Until recently animism – a belief in the soul, from the Greek *anima*, or breath – was prevalent in the West, but the materialistic twentieth century created such an atmosphere of scepticism that to many people today the very existence of an intangible self is questionable. After all, seeing is believing, and if something cannot be seen then it is unlikely to exist.

However, those who have had an NDE have discovered for themselves the reality of the soul, even though they may have been total sceptics before. The lives of many of these people originally had been based on the assumption that the material world and the physical body represented the limits of existence. All that was to change after their visit to the other side of death's door.

'Just fancy dress'

Twenty-six-year-old Alan, originally a motorcycle courier from Wolverhampton, had always regarded the idea of the soul with a vehement scepticism that bordered on disgust. He says:

"To me spirits and life after death was complete nonsense. I'd make myself switch off during funerals because all that talk of heaven made me want to vomit. As far as I was concerned, what you see is what you get. When you died that was that. Gone for ever. How could you have any more experiences when your brain had decomposed? Ashes to ashes and dust to dust and that was the end of it. "

However, Alan was forced to confront what was, to him, an unimaginable experience, which was to change the way he viewed life after death for ever:

"I was zipping through the traffic on my Yamaha one dark and rainy March morning in 1986, my head full of football as usual, when a truck slithered across the road in front of me. I tried to manoeuvre round it but I was going too fast and suddenly the bike went one

way and I went the other. I hit the road with an almighty thud and a massive pain shot up my shoulder. I skidded in front of a car and there was a screech of brakes and a tremendous blow. Then there was a loud popping sound close to my ears.

What happened next was very, very ordinary. Or so it seemed. No trumpets or angels or demons. I was just standing there in the road, looking around. I felt nothing in particular. If anything, I felt free of pain and happy, although to be honest this is what I think about that moment now, looking back. At the time I was just me as usual, standing in the road.

Then I noticed something. It was a twisted body in biker's gear lying more or less at my feet. He had blood on his face and people were gathering round. The truck had stopped at an angle across the road, and the driver was with the others, explaining that it wasn't his fault. I had no particular feeling, except I was interested in what was going on. But suddenly it hit me that the guy on the ground was me. I can't tell you how I felt about that. You'd expect I would be horrified or frightened or confused, but I wasn't. Once I'd seen it, I was vaguely interested, but almost immediately began to want to wander off. My own body just wasn't that interesting any more - imagine that!

I thought I must be dead. There was no other explanation for not being there ... in my body, and I began to feel sort of lightheaded and happy. Straightaway I rose up into the air, and saw the whole scene from above. I saw the ambulance arrive and the paramedics start work on that guy in torn leathers who just happened to be me. And even when they rushed me into the vehicle and drove off fast, sirens blaring, I just couldn't be less interested.

Without warning I was in a field with the sun warm on my face. It was a real field with real sun. Get that straight ... I've had drug trips and they just weren't in this class ... This was very different. I was happy just to wander around looking at the flowers. There was some music, I don't know what, but it was just beautiful. In those days I was a heavy metal fan, but it wasn't a bit like that, I can tell you! But it wasn't like any classical music I've ever heard either. I was totally happy just to wander in the field for ever. Then I saw a couple of guys in long cloaks with hoods, but they weren't a bit spooky. I felt I really wanted to go over and say 'hello' and as soon as I thought it I was by their side. They talked to me although I couldn't see their faces. It was a mind thing. Mind to mind. I just knew what they meant. One of them told me I had to go back, and I couldn't believe it. I just crumbled. I begged them to let me stay, but they said no, go back.

The last thing I saw of that brilliant place was their heads, real as anything, nodding at me and the sun shining like it never shines here. It just made me ecstatic to be there, with them like that. But suddenly I was on a stretcher in the casualty ward with doctors doing things that hurt and being frantic about me. It felt awful, all of it, but especially being back.

I'd broken my leg, dislocated my shoulder and had concussion besides lots of bad cuts and bruises. I was pretty out of it for a couple of days. But after that I started to think about my experience. I had an instinct that I shouldn't tell just anybody about it. I didn't really mind being laughed at, but I thought my experience was somehow precious. I didn't want people demeaning it with their ridicule, or even not bothering to try to understand it. In the end, I mentioned it to the woman who brought library books around - I don't know why, but it was a good choice because she knew all about NDEs. She got me Raymond Moody's book and after I read it I realized what had happened to me. Even though I don't think I had clinically died or even been in danger of dying, I'd had an NDE. It made me glow inside to know that I wasn't alone, and how all those other people felt about their

SPIRITUAL BELIEFS IN ANCIENT EGYPT

The Egyptians believed that each individual had several spirit bodies besides the physical one, each with its own specific tasks. The two major ones were called the Ka and the Ba. Neither is exactly similar to our concept of the soul, but of the two it is the latter that shares the most characteristics with it.

The Ka equates more or less with the mystics' etheric double, whose task it is to stay with the physical body and protect it. Although it could rove around, the Ka was believed to inhabit tombs for as long as the physical body existed. Of course, mummification meant that this subtle body had an extended tour of duty. It was the Ka that wreaked vengeance on grave robbers, causing the 'mummy's curse' to come horrifyingly true.

It was also the Ka that separated during OBEs, and which enjoyed out-of-the-body adventures during sleep and unconsciousness. Special dream temples were visited by the sick, where they were put to sleep by a mixture of drugs and hypnosis and their Ka was freed to discover how to rid themselves of their ailment. The Ka's travels in a variety of other colourful dimensions were also believed to enable priests to discover ancient wisdom direct from the gods themselves.

experiences. Most of them had had their lives turned around by their NDE, and I was no different.

I'd gone from being an atheist – a biker whose idea of a good time was a home win on a Saturday and who thought when you were dead that was it – to being, well, completely different. I was a man with a mission. I came back from the other side knowing that even my life had a purpose and that wonderful angelic beings really cared about me ... I felt as if I had the secret of the universe inside my memory. There's no two ways about it. Our bodies are just a sort of fancy dress. We hand them in when we die and get on with the real stuff. I can't wait. **"**

Alan was so profoundly changed by his NDE that he abandoned all his previous interests and friends, eventually settling in the west of England where he now helps to run a New Age bookshop that specializes in mystical experiences. But to him the single most important thing about his NDE was the basic fact that it could happen. As he says:

"*If you'd have told me before ... that I was going to leave my body lying on the road and not care, and zip off to spend the happiest time of my life as a spirit, I'd have sent for the men in white coats to have you put away. But it happened to me and it wasn't a fantasy and it wasn't a dream. Going out of the body is a sort of reflex action when you're badly hurt, or of course if you're really dying. The real us is only attached to our bodies by the thinnest of threads, and there's nothing to be afraid of when it finally snaps. It's life that's the scary thing, not death.* **"**

Escape of the soul

OBEs have been reported for centuries, although the terms used may differ according to the prevailing culture and personal expectations. The

▲ A South Seas shaman. All tribal shamans can visit other realms in their spirit bodies, returning with the secret of using plants and spells to heal others.

ancient Egyptians believed in the existence of a series of spirit bodies, each of which had at least the potential for a life independent of the body (see page 46). And shamans – the wise men (and sometimes women) of many tribes, from Siberia to the Amazon basin – travelled to another realm in their spirit body in order to be taught which herbs to use in heal-

ing, where to move the tribe to avoid draught or find the best hunting.

Mystics, such as the Spanish St John of the Cross, have described how the soul can flee from physical

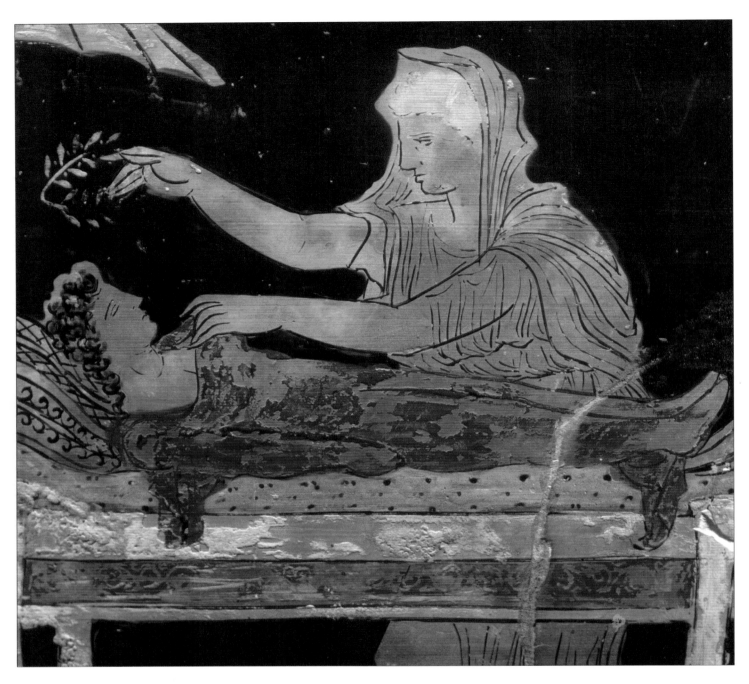

▲ The ancient Greek Mysteries included the use of dream temples. Here people left their bodies to experience otherworldly wisdom, and to be restored in mind and body

trauma, temporarily removing all sensations of pain. Repeatedly tortured by being crammed into a tiny cell for long periods without food or water, St John of the Cross's soul often escaped, flying over high mountain ranges, accompanied by a great rushing sound of wind and a sense of exultation and freedom. Other fortunate people, including the World War II heroine, British Intelligence Officer Odette Churchill VC, have been saved from the full trauma of torture by spontaneous, or even deliberately induced OBEs.

Certain Buddhist practices, involving meditation and visualization, are also designed to remove the consciousness to a point beyond the body in order to lessen either physical or emotional pain. As we have seen, it is said that the so-called heretics of thirteenth-century south-western France, the Cathars (or Albigensians), met their martyrdom by flaming pyre with equanimity – even, according to some sources, actual joy. This was because they were routinely taught a Buddhist-like practice that released the soul prematurely, while the body was apparently suffering slow death by fire.

One such escapee from the horrors of the physical world was Ed Morrell, whose time in the Arizona State Penitentiary in the early years of the twentieth century was marked by repeated sessions of torture during which he was trussed up in a double straitjacket over which water was poured so that it gradually shrank. Morrell said this was like 'being slowly squeezed to death', but fortunately his agonies were spared on several occasions because the torture had the effect of releasing his soul. This may sound like an extreme case of wishful thinking, but there was clearly more to it than that. Later, many of his astral encounters proved to have really taken place. He had even met the woman whom he later married.

Throughout time, many people have believed that the astral body automatically separates from the body while we are asleep, and that our remembered dreams are garbled versions of real OBE adventures. The ancient Egyptians and Greeks encouraged the sick to sleep in specially constructed dream temples, where their freed astral selves were believed to meet with healers (or even the gods themselves) on the astral plane, or perhaps they simply would have dreams that would give the temple priests information about how best to help them. The cream of the Egyptian initiates underwent three-day OBE journeys as they slept in the temples, similar to the drug-induced trips of tribal shamans, during which they claimed that they discovered great secrets.

The crisis apparition

Most, but not all, NDEs begin with a distinct OBE, which appears to be a kind of automatic reflex action, when the individual is faced with a life-threatening trauma. The physical crisis propels the soul out of the body, with a sense of awareness, viewing the world for the first time from an entirely different perspective.

For the most part the OBE/NDE remains intensely subjective, but some of these experiences have actually had witnesses. The first of these categories is the crisis apparition, where an individual is seen by others, often many miles away, at the point of death. There are dozens of such stories on record, not surprisingly many from World War I, when

virtually a whole generation of young men were wiped out. A variation on an often-repeated theme is the following story, recounted by a 90-year-old Yorkshire woman in 1968:

▲ Into the underworld. The ancient Mystery schools created a nightmare world for their initiates to confront, as did some Eastern religions whose view of hell seems similar.

"*My brother Albert was away fighting in the trenches in Flanders in 1916, and we hadn't heard a word about him for about six weeks. It was a terrible time, the worry really got you down, but you had to keep going doing ordinary things. I was in the scullery one morning washing some dishes, not thinking of anything much. There was nobody else in the house. Suddenly I heard the front door go [open] and the sound of a man, like, scraping his boots on the front step. My heart started thudding as if it couldn't stop because*

it was exactly the noise that our Bert used to make when he came in. I rushed to the hall and nearly dropped down in a faint because there he was, white as a sheet, his uniform all covered in muck and blood coming from a big hole in his head all down one side of his face. He seemed odd, sort of vacant. He just looked at me and said, 'Oh, our Maud. Get us a cup of tea, I'm so tired.' I never thought to give him a hug or a kiss – I just flew into the kitchen and put the kettle on. But when I went into the back room to see him he wasn't there. I looked everywhere, calling his name for

▲ World War I gave rise to many accounts of crisis apparitions, where dying soldiers appeared to their relatives at home at the very moment of their death in the trenches.

hours, but there was nobody there. I was so overcome and confused I just lay on my bed and cried and cried. I knew something awful had happened to him. "

Days later Maud received a telegram from the London War Office, informing her that Albert had been killed at exactly the time she had seen and talked to his apparition. As was the custom during World War I, Albert's commanding officer wrote to the family that 'he was shot cleanly through the heart and could have felt no pain'.

Later, however, Albert's best friend, who survived the trenches, told Maud that her brother had been shot in the head, exactly where his ghost had been wounded.

Of course, this and dozens of similar stories are merely anecdotal, and may have become distorted over the years. Crisis apparitions even became something of an urban myth during World War I, and superficially it might appear that any value they might possess is of interest only to psychologists and folklorists.

There are alternative explanations: perhaps Maud's longing to hear some news of her brother was so intense that it created this apparently real hallucination, in which she saw and talked with him. Perhaps she heard a

sound that her mind transformed into the characteristic noise of Bert coming home. Perhaps the entire story was a fabrication for some reason of her own, a moment of glory or a backhanded attempt to bestow on her brother, whose tragically shortened life was otherwise destined to go unremarked by the wider world, some recognition or individuality.

Yet none of these alternative explanations fits the case satisfactorily. Certainly Maud did not fabricate the story in order to get attention or fame, because she waited over 30 years to share it with anyone beyond her own family. And if she had indeed created a story to bestow some glory on poor Bert, why not invent some rousing or poignant speech to have

W.G.WATS

his apparition utter, or some description of a last, heroic action? Instead, it was a story that went nowhere about a man who said nothing except ask for a cup of tea. Its very pointlessness argues against it being a deliberate invention.

However, it is harder to explain away the hallucination hypothesis, except to cite the coincidental detail about the head wound. That, of course, could have been grafted on to the story at a later date. Now that Maud herself and all her immediate family are dead, there is no way of ever discovering the truth. But it is just one such story among many: the SPR has collected hundreds of similar anecdotes over the years, and therefore – as what might well be a major part of human experience – they are worthy of at least a temporary suspension of disbelief. And in the context of other similar cases, this story is entirely plausible.

It is said that the spirit body can travel anywhere instantaneously, just by thinking of it: shot in the head,

dying or perhaps even dead, Bert's last mortal thought may well have been the image of himself arriving home and asking Maud for a cup of tea. Already undergoing the process of separation, his astral body obeyed his desire, and for a short time he made his last wish come true, before disappearing from sight for ever.

Perchance to dream

Mystics and psychics have long believed that the astral body flies free during sleep, although most people ascribe the stuff of dreams to the chemical changes of sleep on the brain, to a sort of film show of random and meaningless images that prepares the brain for the demands of another day. Yet there is evidence that something very strange can and often does happen to the sleeping mind, which may be the result of genuine OBEs during sleep.

The most compelling evidence for this arises from the so-called reciprocal cases, where an OBE was in some way witnessed by another

▲ According to researcher Sylvan Muldoon, this is how the astral body disengages from the physical self during OBEs, although it remains connected by an 'elastic' silver cord.

person. One such case was reported to the American Society for Psychical Research (ASPR) in May 1957 by 26-year-old Martha Johnson from Plains, Illinois. She described a dream she had had just before awakening on the morning of the 27 January 1957, in which she had floated the 1491km (926 miles) to her mother's home in Minnesota. She says:

After a little while I seemed to be alone going through a great blackness. Then all at once way down below me, as though I were at a great height, I could see a small bright oasis of light in a vast sea of darkness. I started on an incline towards it as I knew it was the teacherage [school house] where my mother lives ... After I entered, I leaned up against the dish cupboard with folded arms, a pose I often assume. I looked at my mother who was bending over something white and doing something with her hands. She did not appear to see me at first, but she finally looked up. I had a sort of pleased feeling and then after standing a second more, I turned and walked about four steps. "

She awoke from her dream at 2.10 a.m. Illinois time (1.10 a.m. in Minnesota). Her mother wrote her own version of this event in two letters, the first of which was dated 29 January, just two days afterwards:

" *I believe it was Saturday night, 1.10 a.m., 26 January or maybe the 27th. It would have been 10 after two, your time. I was pressing a blouse here in the kitchen ... I looked up and there you were by the cupboard just standing smiling at me. I started to speak*

and you were gone. I forgot for a minute where I was. I think the dogs saw you too. They got so excited and wanted out, just like they thought you were by the door, sniffed and were so tickled. Your hair was combed nice, just back in a pony tail with the pretty roll in front. Your blouse was neat and light - seemed almost white. "

Martha Johnson confirmed that she had been 'got up' with her hair and clothes as her mother saw her when she 'travelled' that night (although presumably she had not actually gone to bed wearing a blouse and a pony tail).

Louis, from Chicago, discovered in the late 1970s that he had lucid dreams, where the sleeper realizes he is dreaming and can actually control the content of the dream. At first he contented himself with creating exciting epic adventures, becoming his own James Bond character and indulging himself with very realistic scenarios in which he always out-manoeuvred the baddies and always got the girl! But after a while one or two of his real-life friends began to arrive in his lucid dreams, who were clearly not part of the film show, and often just as disorientated and confused as if they really had accidentally strayed on to the set of a movie. Eventually he abandoned the fun to talk to them, and they began to hold long conversations about a range of topics. 'This is real, you know,' his friend Kathy said in a dream. 'I'll prove it to you. I'm not in Canada like you think, but I came back early. I'll meet you in the Tower Cafe at 11 tomorrow morning.'

On waking Louis wrote down every detail of his dream, and noted he had agreed to this meeting, although he believed Kathy really was away in Canada. Yet when he walked by the restaurant the next day there she was, and her first words were 'Now, why am I not surprised to see you?' She had no conscious memory of taking part in his lucid dream, nor of making any arrangement on the astral plane, but clearly some remnant of it had lodged in her unconscious mind and driven her to the right place at the right time.

Dream dialogues

The implications of such dream communication are far-reaching, and certainly appear to reinforce the idea that some part of the consciousness actually separates from the body during sleep. There have been several research projects that experimented with the possibilities of dream dialogues. In the early 1970s, American psychologist Joe Friedman became fascinated with the research that British anthropologist Pat Noone carried out in the remote highlands of the Malay Peninsula in the 1930s. Whereas most of the tribes Noone encountered in that area were blood-thirsty and violent, the Temiar Senoi were peaceful and contented – 'the happy people' as he called them.

AUTHOR EMILY BRONTE'S OBE

The Victorian vicar's daughter whose genius gave the world *Wuthering Heights* led a life of dramatic contrast. During the day Emily Bronte was a gauche tomboy who strode the moors alone in all weathers, returning to supervise the household chores.

But by night, even after putting aside her secretly scribbled novel about the dark passion of Heathcliff and Cathy, she entered another world. For Emily's most private writings reveal her as a mystic, whose many OBEs – whether spontaneous or induced we will never know – swept her away into rapture. The bliss of an OBE, and the pain of its ending, are described in these verses, taken from *Julian M. and A.G. Rochelle* (9 October 1845):

But first a hush of peace, a soundless calm descends;
The struggle of distress and fierce impatience ends;
Mute music soothes my breast – unuttered harmony
That I could never dream till earth was lost to me.

Then dawns the Invisible, the Unseen its truth reveals;
My outward sense is gone, my inward essence feels —
Its wings are almost free, its home, its harbour found;
Measuring the gulf it stoops and dares the final bound!

Oh dreadful is the check – intense the agony
When the ear begins to hear and the eye begins to see;
When the pulse begins to throb, the brain to think again
The soul to feel the flesh and the flesh to feel the chain.

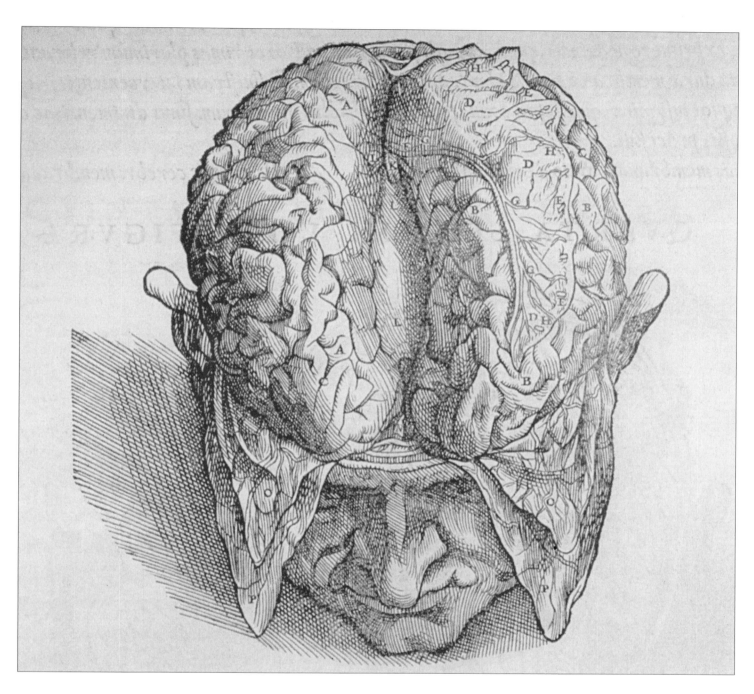

Together with American psychologist Kilton Stewart, he went to live with the tribe to discover their secret.

To their surprise, it was the tribe's attitude to dreams that lay behind their idyllic lifestyle. The Temiar Senoi devoted several hours every morning to sharing their dreams with each other, and talking through their content and meaning. They had developed a sophisticated system for analyzing and utilizing their dreams: for example, children were encouraged to become lucid dreamers in order to confront nightmare pur-

suers. In subsequent dreams these hostile figures became friends, even allies, of the child, and this wisdom was reflected in the everyday life of the tribe.

The Temiar Senoi also used dreams in order to contact the spirits of the natural world. The spirit of the river might tell them where best to catch fish, or the spirit of the forest might reveal where to find the most plentiful hunting.

These people believed that their spirits left their bodies during sleep, and also that the dead could use the

▲ The right half of the brain is said by some to govern all psychic and creative abilities. Does this include the heavenly visions of the NDE? As yet, very little is known about the mechanism involved.

dream time to appear to the living. In effect, the time spent dreaming provided a temporary bridge for two-way traffic to the afterlife. One shaman described to Noone and Stewart how his dead wife had come to him in a dream. He challenged her to prove her identity, believing she could have been a spirit impersonating his wife, but she told him she would give him a dance with which he could heal the sick, and if he performed it correctly a wooden box she had been buried with would appear in the hut. The dance was performed, suddenly a cold breeze swept through the hut, and a box materialized in thin air and fell to the ground. There were many witnesses to this, and the shaman told the story as a matter of fact. It was clear he was not intending to mislead anyone.

Theoretically it makes sense that the dead can impinge on our reality when the noise of everyday life is stilled, and the intuitive, psychic right hemisphere of the brain takes over from the logical and intellectual left half. Relatively little is known for certain about how the brain works – no one has ever been able to discover where memories are stored, for example – and the understanding of the left/right brain functions is still in its infancy. It may be that the membrane that separates one half from the other is more than a metaphor for the so-called veil that obscures the world of spirit from the living – it may do so in a very real way.

Yet Friedman and others were not so concerned with the use of dreams as a form of mediumship, as with creating a telepathic field so that the living could communicate, mind to mind, while dreaming. In London in the early 1970s, Friedman led an experimental group of people aged between 20 and 50 in an attempt to understand the potential of these dream dialogues.

One member of the group, Bill, described standing in a circle with a magician, who reminded him of Tom, another member of the group. 'Tom' told him that he was an 'H' or 'K'. That same night Tom dreamt that he was working in a post office, alphabetically sorting parcels.

The sceptic, of course, has three main explanations for such apparently telepathic communication: deliberate fraud, coincidence, or false memory syndrome. In this case, the protocols of the experiment, where the individual's dreams were first described to Friedman, effectively ruled out collusion in any normal sense, and also made false memory unlikely. And although coincidence is not impossible, the fact that this was only one of many similar dream dialogues recorded by Friedman and others, makes it unlikely.

However, the difference between this case and the story of the shaman's dream of his wife is that in the latter there was a physical factor involved: the materialization of the wooden box, which had been promised in the dream. Bill and Tom's interaction was purely on a mental level, but the tribesman had something solid to show for his dream. The annals of psychical research prove that belief and expectancy create phenomena, and the greater the expectations the more dramatic the results (see the Philip Experiment, page 154). The tribesman had no doubts at all about the power of dream dialogues, whereas the London group were hampered by their own sophistication, the caution imposed by the experimental protocol and the need for proof.

Testing the gift

Many gifted psychics have offered their talents for scientific scrutiny, although this has not always been an easy or a harmonious partnership. One of the most famous of these experimental subjects was US businessman Robert Monroe, who discovered he could induce OBEs at will.

HOW TO INDUCE AN OBE

Robert Monroe passed on his own vast experience of the OBE state through seminars and books. This is the simplified Monroe Method for achieving a safe OBE:

• Choose a warm, dark and quiet room. Lie down comfortably, headpointing north.

• Relax both body and mind by breathing regularly with your mouth slightly open.

• Fix your focus on one simple image as you become drowsy.

• Go deeper into relaxation by focussing on the blackness beyond your eyelids.

• To induce the vibrations that begin the OBE, concentrate on a point roughly 30cm (12in) beyond your forehead, extending it to about 2m (6ft). Visualize a line parallel to your body and imagine the vibrations beginning under it. Make them drop down into your head.

• Control the vibrations by making them flow through your body, first one way, then the other. Once you can make them do what you want, you are ready to separate from your body.

• Simply focus on the pleasurable idea of floating upwards, and your astral self will follow your thoughts.

• To return to your body, all you have to do is want to re-engage, and it will happen.

Monroe was already middle-aged when he had his first OBE, although at the time he thought he was hallucinating and going mad. However, that initial experience appears to have opened the floodgates for him, and he began to enjoy his subsequent OBEs, which he recorded meticulously in an objective, scientific spirit.

He discovered that there were several different openings available to the astral traveller, which he termed 'Locales', each of which had characteristic features and indigenous entities. For example, he described Locale II as follows:

"[It] is a non-material environment with laws of motion and matter only remotely related to the physical world. It ... has depth and dimensions incomprehensible to the finite, conscious mind. In this vastness lie all of the aspects we attribute to heaven and hell ... It is inhabited, if that is the word, by entities with various degrees of intelligence with whom communication is possible."

Like many mystics and mediums, Monroe describes this world as being ideoplastic – where ideas literally create reality. He says:

"Locale II is a state of being where that which we label thought is the wellspring of existence. It is the vital creative force that produces energy, assembles matter into form, and provides channels of perception and communication ... In this environment, no mechanical supplements are found ... You think movement and it is fact."

Unlike many others who have had OBEs, Monroe never actually saw the 'silver cord' that joins the astral and physical bodies like an umbilical cord, but he described feeling something like it 'hanging loosely ... it was body-warm to the touch and seemed to be composed of hundreds of tendon-like strands packed neatly together.'

Monroe subjected his psychic travels to rigorous analysis, presenting his findings in *Journeys Out of the Body*, which was published in 1971. He included many statistics, such as the fact that in 96.2 per cent of his travels, conditions were warm; that 42.2 per cent took place during the day and 57.8 per cent at night; and in 62.4 per cent he had faced a north-south direction. In a clear attempt to give his research some scientific credibility, he also listed hundreds of other statistics, many of which are unfortunately worthless. For example, he tells us that he lay prone for 100 per cent of the experiments, when clearly this was not a discovery but a choice on his part. Nevertheless, Robert Monroe was a major player in the history of twentieth-century parapsychology, although as we will see, the true extent of his role is only just emerging.

He was undoubtedly an inspiration to many would-be astral travellers, taking care to cover all aspects of the experience and share his findings (see page 54). He also founded the Monroe Institute for Applied Sciences in rural Virginia, to teach techniques for achieving altered states of consciousness (ASCs), including OBEs. (One of his students was Elisabeth Kubler-Ross.)

The identity of Mr X

During the 1960s, several scientists devoted their attention to the investigation of ASCs. There is no doubt that the generation that discovered psychedelic trips through the use of LSD and mescalin, while ruining their health in the process, nevertheless heralded an explosion of interest in the possibilities of the invisible world.

In 1961, Celia Green began her extensive work on the OBE at her Institute of Psychophysical Research in Oxford, England, with a survey about the prevalence of the experience. Of the 326 respondents, 60 reported only one OBE, while 21 had experienced six or more. Unlike

Monroe, 80 of these subjects had no awareness of an astral body at all, merely reporting a 'disembodied consciousness'. Others described OBEs brought on by boredom or fatigue.

Another British researcher of the same time was Robert Crookall, who although a senior professor at the Institute of Geological Sciences, was passionately interested in parapsychology. He collected over a thousand cases of OBEs from all over the world, uncovering several common characteristics. For example, he noted that many astral travellers described hearing a loud clicking or tearing sound as they separated from the physical body – reminiscent of the early stages of the NDE – and that this process tended to begin at the feet or hands.

However, it was with the work of psychologist Dr Charles T. Tart in the mid-1960s that the scientific study of the OBE really came of age. While teaching at the University of Virginia School of Medicine, Tart undertook a series of experiments with an individual who had experienced many OBEs, whom he called Mr X. The results were impressive.

Mr X would be settled into a specially equipped room, where his heartbeat, brainwaves and rapid eye movements (REMs), which characterize periods of dreaming, were monitored.

He was asked to project his astral self into the next room, where Tart had hidden a randomly selected five-digit number on a shelf that was too high to be seen normally. The first seven attempts failed, possibly because Mr X was stressed by the laboratory conditions, but his eighth attempt, while not a direct hit, was nevertheless interesting.

His astral self drifted into the adjoining room, and although he did not notice the target numbers, he did spot the absence of the assistant who was supposed to be present, and indeed usually was. Floating into the hall he found her in conversation with an unfamiliar man. Later Tart

checked this with the laboratory technician who admitted that she had stepped outside to have a chat with her husband.

The experiments with Mr X assume a greater significance when it is revealed that he was none other than Robert Monroe, although quite what they prove is uncertain. However, the story of the assistant is strikingly similar to many reports of witnessing encounters and overhearing conversations during an NDE, which later turn out to be correct.

In the mind's eye

Dr Tart found a new subject, called Miss Z, whose fourth attempt to read the five-digit number – 25132 – during an OBE was correct. The odds against this happening purely by chance, or guesswork, are roughly 100,000 to one. However, Dr Tart admitted that the experiment was only a qualified success, because Miss Z may have learned the number through another paranormal function, such as ESP or clairvoyance.

In 1972, Dr Karlis Osis and Janet Mitchell began what was to be almost 18 months of research into the unusual talents of New York artist Ingo Swann. A strong-minded individual, Swann claimed to have had his first OBE as a two-year-old during a tonsillectomy, and could now induce OBEs at will and in normal consciousness. (As we will see, Swann's abilities have attracted a great deal of interest, some from very unexpected quarters.)

Asked to describe drawings or objects set on a high platform while out of the body, Swann was often amazingly accurate, including describing the target picture of a bull's eye with a segment missing, although reversing the colours. On one occasion he failed to make out what was in the box because, as he

◀ The US Pentagon, where secret projects to train people in RV techniques have taken place since the 1970s, although these were not publicly admitted until the 1990s.

reported, the light over the target was broken. Although the researchers claimed that this was impossible, they checked and discovered it to be true.

Osis believed these experiments suggested that the vision of a person while out-of-the-body was limited in much the same way as an embodied person's, and embarked on a series of experiments with Alex Tanous, a psychic from Maine, to test this hypothesis further. Tanous was required to project to a room at the other end of the building and report back on what he found in an optical image device there. But the first runs were failures, although Tanous maintained that this was due to his astral double being too small to see into the device! As he said, 'My projected self, my astral body, as I see it, has hardly any height at all. It's a small ball of light.' Significantly, once Osis had a special platform built for Tanous's double to stand on, the results were immediately much more impressive – 114 hits out of 197 experiments.

Tanous had claimed that his double was occasionally seen by others, although Karlis Osis never had any proof of this. However, over at the Psychical Research Foundation in North Carolina, Dr Robert Morris (now the incumbent of the Koestler Chair of Parapsychology at Edinburgh University) was working with a subject called Keith 'Blue' Harary, who also claimed to be able to induce OBEs. He soon produced spectacular results, not only correctly guessing a sequence of cardboard letters in another room on many occasions, but also identifying members of staff who were, unusually, gathered in another room.

Perhaps most significantly, one research assistant claimed to have actually seen Harary's double during his out-of-the-body travels, in a similar incident to those claimed by Tanous. And even the usually cautious Robert Morris went on record as saying he had sensed Harary's presence in the room.

Even when presented with the positive findings of such meticulous researchers as Tart and Osis, many people remain sceptical, maintaining that the whole concept of a non-physical self is nonsense. Yet the best evidence for the reality of an astral body does not come from the clergy, channellers, mediums or even university laboratories, but from a most unlikely and non-spiritual source – from the US military, and the Pentagon itself.

In 1995, in accordance with the Freedom of Information Act, the US Government admitted that it had allocated at least $12 million (some sources put it much higher) on investigating and utilizing paranormal espionage techniques, including remote viewing (RV). Although there are some differences, this is basically the use of induced OBEs for purposes of invisible spying.

The real X Files

In the summer of 1995, a television programme made by Jim Schnabel for Britain's Channel 4, entitled The Real X Files, revealed the extraordinary background to the US Government involvement with the paranormal. According to this programme, the Pentagon had funded an RV unit for over 20 years, testing and training potential remote viewers for the purpose of invisibly entering enemy installations.

One of its most talented graduates was Major Ed Dames, who now runs his own RV training school as a civilian. He revealed that the main instructor in RV for the army was Ingo Swann, the star subject of Dr Charles Tart's experiments into induced OBEs. This begs the question of just how long the US Government had been investigating paranormal abilities, and which researchers had been unofficially funded by the Pentagon.

It is now known that other governments, including those of the former Soviet Union and Israel, had been routinely using psychic espionage for many years. It appears to have been the threat from the Iron Curtain countries that finally mobilized the US Government into RV research. As Congressman Charles Rose (Chairman, Sub-Committee on Intelligence Evaluation and Oversight) said when presented with the results of early RV testing:

"All I can say is that if the results were faked, our security system doesn't work. What these people saw was confirmed by aerial photography. There's no way it could have been faked ... Some of the intelligence people ... know that remote viewing works, although they still block further research on it ... But it seems to me that it would be a hell of a cheap radar system. And if the Russians have it and we don't, we are in serious trouble."

The implications of such lavishly funded programmes into psychic espionage (which some jokingly refer to as ESPionage) are enormous. Instead of a vague faith in the existence of a soul, here is, arguably, the ultimate confirmation of its reality. After all, military men would not sanction spending a sizeable part of their defence budget on something that does not work, nor would they continue to do so for over 20 years.

In the Belly of the Beast

One of the US Army's star remote viewers was Major David Morehouse, who tells his story in his 1996 book *Psychic Warrior* (subtitled *The true story of the CIA's paranormal espionage programme*). It is a cautionary tale about his meteoric rise as a psychic operative, and his fall from grace due to the dark secrets he uncovered about the remote viewing programme. However, perhaps the most significant aspect of his story is that it really begins with an NDE.

In the spring of 1987, Morehouse was the young commander of the Bravo Company of the 1st Ranger Battalion, 75th Ranger Regiment of

▲ David Morehouse, former US Army Officer who trained in RV techniques as part of the Pentagon's 'psychic spies' programme that began in the 1970s.

the US Army, which was seconded to the Arabian desert in order to train Jordanian troops. The Company was in a valley called Baten el Ghoul (the Belly of the Beast), which the Jordanians believed to be haunted by demons. Of course the hardened and world-weary American troops ridiculed what they regarded as mere superstition, but they were privately uneasy about the place. Morehouse retrospectively describes it as 'an unclean place ... there was something evil in it'. It was in the Belly of the Beast that he was to have the experience that would change his life so radically as to make it unrecognizable.

During military manoeuvres in that strange, haunted place, 'a rogue Jordanian gun shifted into the wrong direction ... and the world turned black'. It is perhaps ironic that Morehouse, until that moment a fairly devout Mormon and idealistic American patriot, had his NDE in that alien, Islamic place. But it was this experience that effectively opened his psychic floodgates for the first time.

Struck by a rogue Jordanian bullet, he came to consciousness in a white mist, not able to feel his limbs. Then

the mist rolled away and he discovered he was standing below a grassy hill, on the top of which was a group of about 12 people, all dressed alike in long white robes. One of them turned to look at him, with a face full of kindness, and beckoned Morehouse to come closer, which he managed to do, although moving 'in some strange way' to the top of the hill. After a few hesitant words were exchanged, the being in white said, 'We called you to give you instructions.'

Unlike many reported NDEs, where the individual becomes almost obsequious towards the entities he encounters, Morehouse's response to the being in white was swift, aggressive and unprintable! He demanded to know, in no uncertain terms, what it was all about, and was told:

"Your choice [regarding a worldly career] is wrong. Pursue peace. Teach peace, and the path to it will be made known to you. You have tasted death ... now bring life."

A great ringing sound filled Morehouse's ears, his eyes stung and his knees buckled. He describes the last moments of his NDE:

"The air was thick as death and heavy. I tried to speak, to cry out, but nothing came from my mouth. All I could do was lie there with the pain, alone and frightened beyond description. The mist crept back around me, masking the hill from my view, and in a few minutes it was completely black."

Most of the NDEs discussed in this book happen as a result of an experience that was truly life-threatening, and in many cases the line had apparently already been crossed between what we think of as life and death. However, in Morehouse's case

▶ The bleak sandscape of the Jordanian desert, where David Morehouse had the fear-death experience that seemed to unleash his considerable psychic abilities.

it was very, almost embarrassingly, different. The rogue bullet that struck him had only penetrated his helmet, although it did make a huge bump come up on his head and give him massive headaches afterwards. Nevertheless, it was odd enough for Morehouse to wonder, much later and in very different circumstances, whether the event had really been the accident it had appeared to be.

After the angel

Morehouse came to think of the being in white as his angel, with whom he was to have several other encounters, some in normal waking consciousness. Then followed his assignment to an Intelligence Unit known as Sacred Cape, from which he was assigned to the bizarre group that was behind Operation Sun Streak. This was what was presented to Morehouse as the Pentagon's RV unit, although it has recently emerged that there were several similar groups operating at the same time, possibly without knowledge of the others.

He discovered that OBEs were a reality, that furthermore they could easily be induced and that information gathered during such expeditions went beyond mere fantasy. As a jittery Morehouse began to plough through his homework – endless documents relating to the RV units – certain aspects became obvious. As he writes:

"The [US] government was funding paranormal research in half a dozen private and as many state and federal research centres across the United States. They were pumping tens of millions of dollars into remote viewing and various related techniques. But the project and those affiliated with it were set into a class by themselves, no longer part of the intelligence community. They were feared, ridiculed, scoffed, mocked and ostracized. Yet somewhere, someone in a position of power was intrigued. Something fuelled the

programme's fire, and from my readings that could only mean one thing: it worked."

In the months that followed, Morehouse discovered a world of espionage and intrigue that seemed to come from the wildest dreams of a science fiction writer. But if he is not deluded or lying – and all the evidence suggests that he is neither – then his story is both a celebration of humankind's hidden potential and a damning indictment of the unethical uses to which it can be put.

A secret history

When Major David Morehouse began his work with Sun Streak he was given a batch of files to read that provided the background to his own role. One thing became quickly obvious:

"I couldn't believe it. This programme had been in existence since early 1974, for nearly 15 years. It wasn't experimental any longer ... they knew it worked – they'd proven that at Stanford, and all the evidence was here. There were books written on the stuff by the researchers involved; nobody paid any attention to them. The books didn't mention the intelligence involvement, but evidence of government funding was all over the place."

In fact, the international parapsychological community had been familiar with the work of the Stanford Research Institute (SRI) of California for years, although its connection with the CIA was merely a matter of conjecture for most parapsychologists. And although most university experiments of a similar nature routinely returned 'just above chance' results, those at the SRI were, from the beginning, simply amazing.

Under the supervision of Harold Puthoff and Russell Targ, many teams of remote viewers were tested at the SRI from the early 1970s. The purpose of the experiments was to

see if it was possible to describe a randomly chosen location while physically miles away from it and with no knowledge of which one had been selected. The subjects were encouraged to sketch any features of the unknown location that came to mind, and these drawings were compared to the real thing later. Time and time again the remote viewers described the target locations with a high degree of accuracy (well beyond either coincidence or chance) and even their doodles matched.

Occasionally, the media would feature the SRI's ongoing remote viewing project, although it only achieved real fame in the relatively small world of parapsychology. But the media had their uses: they demonstrated that absolute beginners could do very respectably in simple experiments with virtually no prior practice. The British scientist and television presenter, the late Kit Pedler, summarized his own experiences in his 1981 book *Mind Over Matter*. Pedler was enthusiastic about the work of Targ and Puthoff, writing:

"... any suggestion that they are dupes, liars or frauds is totally risible.' He noted that the RV researchers had a notice over their laboratory door that read: 'As you enter here you have permission to be psychic.' And while honestly defining at least one Targ and Puthoff experiment as 'weak and untidy in many respects', he nevertheless unequivocally stated: 'I cannot reasonably fault their results, so I must accept them."*

While at the SRI, Pedler witnessed the work of several people trained in RV techniques which greatly impressed him. One of them was Ingo Swann, who together with colleague Hella Hammid, successfully remote viewed the exact position of a large block of masonry on the ocean floor, near Catalina Island, off north California. This was double-checked and physically located by a submarine at a depth of 170m (558ft), and the whole experiment was filmed by CBS TV for its *In Search Of...* series. Pedler even mentions that:

> **"** *[Targ and Puthoff] once had a visit from an irate Pentagon official who stormed into their laboratory and said effectively, 'What the hell do you people think you're doing wasting government money on all this psychic rubbish?' A few days later he had participated in a successful RV experiment. He left slightly chastened.* **"**

It is interesting to note that this little scene apparently in all innocence gave away the fact of the US Government's funding of the RV experiments several years before it was officially admitted! Morehouse categorically states that the SRI experiments were always funded by the CIA: reading between the lines the implication is that they acted as recruiting grounds for useful remote viewers. The enthusiasm of the US and other governments for RV is particularly fascinating because even though they have actually admitted their involvement with it, few people believe them!

Morehouse's psychic awareness rapidly turned into a nightmare, and his determination to tell the public what was going on in his unit plunged him and his family into a darkly threatening world from which they only escaped with his enforced resignation. But obviously his gifts are still intact: he appeared in 1997 on the British television programme *Beyond Belief*, which was presented by Sir David Frost, in a successful two-hander experiment in telepathy with Uri Geller.

The man who died twice

Another retired US Army officer who was an RV operator during the early 1980s – for the then top secret project known as Stargate – is Joe McMoneagle. However, the version of

---

THE HARBINGER OF DEATH

The human double, or 'doppleganger', is well known in folklore as the harbinger of trouble and even death. To encounter yourself is said to mean that you will be dead within a 'moon month'. Perhaps it is true: the poet Percy Shelley met and even spoke with his double on a veranda in Italy and he was dead within four weeks.

One of the most famous of all doppelganger stories is that of the young Emilie Sagée, who taught at a girls' school in the former Soviet Union in the mid-nineteenth century. On several occasions she was seen by multiple witnesses to be literally in two places at once. For example, while the real Emilie wrote on the blackboard, another version stood by her side, mimicking her actions, although only the real chalk made marks. And once she was teaching a class while her double was standing in the garden. As far as we know, she did not see her own double, and thereby evaded the usual fate, although the unenviable weirdness that surrounded her greatly distressed her pupils, eventually causing her to lose her job.

The book *Phantasms of the Living* (1886) by three of the founders of the SPR – Gurney, Myers and Podmore – reflected the Victorian interest in the 'fetch', or double. The fledgling SPR had frequently noted doubles or crisis apparitions. *Phantasms of the Living* included the stories of Lucy Eden and Sarah Jane Hall, whose doubles were seen by several people, but only Sarah saw her self once, with no immediate ill effect.

More recently, the British television series *Strange But True?* featured the story of a man who came face to face with his double while driving in the early hours of one morning. The most disquieting aspect of this encounter was that the double was driving a van exactly like his own, complete with very unusual lettering on the side. However, once again he flouted folklore and lived to tell the tale beyond a moon month.

Engraved by W.T.Fdcn.

Percy B Shelley.

his story told in his book *Mind Trek*, which is subtitled *Exploring Consciousness, Time, and Space through Remote Viewing* (1993), does not include his RV work for the army. In fact, he categorically denies the rumours of his involvement, only to recant and admit it later.

Unlike Morehouse, he learned the technique at the SRI from Hal Puthoff, but their stories share one significant factor: he, too, began his strange career because of an NDE. In fact, McMoneagle was to die twice over a period of 15 years, both times finding himself out of his body, experiencing the other world.

His first NDE, in 1970, changed his life. Succumbing to a heart attack while dining with friends in Germany, he suddenly realized he was watching his companion's frantic efforts to resuscitate him. He says:

"I began screaming at him with my mind while in the out-of-the-body state to 'stop this nonsense, can't you see I'm dead, leave me alone!' ... I then watched them move my body ... I rose approximately 5m (15ft) feet up into the air so I could get a really good view. It was just like being a little kid again ... There was a sadness that I felt for the people who were obviously suffering emotional pain because of me, but I understood very clearly by that time that I couldn't really die ... It was exhilarating."

Rushed into hospital, he witnessed the medical staff trying to revive him, while he wondered: 'Wasn't there a God? Didn't something happen when you died?'

It was then that McMoneagle felt himself being pulled away from the emergency room, fast moving backwards through a tunnel. As he rushed

◄ **The Earth seen from space: many top RV practitioners were routinely given 'off planet' targets. Many successfully reported visiting alien star systems.**

through the ether a blissful warmth spread through his whole being, rising to a continuing ecstasy. This feeling was literally indescribable, but McMoneagle says:

"The closest I can come to giving an example ... is that it was like the peak of a sexual climax 12 times 10 to the 33rd. That would be a 12 with 33 zeroes after it ... It was the most overwhelming feeling I have ever experienced."

He then felt as if he had been absorbed by a being of light, and was overwhelmed by sensations of love, joy and being protected. But he also experienced a total awareness of his faults and mistakes; he was shown his life in terms of lost opportunities and 'non-constructive and non-creative aspects of self'.

Return to life

McMoneagle heard the voice in the light speak to him, pouring out unconditional love and harmony, with no sense of being judged. The voice told him to go back, because he was not going to die. As McMoneagle puts it: 'I, of course, argued with it.'

As a result of his return to life, and his new insight into the realities of the spirit world, McMoneagle enrolled at Robert Monroe's Institute, and from there became involved in Targ and Puthoff's RV programme at the SRI. As we have seen, in his book he categorically denies that the US Government was even interested in using ESPionage. However, even without his later confession there were clues if one looked hard enough. The chain of personnel and places – Monroe/Monroe Institute/Charles Tart/SRI/Puthoff and Targ/Ingo Swann – was too suggestive not to cast doubt on his denial. In 1993, McMoneagle finally revealed that he was an active part of Operation Stargate, retiring in 1984 with a Legion of Merit award for providing information on 150 targets that was unavailable from other sources.

The evidence reveals that RV can be an effective method of accessing information across space, sometimes even outer space. Both Morehouse and McMoneagle describe RV targets on other planets: off-planet work was quite a routine part of Project Sun Streak. But perhaps more significantly, both men describe astral journeys through time, for at least in theory the soul and the mind operate outside both space and time.

One of the implications of the SRI's RV research is that virtually everyone has the potential to develop the technique. The highly sophisticated work of Sun Streak and Stargate reveals just how effective RV techniques can be, even beyond the confines of time itself. Perhaps it is reasonable to assume that what these remote viewers are doing is freeing the soul from its chrysalis and putting it to work. What is alarming is the fact that both Morehouse and McMoneagle have admitted that several governments have developed the technique of *remote influencing*, which is truly a paranormal nightmare, where the astral self controls the mind of distant people (perhaps world leaders), even using psychic energy to kill them.

A detailed analysis of the terrifying world of ESPionage is outside the scope of this book, but the fact that such matters have now moved beyond the imaginations of science-fiction writers shows that human beings are not merely physical bodies and brains, but are equipped with highly sensitive astral selves.

After centuries of relying on the testimony of priests and mystics for evidence of an afterlife it is, as we have seen, ironic that medical science has given us the best evidence for such a state through its sophisticated resuscitation techniques. But surely it is much more ironic that the best evidence for the existence of a soul comes not from churches or visions, but from the cynical and dangerous world of government-funded intelligence agencies.

CHAPTER FOUR

Seeing the Light

In all the thousands of NDEs now on record, the one major characteristic that literally shines through is that of the 'light'. This ineffable illumination communicates 'all good things', as one child said. It is comfort, unconditional love, joyousness, and has been simply described by some as 'God'.

Meeting the light and being enveloped in it is what changes those who have NDEs, and the memory of the light often remains largely undimmed over the years, continuing to comfort and encourage the individual long after the event. As one man described it simply:

"I was in a garden. All the colours were intense ... Everything was lit by a shadowless brilliance that was all-pervading."

A 29-year-old Irish woman said:

"There was a sudden loud ringing in my ears and I went hurtling down a dark, spiral-shaped tunnel towards a brilliant light. I keep thinking about it and wondering why I could look at it - normally I can't bear even strong sunlight and this was oh, a thousand times ... brighter than that. I seemed to spin through the air very fast, but I wasn't afraid or dizzy as you would expect. And as the light got nearer and bigger I began to feel ... oh I can't explain ... this sensation

◀ **Artist Hieronymus Bosch's 16th-century vision of dying seems to be an accurate depiction of the experiences reported by those who return from clinical death.**

of warmth and love, but with a sort of big chuckle in it, like it had a sense of humour somehow. And as I zoomed off towards it this feeling grew until I had this huge grin all over my face. I could feel it like a big bubble of joy, a sort of giggle of happiness, rising to the surface. And all my problems and pain fell away until I was just one big bubble of happiness hurtling towards the light.

When I reached it I was totally enveloped in it and I could feel it soaking into me, into all my mind and washing out all my bad thoughts, until I felt clean. I was laughing with the sheer joy of being in the light, which is where I know I am supposed to be. But then suddenly I was pulled back to my body, because they'd revived me. They thought I was crying with the pain, but I wasn't. I was heartbroken at leaving the light."

Most who have had an NDE report an encounter with the light even though their experiences may not include other 'core' characteristics, such as meeting a guide or religious figure or having a life review. In many cases, the being who meets them at the end of the black tunnel emerges from the light, or

appears to be made of light. Descriptions of this guide vary, not only in identification – some are adamant that they have met Jesus, whereas others are unclear about the identity of the entity who greets them – but also in terms of visual imagery:

"I saw this man coming out of the light and I just knew he was Jesus...' (51-year-old woman);
'The light was the man, and the man was God ...' (25-year-old man);
'There was just this big star thing and I walked up to it and there was this head in the light and it was nodding. It was a man who had black hair and he had bright blue eyes and that's all I can remember. He was fairly nice ...' (child recalling an NDE she had as a baby);
'All good things are in the light' (small child);
'I won't say it was God, but I won't say it wasn't' (man)."

Discovering the light

In the early days of NDE research, it was the commonality of encountering the light that had a far-reaching effect on the researchers. Soon it emerged that the light, in many cases, was the NDE, which is

65

CASE STUDY: 'I FELT RADIANT WITH HEALTH'

One 80-year-old woman recalls that during her NDE, which happened when she was in her 30s, the light took the form of her deceased relatives:

"I was in hospital, very ill after having a miscarriage and losing a lot of blood. I was so weak I couldn't move my head. Then there was a buzzing sound in my ears that annoyed me at first. I thought it was something to do with my illness and was upset that I couldn't move my head to shake it out. Then suddenly there was a popping sound and I went all of a rush to the ceiling. I felt full of energy. I looked down and saw the nurse come up and look at me then shout for help. I saw my white face and thought, 'That's that, then.'

Then, as I turned away from the scene below me I rushed through the air at a tremendous speed, with lots of different colours whirling past, and a sort of cloud of darkness winding itself round me, although the funny thing is I wasn't afraid or upset at all. In fact I was terribly happy. I felt radiant with health and warmth. I was rushing towards a light and as I got nearer I could see people moving around in it, but I couldn't make their faces out.

Suddenly I was standing in the light and felt it enter me and give me such love! I wanted to cry with joy, but I couldn't. Then the people emerged at my side and I couldn't believe it. There was my mother and father, who'd died over 10 years before, looking so well that I hardly recognized them. They had sun tans, which was odd because they always lived in little grey backstreets and never went anywhere sunny. And there was my gran and her dog Ben, and my friend from school, René, who'd died of meningitis when she was nine. 'Just look at you!', I said admiringly. 'Don't you all look wonderful!'. And they all laughed and kissed me and made a fuss. My dad said, 'It's the light that does it. The light takes years off you ...'"

reflected in the titles of the many books written on the subject, including *Children of the Light* by Cherie Sutherland, *Transformed by the Light* by Melvin Morse and *Embraced by the Light* by Betty J. Eadie.

The light may appear to open up and reveal a landscape, which may take many forms, or one may enter the light after encountering the beautiful surroundings. Elisabeth Kubler-Ross (in her *On Life After Death*) lists variations on 'the phase that is totally imprinted with items of the physical world ... It could be that you float through a tunnel, pass through a gate, or cross a bridge ...'

There is a sort of choice at this point. As she says, 'Everyone is met by the heaven he or she imagined.' But the one immutable part of the experience is the light. Dr Kubler-Ross goes on:

"After you have passed this tunnel, bridge or mountain pass, you are at its end embraced by the light. This light is whiter than white. It is extremely bright, and

CASE STUDY: 'I ENTERED A CITY OF GOLDEN LIGHT'

In 1984, Louis, then a 21-year-old student teacher in London, was hit by a car and had an NDE while in the ambulance. On coming back he recalled entering the black tunnel and 'flying' into the light, but nothing more, until he was watching a science fiction movie. He says:

"I can't remember what the film was, but there were a few scenes of space shuttles. This was in the future and another civilization that was more advanced than ours, so the shuttles were as normal as buses to them, and they suddenly made me remember all sorts of things from my NDE. It hit me hard. My stomach turned over just like when you're in love and suddenly you hear the name of your girlfriend when you're not expecting it. It wasn't the same as my NDE, but similar enough to give me a jolt and bring it back.

The space shuttles in the film landed on the top of a tower in a futuristic city. It had very high buildings with lots of glass that shone with a golden light, and it was that, I think, that reminded me. After I'd gone flying into the light, I'd entered another world where there was a city of golden light that shone and sparkled like nothing you see on earth.

My heart soared just to look at it, but I went boldly right among the towers, flying high. I landed on a roof and heard some music and laughter – nice laughter, not cruel at all – but couldn't see anyone. I stood there with a gentle warm breeze in my face and felt totally at home. I wanted to meet the people there but felt I couldn't, as if that wasn't part of the deal. Then I was lifted off my feet by some very loving presence and sent zooming back to my body. Looking back, there was no way I could have imagined it. Flying around that city was a million times better than any special effects."

the more you approach the light the more you are embraced by the greatest, indescribable, unconditional love you could ever imagine. There are no words for it. "

It must be remembered that Dr Kubler-Ross was not merely speaking as a clinician or researcher in this field. She has experienced an NDE for herself.

The light is perceived as having an intelligence, of being almost an entity in itself. Love and comfort emanate from within it and permeate the individual during the NDE, enveloping and accepting him or her totally, without judgment or conditions. When one little girl told Melvin Morse that 'all the good things are in that light', she summed up the experiences of many.

▲ Extremes of darkness and light are reported by many who experience NDEs, although, curiously, both are accompanied by intense feelings of great happiness and love.

Dr Melvin Morse undertook his Transformations study in Seattle because he suspected that those who had NDEs were radically changed by having encountered the light. The results, which he discusses in his

1993 book *Transformed By The Light*, argue persuasively that his suspicions were correct. As he writes:

"The Transformations study neatly documents the fact that people who have NDEs are changed for life. Those changes are most profound in those who have had an NDE who have experiences of light. This is true whether they had a vivid and powerful memory of a flower-filled heaven bursting with light, or just a brief and fleeting memory of seeing the light."

Dr Morse has discovered that people who have had NDEs have a significantly lowered 'death anxiety'; the deeper the NDE, the less they are afraid of death. But more unexpected was the fact that they were also noticeably unafraid of life. The experience had turned them into what Dr Morse calls 'zestaholics', people who seized every day and turned it into a wellspring of new opportunities and adventures. As a paramedic colleague of Dr Morse's said of children who have had NDEs:

"If they die, it probably won't be a fearful experience for them. But one thing is for sure. If they live they will approach life with a new zeal and gusto."

One of the participants of Dr Morse's Transformations study, 51-year-old Dana, explains that her encounter with the light as a child removed all of her fears and enabled her to throw herself unreservedly into life. In Morse's words, she 'wears her NDE with a smile'. She says:

"When I was eight or nine, I was sick with measles. There were no antibiotics in those days and my illness became critical. My parents were taking turns sleeping with me to keep an eye on me. On this particular night, I remember feeling just terrible and waking up. But I wasn't in my body, I was hovering above it, looking down on my mother and I. My mother was awake and she noticed I wasn't breathing. She called for my dad who ran into the room and began shaking me."

Dana began to go up a tunnel towards the light, but heard a voice saying:

"'Let her go back. She isn't ready yet.' I went into this beautiful bright light anyway. It was a beautiful feeling that totally took all my fears of death away. Then I came back."

The experience had a profound and lasting effect on Dana, who went on to marry and raise a family, besides running three beauty salons, a commercial artist business, and other concerns. She also helps out in her local church. Like most others who have had an NDE, her zest for life was greatly increased by her experience, making her aware of the 'here and now', and of the necessity to make the most of her time in the material world.

The value of life

Essentially, NDEs impress people with a deep sense of purpose in life, and an inner knowledge that every life is precious and has its own value

---

CASE STUDY: SWIMMING IN A HEAVENLY SEA

Lynda, a 45-year-old woman from Bristol, England, recalls what happened when she drowned over 20 years before:

"There was no struggle. I sank immediately into a huge sense of security and comfort, even though I was somehow aware that my body was in distress under the stinking green water of the canal. Whatever it may have looked like, I did not actually experience that distress. Instead, the real me was floating some way above the scene. I seemed to be on the bottom of the sea, but it wasn't terrifying. It was a heavenly sea, where the water wasn't even wet!

I was surrounded by a substance that was neither water nor air as we know it. It was much more refined and subtle somehow, and it caressed me as I floated around in it, feeling blissfully happy and content. This water was brilliantly coloured and completely transparent and luminous. It seemed to be divided into layers, the bottom one, where I was, being a delightful vivid green that somehow sparkled and shone. Light permeated it and I could feel light flowing through me.

Then something began to draw me up through the water and as I rose up slowly I went through layer after layer of different colours, each one more beautiful than the last. Up through shades of blue and purple and orange and gold ... and as I rose up the feeling of ecstasy increased. I will never forget it, although try as I might I can't recapture it. It was a feeling that belonged to that magical sea, not to this earth or this body. The last colour I went through was a wonderful vivid pink and I found myself on a beach with golden-pink sand. I sat down and just waited, feeling totally happy, with a magical light shining all around.

I knew I couldn't explore any farther into that magical land, although I saw palm trees behind me and part of me felt inquisitive about what lay beyond. Then I was back in my body, hating it, but knowing at the same time that there is a world of stunning beauty and joy that lies in wait for us when our time has come."

in the overall scheme of things. However, there are no reported cases of a person trying to commit suicide in order to get back to the light, partly because they are imbued with the understanding that suicide is the greatest sin they can commit against God or the universe, and partly because their sense of mission is so strong as a result of their experience that their commitment to their earthly life is total.

This is not to say that those who return from the light have it easy. Sometimes life becomes harder and fraught with problems, some of which can be very grave or tragic. Betty J. Eadie, in her book *Embraced By the Light* (1992), describes how her return was so disappointing, after her wonderful experience, that she actually became agoraphobic, afraid of stirring beyond her own home. It was only by an immense effort of will, and through her love for her family, that she pulled herself together.

However, that was not the end of her difficulties. She fostered a delightful little girl who became the apple of her eye, so beloved that when she was collected by her new adoptive parents Betty felt as if she were being physically riven apart with the pain of it. After months of terrible anguish came the news that the child had been severely damaged through physical abuse, and she was allowed to retrieve the child and look after her once more. It was only after some time of working hard to mend the child's broken body and mind that she realized she had seen her before, as a particularly remarkable spirit, during her NDE. Everything fell into place, and she realized how she had been tested and how everything works out if there is love and dedication.

Others return from the light into severely damaged bodies and lifetimes of pain. In Cherie Sutherland's book *Children of the Light* (1995) there are several stories of children who come back only to be physically and/or mentally handicapped. But

CASE STUDY: A PRAYER FOR HELP

Sometimes the light is experienced on its own, without being part of a full-blown NDE, and occasionally the light is seen by an individual who is not even near death. This is what happened to 60-year-old Patricia Eades from London whose experience happened 25 years before:

"*I was staying with a friend in New York State and was alone in the house one lunchtime. I'd been through a bad time – very hectic and stress at work – and had gone to stay with Rose because I needed a rest. I was beginning to feel very relaxed, and just sat in a comfortable chair with a little light lunch on the side table.*

I put off eating for some reason, although I was suddenly very hungry. I just sat there and drifted into a trance, my senses sort of swimming in the silence, which was broken only by the ticking of a clock. I found that immensely comforting.

Then, without warning, everything went misty. At first I thought there was something wrong with my eyes. Then a white light swirled around me, a beautiful iridescent light with flecks of blue and gold in it. It was like being embraced by someone with total love in their hearts. The

light was somehow intelligent and caring and I felt it knew me of old, and knew me very well indeed. It loved me even though I'd been thoughtless and stupid. I was in the centre of this giant angelic candy-floss that wound around me with such a blissful feeling ... Then it went, just like that, in an instant and I fell deeply and dreamlessly asleep. When I woke up I was totally refreshed and went for a long walk. I'd forgotten completely to have lunch and by now wasn't even hungry!

Since then I've read about NDEs, and what happened to me seems to fit the description of entering the light, but I wasn't anywhere near death as far as I know. I was extremely tired – burnt out – and presumably my body and soul were craving relief. Perhaps the visit of the light came in answer to my unspoken prayer for help. **"**

their ability to cope has been enhanced by the experience, and their wisdom – their understanding of the meaning of life and death – is way beyond their years. One such child was Daniel, who was born with terrible problems, including the condition known as TOF, where the oesophagus is not completely joined, and no opening of the bowel, which had necessitated a colostomy. He was also borderline spina bifida, and as a result of another birth defect he had a bladder problem, which meant he was permanently catheterized.

Besides this, he only had one kidney, one leg was longer than the other, he had reflux asthma and an unusually small digestive system. By the age of 14 he had been operated on

17 times, but he had also had several visions, which were classic NDEs.

Daniel was just four years old when he described how Jesus came for him one night at 10 p.m. He was very precise about times, saying, 'It's all right, you can come back, I just want to show you what it's like.' Later he said to Daniel, 'I'll bring you back. Don't be afraid.'

His mother, Bridget, was 'freaked out' when, as little Daniel was flicking through a religious book, he suddenly said, 'That's not what Jesus looks like.' The four-year-old vehemently argued against the Jesus of the children's book, explaining that he had a black flowing cape, which the child then drew as if from memory. After his NDE, whenever he was in hospital

CASE STUDY: PRAYING TO THE EGYPTIAN GODS

One of the great questions in NDE research is how much personal belief influences the content of the vision. Christians tend to encounter Jesus in the light, whereas others meet relatives, angels or God. But although the NDEs of many atheists and agnostics have been recorded, this is the first known NDE of a modern pagan. It happened in February 1997 to Lucien Morgan, a British television presenter who lives in London. A follower of the ancient Egyptian religion, he says:

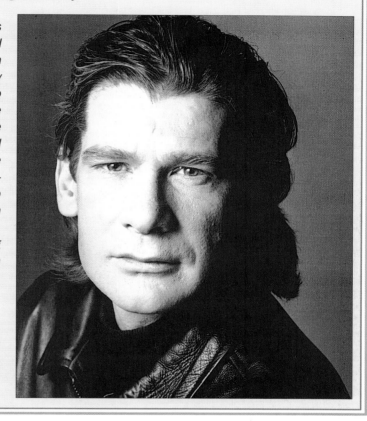

"I was practising lucid dreaming [conscious awareness of dreaming] and was enjoying flying over fields and streams. Then I saw the most wonderful, brilliant light in the distance and I wanted to go towards it with all my heart. I prayed to the Egyptian god of light to let me go to it and suddenly it was coming towards me very fast. The light was brighter than anything I'd ever seen, but the strange thing is it didn't hurt my eyes to look at it. I could hear little demon voices all around me, trying to stop me getting close to the light so they could get me for themselves. Besides, I thought of my girlfriend waking up to find a dead body beside her. So I prayed to Sekhmet [a powerful Egyptian goddess] for help – and came back. Funnily enough, my girlfriend must have known something was wrong, because she'd thrown her arm over me, even though she was fast asleep. She never does that normally. I hadn't wanted to come back, but I knew I had to."

However, Lucien feels changed only in subtle ways by his dream of the light, reflecting perhaps Melvin Morse's idea that the deeper the NDE, the more transformed the person who experiences it. After all, this was just a dream, not a true brush with death.

---

again and Bridget would say, 'I have to leave you now', he would answer, 'It doesn't matter, Mum, – he's with me.'

When he was 10, Daniel said that Jesus had come to take him to heaven, which was a beautiful, serene place full of the light, with wonderful flowers and a river. He met his Nanny and Uncle Neville who had died as a young man, besides some other people. Jesus told him he had to stay, but Daniel replied, 'I can't stay … Because Mum's not ready to let go.' So Jesus took him back to bed.

Bridget was profoundly affected by this story. She felt guilty because perhaps Daniel 'had had enough of

◀ Tiny children who return from death are sometimes confused because the Jesus they met looked nothing like his image in the religious books they were familiar with.

fighting the good fight and maybe he did want to go, and I was the one that was pulling him back.' She went for counselling, and began to take a hard look at her own neediness and its effect on her son. Finally she told him that 'It's okay, I'll be all right now, it's okay to go … I can cope.' However, although constantly battling against his many infirmities, Daniel remained with his mother.

Betty J. Eadie describes how her attitude to her children changed as a result of her own NDE: she realized that they were not hers, and that parents are only given them to look after. They are their own souls with their own individual purposes. Bridget learnt a similar lesson through her son's NDE.

Of course, Daniel himself had been radically affected by his encounters

with the light and with Jesus. When he was just four he went with his mother and some other children to put flowers on his grandmother's grave. The children began arguing about how they would be buried if they were all killed together, when Daniel piped up with, 'I don't know why you're all arguing. I'm going to die before all of you. So stop it.'

Walking through the graveyard afterwards, he stopped to pray by a stranger's grave, saying, 'Down there [in the grave] there is nothing. They're just empty shells.' This was incredible coming as it did from such a tiny child.

Daniel's strength, courage and wisdom has touched a great many people. Bridget is the first to admit that he has totally changed her attitude to death, which originally was one of

real fear. And his influence has extended well beyond the boundaries of his own family. As Bridget says:

"*Daniel doesn't even realize that he has this incredible power. He's not even aware of it. Actually, someone said to me, 'When Daniel smiles it's like the sun shines.*"

The boy himself speaks from experience when he says:

"*Death's all right. I know I could die any time so I live just each day. I'd say to people who are dying, 'Don't be afraid. It's a beautiful place.'*"

Healed by the light

Perhaps the most significant thing about Daniel's story is that he was not expected to live long. As Bridget says, 'his life expectancy was nothing'. The doctors thought he would be lucky to live into his third year. But miraculously he made it to age 14 (when he was interviewed by Cherie Sutherland for her book). Was this just a fluke, or had he been healed by the light with all good things in it?

The evidence suggests that many who have had NDEs are. Melvin Morse believes that it is the light that cures people, even those who are beyond the help of conventional medicine. He tells the story of 'Janet', a 31-year-old woman who had been diagnosed as having basal cell carcinoma. which is a particularly deadly form of skin cancer. She describes what happened to her:

"*Two nights before surgery I was sleeping when I was awakened by a bright light shining in my eyes. I opened my eyes to see a large sphere of light floating about five feet in front of me. There was a light within it that was rotating*

slowly from left to right. The sphere spoke to me: 'You aren't afraid, are you?'"

The light instantly removed her fears and filled her with peace. It seemed to go straight through her. She explains:

"*I was filled with unconditional love, which was so complete and powerful that I would need to invent new words to describe it. I asked that my cancer would be removed. I prayed actually. And the light said that what we think of as prayer is more like complaining and we are frequently begging to be punished for something that we are simply going to do again in the future.*

He asked me to think of my own worst enemy. I did and a sudden burst of light went out of me and returned as if it had been reflected back from a mirror. I became aware of every cell in my body. I could see every cell in my body. It was the sound and the sight of light coming from my being. I was crying, laughing, shaking, trying to hold still and trying to catch my breath.

When I finally recovered, the being of light said, 'Now you have prayed for the first time in your life.'"

Remarkably, Janet's tumour disappeared, and although spontaneous remissions do happen to many types of cancer, it is extremely rare for her particular condition.

Spiritual force field

Melvin Morse believes that the NDE significantly changes the electromagnetic force field of the body, and in this case that 'this woman, through fear and stress similar to that experienced by people on the brink of death, altered her own electromagnetic forces and was able to spontaneously regress this cancerous lesion.'

It must be stressed that Dr Morse is not in any way 'putting down' the mystical aspects of NDEs. He sees the physical side of the experience as being the means whereby the spiritual event can take place.

Elisabeth Kubler-Ross has also noted what she calls 'ask and you will be given' cases, where NDEs work miracles. Her most dramatic case

◀ People who have had an NDE recognize that bodily remains are merely shells. The true self goes on to encounter the light in a realm of intense, unconditional love.

A POETIC NDE

This poem was written by Angela, a 17-year-old trainee hairdresser from Swansea, Wales, as she lay waiting to die in 1983. However, against all expectations, she recovered:

They try to prevent me from going
Back home, where I know I want to be
They weep furtively and talk of
stopping by
With next week's glossy magazines
I won't be subscribing again

I can't explain, they don't understand
That I'm impatient now to go
I'm going home and they have to stay
Like sleepwalkers swimming
underwater
Slow motion puppets – that's life
Me? I'm going home
And that can't be bad

They see me weak and broken
And I catch their pity like a sigh
In their brains, unguarded
I know you, I think, so much fear
Not just for me but for you too
For this way you must come too
One day ... when? Who knows ...
But come it will, oh yes

Your love is warming, thank you
Thank you, oh yes
My love is yours forever too
But please see me waiting for
Lovers of light to lift me up
Going up, going home – that's me

▲ **What observers may see as a lonely or traumatic end to a life may in fact be the moment when the spirit is finally freed, enjoying unimaginable vitality and bliss.**

was that of a man who had 'become a total bum, drinking half a gallon of whisky a day, trying heroin and other drugs' to numb the pain of having lost his entire family in a particularly horrific accident. Their car had been hit by a petrol tanker, which spilled its contents over them and then ignited, burning them all to death. The man became a total wreck, resigning himself to the slow suicide of drink and drugs. In fact, he had tried to commit suicide many times, but had failed. After two years of life on skid row he went to the edge of a forest and lay down 'drunk and stoned', wanting desperately to be reunited with his family. He lacked the motivation even to move when he saw a truck heading

straight for him. It ran over him, leaving him critically injured.

Then this man found himself hovering above his broken body, suddenly aware of a great light in which he saw his family, radiating love towards him. As Dr Kubler-Ross writes:

❝*He was so awed by his family's health, their beauty, their radiance and their total acceptance of his present situation, by their unconditional love. He made a vow not to ... join them, but to re-enter his physical body so that he could share with the world what he had experienced.***❞**

Amazingly, when he was taken by ambulance into the hospital he re-entered his body, tore off the restraining straps and walked out unaided. Moreover, he never suffered any ill effects or withdrawal symptoms

from his alcoholism and drug abuse. As Dr Kubler-Ross says:

❝*He felt healed and whole, and made a commitment that he would not die until he had the opportunity of sharing the existence of life after death with as many people as would be willing to listen ... We do not know what happened to this man since [his meeting with Dr Kubler-Ross], but I will never forget the glow in his eyes, the joy and deep gratitude he experienced.***❞**

This man had been through a living hell, but was reborn through his NDE in which the great secret of life after death was revealed to him. Not only did it remove all his loneliness and anguish, proving to him that his family were more alive than they had ever been, but he was also physically and spiritually reborn and given a sense of mission. Out of that personal tragedy came immeasurable hope and healing.

The beings of light

As we have seen, many people encounter beings in the light. Sometimes there is only one, ineffably beautiful and kind, who they perceive or somehow know as Jesus. In other cases the being is a deceased relative or friend, and sometimes Jesus and other beings are there in the light to greet the person.

The identification of the being of light as Jesus is somewhat controversial, as some believe that their meeting with him proves that Christianity is the only true religion, and that entrance to heaven is exclusively through his mediation. Betty J. Eadie in particular is very emphatic on this point, taking care to point out that before her NDE she was not a great believer, but that her encounter with Jesus revealed that the only way was that of Christianity. However, it must be stressed that the vast majority of those who have had NDEs become less dogmatic and more concerned with spirituality in a wider sense after their experiences. One man described his feelings about the different religions in terms of people choosing to support different football teams – whichever they choose, the game is still the same.

This is perhaps the one area of NDE research that is most problematic in terms of sorting out subjective beliefs and expectations from the overall, objective pattern of the NDE. Researchers have to be on their guard against leading questions. For example, one British NDE researcher, who was himself a convert to Catholicism, tried hard at a seminar to make a woman say she had encountered Jesus in the light, but she rebuffed him, unequivocally stating that she had met God. Even that identification may be going too far sometimes: one man cautiously said, 'I won't say the light was God, but I won't say it wasn't.'

CASE STUDY: THE MAN WITH THE GOLDEN HALO

Betty J. Eadie has no doubts about what happened to her when she died on 18 November 1973, while in hospital for a partial hysterectomy. She left her body and was met by many loving, supportive people in the spirit who she felt she had known 'before', in some spiritual pre-existence. But one of these beings of light stood out. To her he was Jesus. This is how she met him:

"I saw a pinpoint of light in the distance. The black mass around me began to take on more of the shape of a tunnel, and I felt myself travelling through it at an even greater speed, rushing toward the light. I was instinctively attracted to it, although ... I felt that others might not be. As I approached it, I noticed the figure of a man standing in it, with the light radiating all around him. As I got closer the light became brilliant – brilliant beyond any description, far more brilliant than the sun – and I knew no earthly eyes in their natural state could look upon this light without being destroyed."

She knew instinctively that only spiritual eyes could survive such brilliance. Approaching the man she:

"... saw that the light immediately around him was golden, as if his whole body had a golden halo around it, and I could see that the golden halo burst out from around him and spread into a brilliant, magnificent whiteness that extended out for some distance. I felt his light blending into mine, literally, and I felt my light being drawn to his. It was as if there were two lamps in a room, both shining, their light merging together. It's hard to tell where one light ends and the other begins; they just become one light. Although this light was much brighter than my own, I was aware that my light, too, illuminated us. And as our lights merged, I felt as if I had stepped right into his countenance, and I felt an enormous explosion of love..."

Sometimes beliefs are unexpectedly checked in the NDE: one man described how he had explained to a being of light that he expected to find Jesus on the right-hand side of God and St John on the other, although as he said this he wavered, changing this to St Peter. But the being asked him why Peter should come before John? Perhaps his instinct was right in the heaven he encountered.

Children frequently report meeting Jesus, although sometimes he looks very different from what one girl called 'the holy photos', or the pictures in religious books. One little boy described him as wearing a flowing black cloak, while another had him with a red hat and a round belly.

One child in Cherie Sutherland's files, Hal, had an extraordinarily detailed NDE, during which he met a deceased school friend called Edward, who told him many things about heaven. Hal said:

"He'd already said to me, 'Come with me, you're going to go back, but before you go back you have to meet the light ... I said, 'Who's the light?' And he said, 'Oh, that's the supreme being.' I said, 'You mean God?' He said, 'Oh, if you like.' He seemed a bit vague about that. I said, 'Is he the boss? There's no one higher or mightier?' He said, 'Yes, he's the supreme being. He's the boss.' But he wasn't going to call him God. That was the word he used – supreme being."

As we will see, little Durdana Khan encountered 'God', whom she always described, simply and invariably, as

being 'blue'. Aged two-and-a-half, she visited him 'in the stars' until she was resuscitated.

But surely the most bizarre other-worldly encounter was with Elvis Presley! The woman involved had met him when she was a child, so perhaps the meeting was not so unlikely. But as Melvin Morse writes:

"... When the woman in the Midwest saw Elvis, she was probably projecting him on to the bright light that others have described as God or Buddha or have been unable to describe at all. Meeting Elvis as a child may have inspired the same awe and respect she felt when she met the light as an adult."

Some children report meeting deceased people they have known, especially much-loved relatives. Significantly, not one child has described meeting a parent who was still alive, which seriously undermines the accusation that NDEs are exercises in wish fulfilment.

It appears that identifying the being of light may be an embellishment of the central pattern of the NDE – a personal touch somehow created to make the message stronger for the individual. But, as Melvin Morse says, '... the persistence of the core experience demonstrates that the entire experience is not embellished.' Clearly what really matters is the light itself, which is 'full of good things' and which bestows unconditional love and healing for the body and spirit.

Music of the spheres
Mystics have often spoken of the mysterious 'music of the spheres', which is normally out of the reach of human ears. Is this the celestial music so frequently reported by those such as biker Alan. Hannah, one of Cherie Sutherland's interviewees, said:

◄ Are NDEs wish fulfilment? One women met Elvis Presley in the afterlife; he had been her great hero since she met him as a teenager.

"I can't describe it in earthly terms. I still hear it sometimes. It's like pan pipes but beyond anything here. I was in darkness. Then the darkness changed into a passage and then it was light and peaceful, like being in a big smile."

Another, Helen, who had her NDE due to an asthma attack when she was a teenager, said:

"I heard this music but I don't know where it was coming from, and I can't even describe what it sounded like. It was sort of like instruments, or voices, I don't know. But I remember listening to it and I was thinking, 'I didn't know there were so many notes between all the notes that we know.' And it was like they were all in harmony. And I was listening to this and it was making me feel very happy. It was really beautiful music."

This music does not reflect personal taste. As we have seen, biker Alan, a heavy-metal fanatic described hearing something quite different during his NDE, and returned as a convert to more soothing music. Tod, from London's East End, who was 27 years old when he had his NDE, writes:

"I had this idea that if there was an afterlife it would be very serious and sort of gloomy, full of earnest do-gooders. I remember watching the Festival of Remembrance [annual British ceremony to honour the war dead] on television and somebody read a poem about the death of a soldier in World War I. I went cold and shuddered for some reason when they got to the line 'And all the trumpets sounded for him on the other side'. I had this mental image of some white-faced public schoolboy in a bloody uniform being saluted as he climbed out of his grave. It was horrible, somehow.

But about a year after that my bike was hit by a car and I shot out of my body like it was just a reflex action - really natural. And all around me there was this golden light and this indescribably beautiful music. Not spooky or military, but somehow sweet without being cloying. It was utterly gorgeous and I sort of bathed in the light and the music, floating above my body without a care in the world and not a white-faced soldier in sight! It was a real blow being revived by a passer-by. I can't watch the Remembrance ceremonies now. They've got it all wrong. Death isn't cold or spooky or grotesque, it's the best thing that ever happens to us."

Home from home
A few people describe seeing unearthly cities during their NDE, which are often described as 'cities of golden light' or made of glass or some unknown sparkling, iridescent material. This transcendental place or its inhabitants may appear strangely familiar, and may give the person a sense of 'coming home'. Just to look at the buildings is to experience profound sensations of exaltation and bliss.

During his or her NDE a person may leave the ubiquitous heavenly garden to be shown buildings – in Betty J. Eadie's case they were 'exquisitely built and appointed' – in which people are carrying out certain tasks. One woman encountered her deceased mother who was dressmaking (something she'd never done when alive), while another met her father who (being British) offered her a 'nice cup of tea'.

Some have described schools and colleges, even workshops that produce beautiful handicrafts and clothes. Everyone is radiant with happiness and contentment, and no one seeks to set him or herself above the others. And everywhere and everyone is permeated with the brilliant light, which is love.

CHAPTER FIVE

Life After (Near) Death

Since the term 'near-death experience' was coined by Raymond Moody in the 1970s, it has become apparent that the experience bestows many benefits, some of which are radically transformative. The events that produce the NDE – accident, heart attack, attempted suicide and so on – may be unimaginably painful and traumatic at the time, but the after-effects are quite the opposite.

The NDE itself almost always has a lasting effect that is totally positive on those who experience it, and often on many who come into contact with them. Tania tells of how her life changed as a result of having had an NDE at the age of 21:

"In the days following my experience I was in an unhappy haze. I'd visited a world of light and love where there was no pain or unhappiness. I'd met my beloved dad who'd died horribly of cancer years before and yet there he was strong and healthy and full of laughter. He'd shown me round a beautiful garden and we'd sat and talked among wonderful flowers and amazing music. When he'd broken it to me that I had to return, I sobbed and sobbed to be allowed to stay, but suddenly I was back in

◀ **The age-old belief in angelic beings appears to be justified: many who have NDEs describe encounters with entities who reveal themselves as guardian angels.**

my body. The medical staff [I had been in a car crash] thought I was depressed because the man in the other car had been killed, but although I was sorry to hear it, that wasn't the reason.

But as the days passed I began to realize I'd been very lucky. I looked around at everyone else and saw a great unspoken fear on their faces. Whether or not they knew it consciously, they were all afraid of death, and it showed in the way they carried themselves, like victims, and like a great cloud over their heads. But I wasn't like them. I'd been to heaven and met my dead dad and he was better and happier than he could ever have been alive. I saw there was nothing to be afraid of."

All NDE researchers have been forcibly struck by the sheer power of the NDE and by the strength of its continuing influence on the lives of those who have had one. Often it is recalled with great clarity many years after the event, and is spoken of in terms that evoke a spiritual rebirth and, as Margot Grey writes, 'a personal sense of renewal and a search for purpose and meaning (usually accompanied by personality and value changes with enhanced self-esteem).'

Later, Dr Grey added:

"Other after-effects [of the NDE] include a sense of rebirth and renewal, a renewed sense of purpose, a new-found inner strength and an increased self-confidence, together with unconditional love and a sense of service."

The great awakening

The life-changing potential of the NDE should not be underestimated.

As one man said:

"Let's not beat about the bush. I'd died and come back – I had been resurrected and nobody can tell me that isn't the biggest, most significant thing that can happen to you."

Sometimes the experience can provide a much-needed jolt and turn around a dissolute and largely negative life completely. In *Saved by the Light* (1994) by Dannion Brinkley and Paul Perry, the story of Dannion's rebirth through two NDEs is told.

On 17 September 1975, 25-year-old Dannion was talking on the telephone during a thunderstorm in his home in Aiken, South Carolina. Without warning, lightning coursed through the apparatus, throwing him ceiling high and causing explosions of agony to surge through his whole body. But abruptly the pain vanished, leaving him with 'a glorious calmness'. He found himself viewing his burnt body from above, watching his wife desperately trying to save him.

On his way to hospital he found himself being drawn into a tunnel towards the light, where he was met by beings of light who bathed him in love. They showed him a life review,

in which he felt the full effects of his bullying and rages on others, and knew their fear and resentment. It was as if he had become all the other people he had hurt and insulted, and he found himself feeling profoundly guilty and ashamed for the first time in his life. Far from being a vague, otherworldly experience, it was a stiff dose of reality, and one that was to change him completely.

Dannion was then taken into a 'city of cathedrals … a monument to the glory of God'. The very fabric of the buildings, which seemed to be somehow made of living glass, pulsed with the power of learning. There he encountered a panel of 13 beings of light, who answered his questions telepathically, filling him with a glow of knowledge. Later Dannion confided 117 predictions (concerning global events) to Dr Raymond Moody, and later it is claimed that 95 of them came true up until 1993. These

included the Chernobyl disaster and the break-up of the Soviet Union, neither of which could have been guessed at in the 1970s when Dannion had his experience.

However, some of Dannion's predictions have failed to materialize, including a war between Russia and China, although the beings of light had impressed upon him that these events could be avoided if mankind had a change of heart.

One of the beings told Dannion that his personal mission was to help people to overcome stress, and revealed to him how to build equipment that would combat this killer condition. Meanwhile, his body had been pronounced dead, and it was a full 20 minutes later that he began breathing again.

The lightning strike had ruined his body, frequently causing him to black out. In May 1989, his weakened condition resulted in him dying once

---

CASE STUDY: AN INSPIRING TALE

NDEs are frequently inspirational to others, but rarely are they also of such practical use as in the following story told by British author Lynn Picknett:

In the early 1980s I was working as deputy editor on the weekly publication *The Unexplained*. It was my job to commission the material that would fill the pages, but one week a particular article didn't arrive. And for once there was nothing else on file. I went hot and cold with horror when I realized the unthinkable would happen – there would be blank pages in the magazine!

I remember standing there silently praying for help as I automatically started opening the day's mail. The last thing I opened was an ordinary-looking brown envelope that was literally to change my life. It contained an unsolicited typescript by a Dr A.G. Khan, telling the story of his daughter Durdana's NDE when a small child in Pakistan some 12 years previously (see page 122).

I skimmed through it and nearly burst with amazement and relief. It was an editor's dream come true! Not only was the content of the article exactly what we needed, but it was written so well that it hardly needed any editing. In fact, it actually fitted the allotted space perfectly. And there were stunning illustrations to go with it!

But much more significantly, Dr Khan's package had another, more profound effect. My father [Cyril Picknett MBE] was slowly dying of cancer at home in York and his

thoughts had begun to turn to the question of an afterlife. He was troubled because he felt that the Church of England had let him down, and that there were no answers. And he urgently needed some comfort.

That weekend I travelled home with Durdana's story, and read it to him. I was careful to say, 'I don't know if it's proof of life after death, Daddy, but it's very impressive.' He smiled for the first time in ages. 'It's wonderful,' he said. 'I like the bit about the garden. I hope I'll be allowed to work in it.' (He loved gardening.)

I have no doubt that his last days were helped enormously by Durdana's story. The doctors had warned me that his death would be agonizing, but when it happened it was totally peaceful. He just slipped away in his sleep, smiling a little. I fully believe that his mind had been opened to the possibility of an afterlife, and he welcomed his entry into it so much that he left all pain behind very easily.

A few months later I dreamt that I went to see him in heaven. He looked very healthy and happy and made me a cup of tea in his own house made of light. Then he showed me round a wonderful garden very proudly. 'They' must have let him work in it after all.

THE CREATIVE POWER OF DREAMS

To the majority of people, dreams are the nearest they get to the flashes of inspiration and enlightenment reported by people who have had NDEs. Many celebrated achievers have admitted they owe their genius to the stuff of dreams: among them were Charles Dickens, whose afternoon dozes frequently presented him with his plots and characters complete, and Samuel Taylor Coleridge, who dreamt his epic poem *Kubla Khan* only to be interrupted the next morning while feverishly copying it down from memory, and losing most of it for ever.

Scientists, too, have had cause to be grateful to dreams – 'the royal road to the unconscious'. James Watt, the inventor of the steam engine, dreamt how to make lead shot by dropping molten lead into water from a great height. His actual dream imagery was of falling rain, but Watt was so perfectly in communion with his unconscious that he interpreted it exactly. Similarly, when the nineteenth-century German chemist August Kekulé was confronted with the problem of how hydrogen and carbon atoms were linked together in benzene, he dozed off and saw the benzene molecules in the form of a snake, swallowing its own tail. On waking he realized that the carbon atoms would form a ring, which proved to be the case.

Closer to our time, Angus Lavery, expert on Rubik's inventions for the world-famous London toy store Hamley's, dreamt the solution to Rubik's Clock, which has a hundred billion permutations, eight weeks after he first saw it at a toy fair in 1988. He can now solve the problem posed by the clock in 18 seconds.

The music for one of the world's all-time favourite songs was dreamt by its composer. He woke with a refrain running through his head that seemed so insistent and familiar that he contacted all his musician friends and asked them what it was. When he realized no one knew, he recorded it. The composer was Paul McCartney, and the song was *Yesterday*.

▼ **Charles Dickens was one of many creative geniuses whose ideas came fully formed during day dreaming or sleep.**

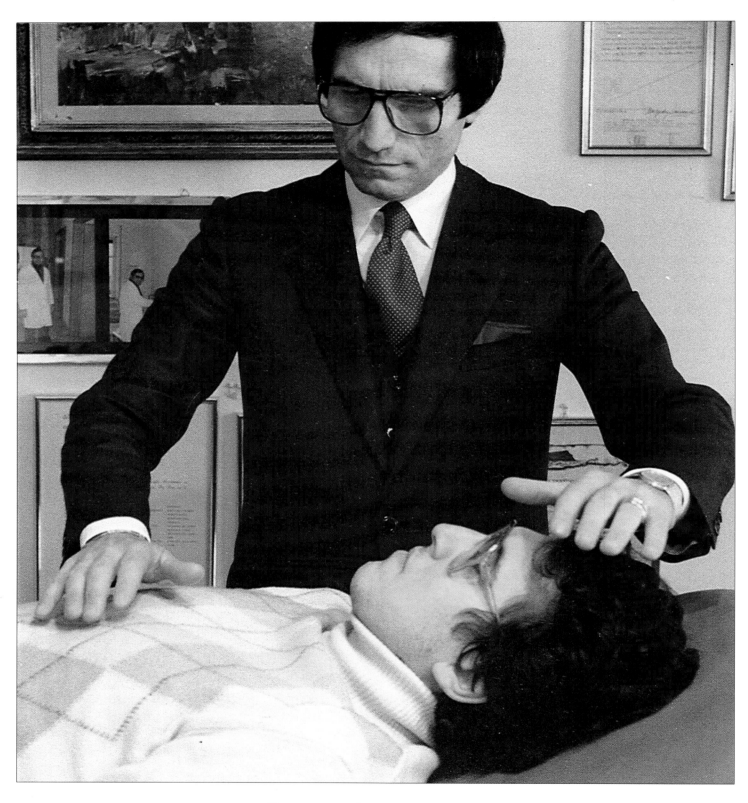

Paranormal powers

more due to a heart attack, and this time when the being of light met him at the end of the black tunnel, his life review was not such a shameful experience. Thanks to his NDE 14 years before, he had radically reassessed his life and changed his ways for the better.

Dannion also discovered that he had become psychic. Just by touching someone he saw key events in their lives – the moments that had made them the person they became. Dr Moody witnessed Dannion's extraordinary ability to understand people's

▲ The Italian psychic Nicola Cutolo is one of many naturally gifted healers. Some people also discover that they have become healers after their NDE.

secret selves simply by touching them and then helping them to deal with the emotional issues that had

POSITIVE BENEFITS OF THE NDE

After an NDE, a person becomes different from others as a result of his or her return from death. These are some of the main changes that have been noted by researchers:

- Greatly reduced fear of death. According to Melvin Morse, those who have had an NDE have approximately half the average anxiety about death.

- Improved intelligence and inexplicably greater knowledge. Sometimes the person just knows the answer to a problem, or has specific information simply pop into their head. Occasionally they are taught obscure facts during their experience that later proved to be correct.

- A greater zest for life. As Dr Morse says, these people 'are not afraid to live or die'; they are 'zestaholics'. They exhibit all the positive characteristics of the type-A personality, becoming relentless but not ruthless in the pursuit of their goals, but without treading on others on the way up, and without the anger and frustration that otherwise often results in 'burn out' and coronaries.

- A discovery of personal destiny and purpose. After an NDE, many people report that they have been sent back to earth with words to the effect of 'we have plans for you'. They return to consciousness knowing that every individual has work to do in this life, and cannot leave it until that mission is completed.

- Increased psychic abilities. Many people become clairvoyant (able to see into the future) after an NDE, although this is a mixed blessing. Some become talented healers.

- More spiritual. Almost always, those who have a brush with death become more tolerant, altruistic and loving as a result. However, their visit to heaven often reveals that no one religion is right, and so they tend to become much less narrowly religious in the denominational or dogmatic sense.

- An inspiration to others. Their stories, and their example, have proved immeasurably inspiring and comforting to others, particularly those who are dying. Those who have experienced an NDE can tell us what God is like.

- The knowledge that suicide is wrong. No matter how inviting the world of light may appear to be, those who have been there return with the firm understanding that to take life, either in an act of murder or suicide, is the gravest possible sin and crime against God and the realm of love. Those who have had an NDE also understand that all physical and emotional pain will end naturally with entry into the light.

been revealed spontaneously to him.

This sudden burst of psychic power is not confined to Dannion Brinkley. Many who have had NDEs discover that the doors of their inner minds are opened, that they possess a profound awareness of the unseen world where past, present and future are almost equally accessible. Ruth, a 32-year-old whose NDE in 1987 completely changed her life, says:

I was very quiet and introspective after my operation. People thought it was because I'd been so ill, but that wasn't it. In fact I got better almost miraculously quickly, but my experience wasn't something I wanted to shout about. I knew I had died ... I kept repeating it to myself over and over: 'I've been dead, I've actually been dead ...' and trying to get my mind around it.

I'd been dead, and come back and I didn't want to share it with anybody then because it seemed such a precious thing to me – a lovely, lovely gift somehow. But just a couple of weeks after I went home to recuperate I noticed something very unusual. At first I thought it was an optical illusion. I was lying on the sofa and my eye caught the doorknob - very prosaic, I know! And it seemed to shimmer as if it was alive. I looked around the room and saw the huge bunch of 'get well' flowers exploding with light and colour. I just sat there and blinked and rubbed my eyes, but nothing changed.

Everything in the room, even the really ordinary things like magazines or coffee mugs, were alive, buzzing and fizzing with life. It was wonderful. Then my neighbour popped in to check on me and I just sat and stared because there were coloured lights bursting from her head and hands and I felt a bit embarrassed. It was as if I was seeing something very intimate.

Since then I see what I now know to be auras around living things, including animals and trees, and I can tell just by looking if someone is ill or depressed. And I've discovered that I can make them feel better by visualizing their auras getting bigger and brighter. I'm not saying I can dramatically heal them and I never tell them what I'm doing, but I've seen it work time and time again. One minute they're really down, with feeble little bits of light coming from them, and after I've done my 'visualization thing' they get these 'light shows' around their heads and start to smile for no apparent reason. I've talked to a few other people who've had such experiences and they've had something similar. I wonder just how many of us there are, quietly helping people in this strange way. **"**

In several notable cases, NDEs have triggered a greater ability to heal. One woman, 'May', discovered that she could relieve her friend's cancer pain simply by directing her attention to it and asking for the light she had known in her NDE to flood the whole area.

At first both May and her friend put it down to coincidence, but after a few days, when the pain responded every time to May's attention, the connection became too obvious to ignore. This was only the beginning, for the tumour was shown to be shrinking fast, and completely disappeared, against every prognosis, within a few weeks. May says:

"It was not me doing it. I'm sure my experience had somehow opened me up to become a channel for that wonderful loving light. You can't fight its goodness and you don't want to. It doesn't know the meaning of impossible and all it wants is to create perfection and get rid of anything ugly or hurtful. I think that's why sinners can't get close to God. It's nothing to do with him hating them, it's just that what they do and what they've become is too ugly and dark to be able to stand close to his light, that's all. But they, too, can be transformed by it if they take the tiniest step towards it. God wants them to.

I haven't taken up healing as a profession like some do. I couldn't cope with the raised hopes. But I have managed to help quite a few people with chronic pain, and

have, I believe, eased the passing of several people. Part of that process seems to be just telling them about the time that I died and came back, and what a wonderful place they are going to. I know they believe me and I love seeing the peace that comes over them then, when their anxiety goes and they relax into the transition. Then their death can be beautiful, as it was meant to be. **"**

A timeless experience

More than any other NDE researcher, it is the work of Melvin Morse that has revealed the full extent of the transformative effect of the NDE, which had largely been marginalized by other workers in the field. The overwhelming response to his earlier book *Closer To The Light* (written with Paul Perry), had presented him with abundant subjects to interview, and what struck him most forcibly about them as a group was the way their experience had changed them in almost unimaginable ways.

Other researchers, such as pioneer Raymond Moody, and Margot Grey, had noted that, on the whole, people became more loving and tolerant, and often evinced greater psychic powers than before their NDE. In his survey, Morse also discovered enhanced paranormal powers in people after an NDE, finding that their psychic abilities were four times higher than average.

Morse cites many cases of people who began to predict future events as a result of their NDEs, but it was not always a happy development. One woman became so distressed by her new-found abilities that she made sure she took prescription drugs most of the time in order to dull her senses and keep the unwanted paranormal gifts at bay.

There were other, more subtle reactions to the experience. As Morse says:

"Some were very profound … Others were subtle. For example,

many cannot wear watches because something keeps breaking them. Some of these people reported guardian angels who stayed with them long after the frightening experience of almost dying.

I was fascinated by the help they received from these merciful companions. **"**

One British woman, Elaine, who 'could never wear watches', discovered a childhood NDE she had forgotten by taking part in a hypnotic regression experiment:

"I could never wear a watch. If I tried they just stopped immediately. I had other weird things with clocks as well. I would go into a room and the clock would stop, or I would suddenly wake up having just dreamt that my bedside clock had stopped and the ticking would stop immediately. I thought it was just one of those things, but I think now it had a deeper connection with something I had buried deep in my unconscious mind.

In the late 1980s, I took part in an experiment in hypnotic regression with a couple of my friends who were training to be hypnotherapists. I agreed to be their guinea pig because they were very concerned with doing it properly. I felt I was in good hands. One of them, Tim, took me back to my early childhood to a specific event and I startled him by telling the story of how I'd died of measles and floated out of my body, looking down on myself in the bed. I described going hand in hand with a 'nice lady dressed in light' through a lovely field and feeling very happy. She showed me the whole town below - the field seemed to be up in the sky - and I could see it change over the space

▶ **Someone to watch over me – this highly sentimental Victorian scene may actually be closer to the truth than we might think. It seems we all have guardians.**

of many years. She said I would live a long time and have many ups and downs, but there was nothing to be afraid of because I'd been shown a great secret. Then suddenly I was back in my body and my mother was kissing me and crying, glad I was alive again.

The interesting thing is that although I knew I'd nearly died of measles when I was little, I had no idea it had been such a close call. And I couldn't remember being out of the body. Since the hypnosis session I've read a lot about such experiences, and I recently heard that you can't wear watches afterwards. Somehow that was the extra bit of proof I'd been looking for. I now know that I had died, and that I did come back. **"**

Guardian angels

After an NDE, many people describe meeting their guardian angel while in heaven, and some continue to feel his presence afterwards in very tangible ways. Betty J. Eadie encountered three men in 'beautiful, light-brown robes... A kind of glow emanated from them ... [they] appeared to be about 70 or 80 years old, but I knew somehow that they were on a timescale different from earth's.'

She recognized these beings as her 'choicest' friends from a pre-existence in a spirit world, and says that 'they had chosen to be with me'. She describes how she 'felt their love ... experienced their feelings. And this filled me with joy because they loved me so much.' Later she realized that she had more guardian angels, but that these three had elected to welcome her into her NDE and help her understand its implications for humankind as a whole.

Sometimes the angels prove remarkably useful in practical ways. One respondent in Melvin Morse's Transformations group was a well known American writer who chose to go by the name David. He first met his guardian angel during a serious bout of hepatitis when he was young.

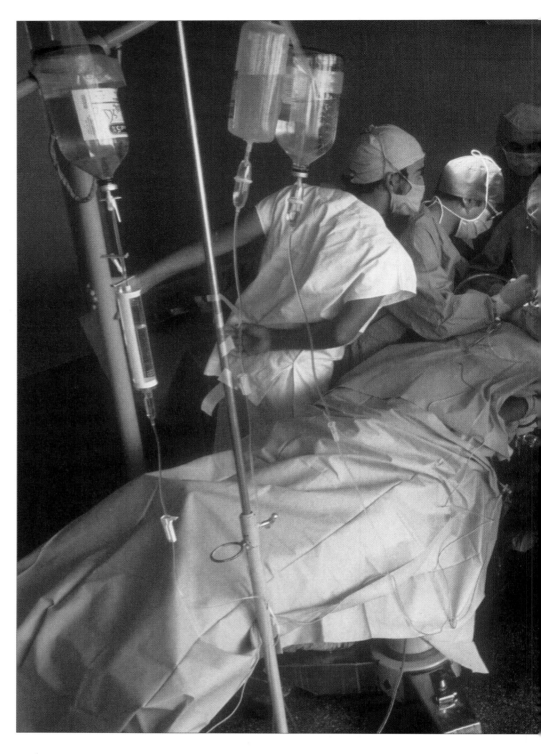

▲ People undergoing surgery – and in effect dead to the world, sometimes for hours – often become surprisingly alive and full of energy during their OBEs.

He saw her distinctly standing behind his parents and the doctor, then he stood with the angel during a brief OBE. Although he has never seen her again, he frequently feels her presence 'like someone standing in the room', and he maintains that she has often helped him with his writing. He knows she is doing so when he seems to lose control:

"*It happens to me a lot on the stuff I write. I wrote something last night and I don't know where the hell it comes from. My wife can go through my manuscripts with a red pen and circle the stuff that*

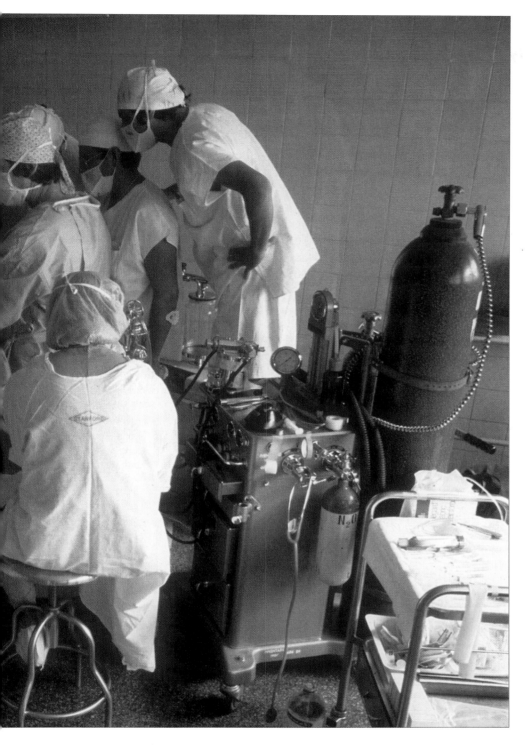

up and take a break and then read the work, and it's as though someone came through the window and stuck it on my computer. "

However, this mysterious kind of inspiration is not quite so unusual as it may appear. Throughout history, artists, composers, writers and scientists have believed their work to come from somewhere – or someone – else, or have awoken from a dream or trance-like state with the whole work complete in their minds, without any conscious effort on their part (see page 81). The question is, does the NDE somehow unlock the latent abilities of the unconscious mind? Is the experience therefore analogous to a profound dream? Or is there something objective and external involved, such as a real guardian angel?

Certainly the sudden ability to do 'automatic writing', where the pen seems to move by itself, is not unknown in NDE cases.

One man, a respondent of Margot Grey, said:

" *I was directed to pick up a pencil and a piece of paper, and as I started to write I felt as if someone was writing through me, as if I was taken over by a higher source. I was given answers to many of the problems of life and understood many things that were due to happen. I had never been able to do this before my experience.* "

Fast-forward video

The early accounts of NDEs frequently included a life review, in which the individual is confronted with his past, but the later work of Dr Grey and others revealed that some people were also shown previews of what was yet to come in a sort of fast-forward video show. (Kenneth Ring calls this a Personal Flash Forward, or PFF.) This alone gives the aftermath of the NDE a paranormal aura, especially when the scenes shown come true.

One man who had died during a heart-bypass operation said:

doesn't look like my own. And I don't know where it comes from. It's the most powerful imagery in the world. But where am I when this stuff is coming out? I'm not sitting in the chair, I'm gone. When I'm done I frequently feel like I'm going to faint. I need to get a cup of coffee or talk my wife into giving me a back rub. Then I sit down and read my stuff and it's the first time

I've read it. I don't know where it's coming from. It happens with such frequency that I feel like I'm a fraud. I don't feel like it's coming from me and it leads to some spooky times. I know my fingers are moving and I know words are appearing on the screen, but it's as though they aren't coming out of my head. And I have a very strange, detached feeling. I'll get

▲ American psychologist Dr Kenneth Ring has inspired many other NDE researchers, including Dr Margot Grey whose work in the UK largely reinforced his own.

"I was jumping up and down and punching the air with joy in that place of love and light, but soon had to stand quietly when they [beings of light] showed me a sort of movie show of my life. It was … like a series of very brightly lit scenes of events that hadn't neces-sarily seemed very important at the time, things I had forgotten but remembered with a huge overflow-ing sense of familiarity when I saw them again. There was … me having a row with my brother when I was about eight years old and kicking his kitten when he went out of the room. Not only was I full of the worst kind of shame – I thought I would explode with it – but also I seemed to feel the kitten's pain. It was a dreadful mixture of physical hurt, shock and perplexi-ty about how a human she had trusted could do such an appalling thing, a moment when her total innocence was violated by my big boot on her ribs.

But it wasn't all bad. I returned to the day when I saw the apart-ment opposite explode in flames and my neighbour escaping with just his pyjamas. He lost every-thing and my heart went out to him, so I made a parcel of some of my stuff, including some really nice things, and took them over to him. Then I organized a collection in the neighbourhood and let him stay at my place until he had somewhere to go. I knew I'd done the right thing, and the beings beamed their delight at me.

Then, suddenly, came scenes from my future, with me looking older and a bit bigger around the middle. I was sitting in a room I didn't recognize with my arm around a lady who was a stranger to me, although I somehow knew she was called Ray, which struck me as strange because it's a man's name. I could hear, and somehow even smell, the sea, although I didn't live anywhere near it at the time of my experience. I knew I was happy in this future existence, but that everything was very different from the life I had at that time.

Since I had my NDE my mar-riage … fell apart. It was very sad, but I was a different man because of going to the light and my [first] wife and I couldn't see eye to eye. I became very restless and travelled extensively around the world. I suppose I was looking for some-thing, or perhaps for someone. About 10 years after my NDE [which was in 1975] I was sitting in the Departure Lounge at Heathrow Airport in London wait-ing to get on a plane for New York *when a pretty lady asked if she could borrow my newspaper. There was something familiar about her ...you've guessed it...well, the long and short of it is that we're married now and live close to Sydney, Australia. And her name really is Ray - it's short for Raylene.* **"**

One of Dr Grey's respondents who had nearly died during childbirth said:

"*During the experience I was aware that I already knew everything that was going to happen to me. But afterwards I could only recall fragments. I do remember that it was communicated to me that when it was necessary for me to know certain things I would be able to recall them. I have since found this to be the case, as sometimes when things happen I realize I already know how it's going to work out.* **"**

Another female respondent told how in her life preview she had seen herself and her family in many years time, the vividness of the scene being reinforced by the fact that she could smell. Later, when the scene took place in real life, it was the detail of the odour that specifically amazed her:

"*Particularly striking was the smell of the salad I was producing ... mingled with the smell of evergreens growing around the house and the odour of freshly cut grass. Also, I could detect my own cologne and soap from the shower my husband had vacated. This picture was only a glimpse, but it made a huge impression on me. I must have vowed right then never to forget it, because I certainly have not.* **"**

Recent research has shown that certain odours trigger memories in a more immediate way than any other association. The scent of old-fashioned lavender cologne, for example, can instantly bring back childhood visits to an elderly neighbour, or the

smell of chalk cam revive memories of a traumatic first day at school. Was this PFF 'stage-managed' in order to carry the maximum memorability for this woman? Certainly it made a lasting impression of total reality, so that when the event came true it was immediately recognized.

The future of the world

Some 'flash forwards' go beyond the individual's future life. Like Dannion Brinkley, many report being shown global events during their experience, although sometimes they are told that these are not 'written in stone', but are likely to happen if humankind fails to change its ways. Others become prophetic after their NDE, so it may be reasonably supposed that the ability to see the future came about as a direct result of their experience. These Prophetic Visions (PVs) have been noted by several researchers, notably Kenneth Ring and Margot Grey.

Dr Ring summarized the extent and content of most PVs as follows, although he was careful to say 'Any

overall account must be regarded as extremely provisional':

"*There is, first of all, a sense of having total knowledge, but specifically one is aware of seeing the entirety of the earth's evolution and history from the beginning to the end of time. The future scenario, however, is usually of short duration, seldom extending much beyond the beginning of the twenty-first century. The individual reports that in this decade there will be an increasing incidence of earthquakes, volcanic activity and generally massive geophysical changes.* **"**

These natural upheavals will lead inevitably to social disruption, made worse by man-made disasters:

"*There will be resultant disturbances in weather patterns and food supplies. The world economic system will collapse, and the possibility of nuclear war or accident is very great (respondents are not agreed on whether a nuclear*

CASE STUDY: FINDING TRUE PEACE
Dr Elisabeth Kubler-Ross's terrifying 'initiatory' experience of reliving the death agonies of her thousand patients (see page 100) was preceded by an OBE from which she returned with the dim memory of the words 'Shanti Nilaya'. She had no idea what they meant. After her extraordinary descent into the agony of others, she slept briefly then awoke in a state of mystical awareness. In her book *On Life After Death* (1991) she describes what happened next:

"*It took several months before I was able to verbalize my experience and share it with a beautiful, nonjudgmental, understanding group ... After I shared my experience, I was given a label for it. It was called cosmic consciousness ... I was also told at that moment that as I merged into this spiritual energy, the source of all light, the words that were given to me, Shanti Nilaya, mean the final home of peace, the home all of us will return to when we have gone through all the agonies, the pains, the sorrows, the griefs. It is where we will be able to let go of the pain and become what we were created to be, a being of harmony between the physical, the emotional, the intellectual and the spiritual quadrants, a being that understands that love, true love, has no claims and no 'ifs'. If we could understand this state of love, then all of us would be whole and healthy, and all of us would be able to fulfil our destiny in a single lifetime.* **"**

catastrophe will occur). However, all of these events are transitional rather than ultimate, and they will be followed by a new era in human history, marked by human brotherhood, universal love and world peace. Though many will die, the earth will live. While agreeing that the dates for these events are not fixed, most individuals feel that they are likely to take place during the 1980s.

Many respondents of both Kenneth Ring and Margot Grey described remarkably similar scenarios of the earth's future, including earthquakes, volcanic activity, social unrest, meteorological changes, food shortages, disease and nuclear war. Interestingly, whereas war and social unrest are regrettably easy enough to predict, in the 1970s when many of these respondents made their predictions, disease and meteorological changes were not much debated, nor widely considered as major global prognoses.

However, there is a problem. Many respondents predicted that a variety of cataclysms – from World War III to widespread pestilence – would take place in 1988. Writing in the early 1980s, all Kenneth Ring and Margot Grey could do was faithfully record what their respondents predicted. Now, as the twenty-first century looms ever closer, and 1988 is already a dim memory, are we not justified in assessing these PVs more critically? Perhaps, like many other psychics, these NDE cases found it difficult to be accurate about specific dates, although the content of their predictions was essentially correct. However, one thing is for sure: the non-arrival of these disasters is hardly the result of humankind changing its ways!

◄ **Drought in Africa – but is this just the start of many worldwide disasters predicted by those who have experienced an NDE, whose visions often include doomladen global prophecies?**

CASE STUDY: NEVER-ENDING LIGHT

This is how Jaimal Lovitt, a high-school student, described an NDE to Dr Melvin Morse:

"I once saw the light, it was not like anything you could imagine, for it was like a sound that existed only in the silence of pitch black.

It is like the sound of life searching for a place to lay and rest, almost as if it was everybody's existing energy taken and mixed together to form a white ball of light that rings the sound of life as loud as it can, but so faint that the unaware don't hear it and the aware only think they do.

The light is a pattern that some call life. The ups and downs, the happy the sad, the good the bad, the only thing that is real and not quite in our reach, the people who talk and then lost their speech. The quiet of the afternoon, the thought that the end is soon. The calling of the world to shout out and scream 'I'm alive, can't you see, so give me the power to hear the great sound for I've heard it once it won't let me down.

I shall see the light as white as it may be, but when I die it shall always be with me.

For when it's all over and I'm old and turned grey, my light will be there forever to stay because it is never-ending, eternal and sharp, and it will always be with me even in the everlasting dark. **"**

Incredible knowledge

Perhaps the most significant discovery that Dr Morse made about NDEs was that those who have them tend to become more intelligent as a result of their experience. Some even returned from death with incredible, otherwise inexplicable knowledge. One such person was Olaf Sunden, the results of whose experience were, Dr Morse admitted, 'too complex for me to comprehend'.

During a routine tonsillectomy when he was 14, Olaf was accidentally given an overdose of ether and stopped breathing. He describes what happened next:

"Suddenly I rolled into a ball and seemed to smash into a wall into another reality. The passage from this side to the other was extremely painful, a suffocation. The forces which brought me through the death barrier were terrific and the boundary barrier was extremely strong.

Suddenly I was on the other side, and all pains were gone. I had lost all my interest and attachment to my biological life. [I realized that] the boundary between life and death is a strange creation of our mind. It is horrifying and real when perceived from this side [the side of the living] and yet is insignificant when perceived from the other side.

My first impression was a total surprise. How could I exist in such a comfortable way, and how could I perceive and think while being dead, and yet have no body?"

The universe appeared to him to be without boundaries. He saw it as (in Melvin Morse's words) 'a system of shrinking bubbles, one in which the bubbles appeared in spherical, concentric trains that moved in intricate patterns that he completely comprehended'. This perception was to prove quite astonishing in the years to come.

In his OBE state, the young Olaf stood in a bright orange light, which he called 'the point of annihilation'. It was frightening, but it opened up his understanding like nothing else in his short life. He says, 'I felt I had a total comprehension, which made everything understandable'. Then he had the

CASE STUDY: AN ANGEL'S HELP

Four-year-old Russ fell from a treehouse,
and as he fell he met an angel:

"I looked up and suddenly I was falling, but it felt more like I was floating. I heard a voice tell me not to be scared, but to hold very still and to look up and not move my neck. It said that it would hurt but I would still be okay.

I saw a little girl floating in the air next to me. She was all bright, but it didn't hurt my eyes to look at her. I did what I was told and landed hard and broke my collarbone.

When I got to the doctor, I heard him tell my mother that if my head had been turned to the left or the right, I would have snapped my neck. I did just what the little girl told me to do and walked away okay. **"**

sensation as if his 'mind [was] splitting into two parts', and the newly omniscient part disappeared above him as a burst of light. The other part of him was sent back into his body. Olaf says:

"I remember thinking, 'please let me understand this new physics of relativity'. Then I felt a bump and was caught up in a channel and transported with tremendous force back into my body. I collected all my power to remember the cosmic comprehension of the universal machinery. **"**

The immediate aftermath of his NDE was hardly typical. Before his experience he had been an average to below average student. Now he was arrogant in his new-found intelligence, refusing to accept standard scientific thinking and constantly offering his own theories. How could he explain that he could explain the theories of Albert Einstein because of the knowledge he had been given when he was dead?

However, this is by no means the end of the story. In the 1960s, when Olaf was in his forties, the news was made public about scientists discovering the neutrino, a nuclear particle that can travel through the enormous heart of a star without being changed in any way. This was staggering news to Olaf, because he realized that he had been given prior knowledge of

this in the 'bubbles' that passed through solid bodies in his NDE.

As a direct result of the knowledge that freed him from conventional thinking, Olaf has made a success of his life. He is an innovative research scientist, an engineer holding a hundred patents, including a method of making paper that reduces the need to destroy trees by 25 per cent.

But Olaf's 'cosmic gift', as he calls it, was to prove of immeasurable benefit in his own life. In the 1970s his teenage daughter was terribly hurt in a road-traffic accident, and it was thought that she would live out her days in a vegetative state. Olaf believed she was by then on the other side, but perhaps not yet totally out of reach.

Drawing on his wellspring of intuition, which he had learned to trust totally since his NDE, Olaf gave his comatose daughter a caffeine-like substance he had experimentally used in order to improve memory functioning. The first dose provoked an immediate, dramatic effect. The girl abruptly tried to sit up and kept up this struggle for a full 15 minutes, before collapsing once more into her coma. But a second dose established a definite return to life, and after four weeks she became conscious enough to answer mathematical questions by pressing her father's hand. One month later this girl, who doctors believed would be little more than a vegetable for the rest of her life, passed

an examination in mathematics!

Although she had eye problems and is still partially paralyzed in one leg, Olaf's daughter is now a successful architect and mother of two children thanks to the insights her father learned during his brush with death.

As Olaf said to Melvin Morse while they were having dinner:

"I no longer think I am crazy or a crank because of what happened. I know that my experience was real and not a fantastic dream. But the question I have is this: Did that

knowledge come from inside my own brain or did it come from someplace else? And this universe that I entered. Did I really go to an altered reality? **"**

The power of love

NDEs happen to people from all races, creeds and walks of life yet the effect they have can be summed up

in one word: love. Before an NDE, a person may have been embittered by the hardships and pain of life, but after they have been touched by the light their attitude significantly changes.

In his book *The Return From Silence*, D. Scott Rogo tells the story of Helen Nelson of New Britain, Connecticut, who in 1975 was pronounced dead after having a heart attack and lying alone for four days. As the medics finally began their desperate attempts to resuscitate her, her NDE began. She said:

"*I could feel myself going through this tunnel ... And there was this light at the end. God, it was so bright! As I neared it I could feel this warmth enveloping me. I could feel ... it was like velvet suddenly creeping over me, the softness and this warmth. And I suddenly got into this spot and it was like a jolt, and I'm standing and I'm looking around me and I see all this beautiful golden light! Again I have to say, if you ever remember being touched by warm velvet, that beautiful caressing feeling.* **"**

▼ Olaf's daughter was badly hurt in a road accident, but he knew how to help heal her, thanks to the knowledge he had acquired as a result of his own NDE.

▲ The Earth seen from a space shuttle: this is also the perspective from which many who have had NDEs view their home planet, a profoundly moving experience.

Mrs Nelson discovered she was in a marble building in which she recognized her deceased relatives and other spirits floating around. She was particularly pleased to encounter her mother and her father:

"They seemed to welcome me. They looked as they had looked when they were quite young. I know we communicated a great deal. But I don't remember exactly what was said. I know I was given a tremendous knowledge, a tremendous understanding of reality. Every once in a while it's like a faint whiff of perfume. I get an inkling of it. And it's so delicious!"

Her father then told her she must go back, and she pleaded to be allowed to stay. However, he was not to be swayed, replying, 'There is something very important for you to complete.' Then Helen found herself back in her body, suffering terrible agony:

"I felt as though every limb, every bone in my body was being crushed or torn from me. I saw a

lot of energy, a lot of electrical energy. It was like a bang! I heard someone saying, 'Helen, Helen'. And I looked up and noticed my two ministers and my doctor. I kind of chuckled! I wasn't aware I had all the life supports going and I couldn't speak. But I chuckled. I thought I was at my funeral! Because I knew I had died! The reality that I was alive wasn't there yet. Then back into the coma. And that's what it was for quite some time - in and out of coma. The moment I would come out of the comatose state it would hit me what had happened."

Helen was in no doubt about the effect the NDE had on her life, and on her whole attitude. She said:

"I came out of this NDE with the one positive knowledge that is constantly magnified in my life, and that is that love is the innermost core of our entire being, the core of what life is really all about."

Time and time again those who return from the 'valley of death' tell of the overwhelming feeling of love they have experienced. Death is not cold, grim nothingness. According to these adventurers of the soul it is quite the opposite – bright, light and totally alive with love.

One of Dr Kenneth Ring's respondents, the noted anthropologist Professor Patrick Gallagher, had a terrible car crash in the aptly named Death Valley, California. He described his NDE to Dr Ring in these words:

"I was floating in the air above the body ... and viewing it down a sort of diagonal angle. This didn't seem to cause any consternation to me at all. I really was completely dead but that didn't cause [me] any emotional difficulties.

Then, after that, I realized that I was able to float quite easily, even though I had no intention of doing that ... Then I very quickly discovered

---

THE WISDOM OF THE PROPHET

This excerpt from *The Prophet* by Kahlil Gibran was read by Cherie Sutherland at the graveside of her son Patrick. It was his death that prompted her to research NDEs, and which led to the publication of her findings in *Children of the Light* (1995).

For what is it to die but to stand naked in the wind
and to melt into the sun?
And what is it to cease breathing but to free the breath
from its restless tides that it may rise and expand
and seek God unencumbered?

Only when you drink from the river of silence
shall you indeed sing.
And when you have reached the mountain top,
then you shall begin to climb.
And when the earth shall claim your limbs,
then shall you truly dance.

---

also that not only was I floating and hence free from gravity but free also from any of the other constrictions that inhibit a flight ..."

He flew at a phenomenal speed, with a feeling of elation:

"... Then I noticed that there was a dark area in front of me and as I approached it I thought that it was some sort of a tunnel and immediately, without further thought, I entered into it and then flew with an even greater sense of the joy of light ... [After] what now I would imagine to be a relatively short period of time - although again time was dispensed with - I noticed a sort of circular light at a great distance which I assumed to be the end of the tunnel as I was roaring through it ... and the light - the nearest thing I can barely approximate its description when one can look at this object without any of the usual problems that staring at the sun causes.

The fact is, this seemed like an incredibly illuminating sort of a place, in every sense of that word, so that not only was it an awesome brightness ... with a tremendous beauty, this kind of yellowish-

orange colour, but it also seemed a marvellous place to be. And so this increased the sense of joy I had about this flight."

After that he went through a tunnel into a different state of being, which was still:

"illuminated by that same light, and uh, I saw other things in it ... I saw my father there, who had been dead for some 25 years ... I also felt and saw of course that everyone was in a state of absolute compassion to everything else ... It seemed, too, that love was the major axiom that everyone automatically followed. This produced a phenomenal feeling of emotion to me ... because it made me feel that ... there was nothing but love ... It just seemed like the real thing ... this sense of total love in every direction."

Or as one 48-year-old British woman who had her NDE in 1983, cheerfully put it: 'After you've done your work on earth you get your reward – and that's death, which is total love and happiness. Having had a glimpse of it, I'm happy to wait and I'll be even happier to go!'

CHAPTER SIX

To Hell and Back?

Classic NDEs centre on entering a heavenly realm, and are believed to provide a foretaste of a more permanent state of rapture that may greet us when we finally leave our bodies for ever. In many ways, the NDE has vindicated the age-old belief in heaven – but has it also done the same for hell?

Raymond Moody's pioneering research into NDEs failed to come up with any reports of a realm that matched the 'fire and brimstone' concept of hell. At first it seemed that this must be because there is no hell. Nearly all his respondents described, if not technically an afterlife, then certainly an otherlife, that was synonymous with heaven. It seemed as if virtually every brush with death automatically guaranteed a visit to a place of celestial music, poignant encounters with loved ones in a stunningly beautiful environment, and sensations of ineffable joy and comfort. Soon, however, darker hints emerged that suggested that the temporary cessation of a heartbeat did not, as previously thought, guarantee entry into paradise.

Within two years of publishing his *Life After Life*, Raymond Moody wrote of people who had experienced less-than-heavenly realms when clinically dead. He reported that several of his original pool of respondents had encountered even more distressing and thought-provoking

◄ **Sixteenth-century artist Pieter Huys' vision of the underworld, which is now seen to correspond with 'Winterland' described in some NDEs and also by mediums.**

planes of existence, which some went so far as to call a 'realm of bewildered spirits'.

Where confusion reigns

In his *Reflections on Life After Life* (1977), Dr Moody recounts the experience of one of his correspondents who had entered a very different world from the expected heaven of most NDEs:

"These bewildered people? I don't know exactly where I saw them … But as I was going by, there was this area that was dull – this is in contrast to the brilliant light. The figures were more humanized than the rest of them were. If you stop to think of it in that respect, but neither were they in quite human form as we are.

What you would think of as their head was bent downward; they had sad, depressed looks; they seemed to shuffle, as someone would on a chain gang. I don't know what they were, but they looked washed out, dull, grey. And they seemed to be forever shuffling and moving around, not knowing where they were going, not knowing who to follow, or what to look for."

These depressed people didn't even raise their heads as he went by. They appeared to be too apathetic to be curious about the newcomer or to do anything to change their own dreadfully bleak prospects. He says:

"They seemed to be thinking, 'Well, it's all over with. What am I doing? What's it all about?' Just this absolute, crushed, hopeless demeanour – not knowing what to do or where to go or who they were or anything else.

They seemed to be for ever moving, rather than just sitting, but in no special direction. They would start straight, then veer to the left and take a few steps and veer back to the right. And absolutely nothing to do. Searching, but for what they were searching I don't know."

(One suspects that the inhabitants of that hopeless world didn't know what they were searching for either. All hope, motivation and determination had been wiped out.)

Interestingly, this man described those poor wretches as not quite human, and their behaviour does suggest some kind of sheep-like animal, or zombie. Clearly, the sense of oppression and hopelessness that

▲ Although most people who experience an NDE report a life review that was non-judgemental, some have described much more hostile and terrifying trials of their soul.

accompanied this experience was intense and lasting, but was it a real, astral visit to another realm, or just a kind of dream?

The dream-like sense of oppression also comes through clearly in this report from Amanda, whose NDE in 1986 happened as a result of an accidental drug overdose:

"I had a huge feeling of unease as I seemed to be high up, looking down at my body. I knew something wasn't right … the scene seemed to fizzle out into a greyish mist, and I felt so depressed all of a sudden that I wanted to call out for my mother like a little child. There was a bit of a breeze, but such

damp, stuffy air! It smelled awful, a mixture of bad drains and mildew. It was a neglected place, a place of decay where things were forgotten and left to rot.

How can I describe that dreadful place? It's difficult because it was somehow in my mind as well as 'out there' before my eyes – although, of course, I'd left my body behind. But it was a sort of large cave, full of broken greyish

▲ The poet Dante shows a pope around the infernal regions of his vision. It seems there is no escape for the wicked.

rocks and a grey-brown dust.

I looked round, and the terrible feeling of hopelessness got to me. I could hear a sort of sobbing and moaning from deeper into the cave somewhere, and then I saw a man sitting on a rock quite close to me. He was almost transparent, completely colourless like a ghost. He looked up at me with an expression of complete despair. I'll never forget it. He didn't say anything, but he didn't have to. We were both condemned to that place and there was nothing we could do about it. At that point I was revived by the paramedics, and the first thing I did was get a lungful of good, clean air. And as soon as I could I had a bath to wash off the memory of that place. Perhaps it wasn't actually hell, but it came very close. "

Although several people had admitted to Raymond Moody that their NDEs were in quite a different category to the heavenly variety, his published work certainly never stressed this kind of experience. Indeed, the whole concept of the 'negative NDE' was apparently marginalized by the early researchers, and is still largely

CASE STUDY: NIGHT OF A THOUSAND DEATHS

Pioneering thanatologist Dr Elisabeth Kubler-Ross writes of an extraordinary personal experience in her short book *On Life After Death* (1991). Some years ago she took part in an experiment into OBEs in Robert Monroe's lab in Virginia. She was successful – too successful. That night, alone in her hotel room, she realized she had 'gone too far' and had to 'accept the consequences of my own choices'. She then experienced a night of living hell:

"*I literally experienced the deaths of my thousand patients. It was a total physical, spiritual, emotional and intellectual agony causing the inability to breathe, a doubling-up of my body, an agonizing pain and a total knowledge and awareness that I was out of the reach of any human being.***"**

During that long night, Dr Kubler-Ross was only granted a few reprieves, during which she begged for an end to the agony. Once she begged for a hand to hold, and at another time for a shoulder to lean on, but a 'deep, compassionate and severe voice' said, 'You shall not be given'. In the end she stopped fighting and rebelling, and gave in. At that moment the pain stopped and she entered a world of light and mystical vibration. Afterwards she slept profoundly and woke up reborn, and convinced of the existence of a great universal love. She accepted her experience had opened her up to the mystical bliss of the light.

sidelined, or even totally ignored today. But although descriptions such as those given above may have been 'negative' in the sense that they did not fit the ideal picture of the NDE with its ineffability and lasting sense of comfort, they were not completely hellish. Their lack of hope and deadening sensations of grey, never-ending dullness are depressing rather than actually menacing or painful. But the discoveries of one particular researcher was to shatter the complacency of his peers and provide some very disturbing evidence for the existence of hell itself.

In 1978, Dr Maurice Rawlings, then a clinical professor of medicine at the University of Tennessee, published his ground-breaking book *Beyond Death's Door*. It caused a storm then and is still regarded by many researchers as controversial.

A specialist in cardio-pulmonary resuscitation, Dr Rawlings had witnessed at firsthand many NDE cases, usually immediately after they had taken place. This put him in a unique position where NDE research was concerned at that time; most of the others in the field gathered their data when the person had recovered from his or her trauma, sometimes days or even months afterwards. But here was a highly respected medical professional whose data came from just moments after the NDE had

happened. And many of those he resuscitated talked of hell with abject terror etched into their faces.

His first case was that of a postman who had a cardiac arrest while undergoing a routine medical test. As Dr Rawlings tried to resuscitate him, the patient suddenly screamed 'I am in hell!' Repeatedly slipping away and being revived, his ordeal continued. As Dr Rawlings wrote: 'each time he regained heartbeat and respiration [he] screamed "I am in hell!"' And Rawlings could not fail to notice the man's extreme horror. Clearly, he was reacting to some profound nightmare that traumatized him every time he slipped back into unconsciousness.

Beautiful peace

The postman later had a more conventional NDE in which he felt peaceful and, leaving his body, entered a beautiful world where he encountered his dead stepmother and mother. But when Dr Rawlings interviewed him a few days afterwards, all he could remember was his wonderful OBE. Despite his obvious trauma at the time, he had no memory of shouting 'I am in hell!' or of any kind of negative experience.

In the following months, Dr Rawlings collected many accounts of hellish NDEs, but they tended to be much more different and individual

than the more 'positive' experiences (which almost conform to the well-known pattern). Some of Rawlings's cases appear to fit a Dante-like scenario of many levels of hell, while others are the classic 'hellfire and brimstone' scenes often cited as the ultimate destination of sinners by fundamentalists. Rawlings also draws on other writings to make his point, quoting among others the NDE of Thomas Welch (also told in his own book, *Oregon's Amazing Miracle*, 1976). Welch fell off a logging trestle into a river, and he tells of what happened next:

"All I can remember is falling over the edge of the trestle. The locomotive engineer watched me go all the way down into the water. The next thing I knew I was standing near a shoreline of a great ocean of fire. It happened to be what the Bible says it is in Revelations 21:8 ... It was the most awesome sight one could ever see this side of final judgment."

Welch then experienced a replay of his whole life – the classic panoramic life review – and encountered a

► A twelfth-century icon showing the precarious 'Ladder of Climax', a medieval Christian idea that the road to heaven was only for a select few.

THE SOUL'S GLIMPSE OF HELL

Spiritualists believe that most ordinary people find themselves in the ideoplastic world known as 'Summerland' when they die. But this is not the destination for everyone: some are earthbound and some enter the dark, unhappy plane called 'Winterland'.

Here, drunkards, gluttons and drug addicts mill around aimlessly, seeking the object of their obsession but never finding or possessing it. They may look through the window of a bar or restaurant and see the tantalizing displays of food and drink, but it is always just out of their reach. Similarly, the drug abuser will only catch glimpses of the ever-elusive fix, and suffer unrelieved withdrawal symptoms.

This type of judgment may seem draconian to our enlightened era, when addictions are seen as illnesses to be treated, not punished. However, it is stressed that those in Winterland are given every opportunity to leave it.

Kind emissaries from the heavenly regions are on hand to take the inmates out of that profoundly miserable existence into the light – if they are willing to give up their obsessions. We are told that some do leave Winterland in this way, but many choose to remain in the hell of their own making.

Christ-like figure who talked to him. Almost immediately afterwards he was revived by his colleagues.

Significantly, Welch's own uncomplicated Christianity comes clearly through in his account, as revealed in his obvious familiarity with the New Testament and reference to 'final judgment'. But had his beliefs and background in some way actually created the experience? Or was the lake of fire objectively real, a place where anyone, of any religion or of none, might find themselves?

Rawlings's findings were savaged by other NDE researchers, particularly Dr Michael Sabom, who is also a cardiologist. His findings are in direct opposition to those of Rawlings; he says his work has resulted in 'a complete failure to obtain any cases suggestive of a hellish experience', a position echoed by Kenneth Ring. At first Rawlings seemed isolated by his hostile peers who attacked every aspect of his research: among the many criticisms levelled at him was the accusation that the majority of his cases were drawn from the heartland of Christian fundamentalists, where a strong belief in hell may have coloured their near-death visions. However, his later research was taken from a much wider geographical area – and still he found the same proportion of hellish NDEs.

Then came the greatest blow to those NDE researchers who denied the existence of negative experiences: Dr Rawlings's findings were confirmed by a few others in their own studies, one of whom was working in a different country.

The heat of the moment

In her *Return From Death*, British psychologist Dr Margot Grey writes:

"While the principal emphasis in most reports of near-death research has been on the celestial quality of the experience, I nevertheless found indications that pointed to the fact that negative encounters, while infrequent, do definitely exist."

Like Dr Rawlings, she discovered that 'negative experiences are most likely to be obtained immediately after the event ... [while] retrospective research such as my own ...

almost invariably produces positive reports. The following two cases are taken from Dr Grey's study; the first describes what happened to a woman who had a brush with death while undergoing a routine hysterectomy:

"I went to St Giles Hospital in London to have an operation. Sometime while I was under the anaesthetic, I became aware that I was hovering above my body looking down at myself on the operating table. I felt very frightened and began to panic. I wondered why I was no longer in my body and thought I must be dead. I next found myself in a very frightening place, which I am sure was hell. I was looking down into a large pit, which was full of swirling grey mist and there were all these hands and arms reaching up and trying to grab hold of me and drag me in there. There was a terrible wailing noise, full of desperation. Then suddenly I found myself rushing through this dark tunnel and I found myself back in my body in the hospital bed. As I went back into my body it felt like an elastic cord, which had been stretched to its limit and then let go. I sort of snapped back again and everything seemed to vibrate with the impact."

(Note the classic description of the 'silver cord' stretching as the spirit separates from the body.)

This woman's experience conforms more to the negative NDE, with its grey mist and overwhelming sense of desolation, than to the out-and-out hell experienced by some, although, tellingly, she herself was sure she was in hell. This illustrates the difficulty faced by the researcher in categorizing such emotive experiences. Is it possible to label one person's living nightmare hell, while another's is simply a 'negative' experience? How do you measure terror?

The other case in point cited by Dr Grey was described as follows:

"I was working in the nursing home where I have a part-time job. I am a partially trained nurse. I had spent the day on the beach. It was a glorious hot day, but I am used to the heat having lived in Khartoum, Sudan for about 16 years. I was in the kitchen supervising the evening suppers, when I was overcome by the heat from the Aga cookers. I rushed outside the back door feeling faint and sick. I remember going down three or four steps. I don't remember falling, but the next thing that happened was that I had this experience.

I found myself in a place surrounded by mist. I felt I was in hell. There was a big pit with vapour coming out and there were arms and hands coming out trying to grab mine ... I was terrified that these hands were going to claw hold of me and pull me into the pit with them. As I lay there worrying about what would happen next, an enormous lion bounded towards me from the other side and I let out a scream. I was not afraid of the lion, but felt somehow he would unsettle me and push me into the dreadful pit. I remained in a state of semi-consciousness for about three days. I have never believed in hell. I feel God would never create such a place. But it was very hot down there and the vapour of steam was very hot. At the time I did not think very much about it, but in the intervening years I have realized both good and evil exist. The experience has transformed my life."

The similarities with the previous case are striking: the large pit and clawing arms and hands, the all-pervading sense of doom-laden terror. In fact, Dr Grey's research, unlike that of Maurice Rawlings, suggests that it is possible to discern a consistent pattern among nightmare NDEs. In *Return From Death*, Dr Grey lists the stages of the prototypical negative/hellish NDE as follows:

ARE ALIENS DEMONS IN DISGUISE?

Is there a connection between the classic idea of the demons from hell and the aliens who allegedly abduct thousands of humans for their own evil purposes? The similarities between negative NDEs and the abduction experience are outlined below:

- Many abductees only recall their ordeals under hypnosis. Like the NDE subjects of Maurice Rawlings's study, their initial memory is immediately buried very deeply.

- The aliens are most often described as being 'evil' and 'demonic', subjecting the abductees to physical abuse that amounts in some cases to actual torture.

- The 'greys' are frequently described as giving off a stench of sulphur – the smell classically associated with the regions of the damned.

- The 'men in black' who threaten UFO witnesses are reminiscent of the old man in black himself – the devil.

Phase 1. The subject feels fear and feelings of panic instead of peace and joyfulness.

Phase 2. Just as with the more classic NDE, the subject experiences leaving the body.

Phase 3. Again similar to the classic NDE, the dying person enters into a dark region or void.

Phase 4. Instead of experiencing the presence of comforting religious figures, friendly deceased relatives, or a great white light, the subject is overwhelmed by a sense of foreboding and senses the presence of an evil force.

Phase 5. The subject finally enters a hellish environment, which is completely different from the beautiful and peaceful Elysium [heaven] of the classic NDE.

The guilt factor

Both Maurice Rawlings and Margot Grey noted that their respondents were ashamed of their negative NDEs, seeing them as a reflection of their moral status, just as if they had finally been judged, found guilty and been sent permanently to hell. Margot Grey writes:

"It seems that individuals who have had a negative NDE can sometimes feel that the occurrence must in some way have happened because of the hidden guilt feelings they are not anxious to disclose. This is in obvious contrast to the people who had experienced a

positive NDE who, aside from the fear of ridicule ... were usually very pleased to be able to share ... an experience they felt had immeasurably increased their feelings of confidence and self-worth. **"**

Obviously the guilt factor is a major motive behind much of the reticence about negative NDEs, so there is no way of estimating how many there are. The inference is that there are many people who are so ashamed by their negative NDE that they never tell researchers about it, nor perhaps any living soul. Those who do confide in researchers tend more than those who have positive NDEs to request anonymity, although they often find a great sense of release in finally 'confessing' their story.

One woman from Bradford, Yorkshire, says:

"*I'd lost a lot of blood after a miscarriage and was lying semi-conscious waiting for an ambulance. I drifted in and out of consciousness and saw myself lying on the sofa, with my next-door neighbour patting my hand and her husband pacing up and down willing the ambulance to get there fast. I looked so pale and unearthly I was frightened, and tried to get back in my body, but a sort of dark cloud came between me and it, and I kept being pushed back upwards. I got more and more frightened and the ceiling seemed to open up into a big gloomy hall, with people in black robes with hoods over their faces. I could feel, rather than see, them staring at me disapprovingly. One of them said in such a cold, cold voice, 'You're no good, you know, that's why you're here. You've lost the child and you're dying. But we don't want you. Get back!' And I opened my eyes with a jerk as I was being carried into the ambulance.*

I was so frightened and so ashamed. Even the demons in hell didn't want me. It took me about two years to get over the shame, and then I could only talk about it to a couple of friends. One of them helped me by saying it was a nightmare, I'd been dreaming, delirious. She suggested that we have two versions of ourselves and every event that happens to us – one light and one dark – and that I'd slipped into the dark one. Maybe heaven exists, but I'm certain that hell does. **"**

This story is strongly redolent of the guilt that the woman felt at losing her baby through miscarriage: perhaps it even created her nightmare, although whether it was merely an episode of delirium or a true NDE we will never know, because the experience took place before the arrival of the paramedics. Was she ever clinically dead? At this stage it is impossible to know for certain, but the similarities with other negative NDEs suggest that she was at least very close to death when she slipped down the dark road.

It may be that guilt is a powerful factor in deciding what kind of NDE is experienced. As we have seen, Thomas Welch witnessed a burning lake that was reminiscent of certain scenes in the Book of Revelations, although it was not his fate to discover its torments the hard way. His NDE ended with a conversation with Jesus, all of which confirmed his belief in Christian salvation. Whether it was an objective or strictly subjective experience, Welch's NDE reinforced his belief that he was following the right path: there was little, if any, personal guilt involved.

Breaking the rules

However, there is one group of people whose experiences characteristically lack the total joy of the classic NDE. These are the attempted suicides.

JOURNEYS INTO THE AFTERLIFE

The great Swedish polymath Emanuel Swedenborg (1688–1772) was also a mystic and a medium with a unique insight into the afterlife: whereas usually the spirits enter our world in order to converse with mediums, he was allowed into theirs.

Swedenborg's visits to the otherworld revealed the existence of three heavens and three hells, exclusively peopled with deceased human beings. There were no non-human entities: even the angels and demons had once lived on the earth. He said that the afterlife invisibly co-exists with this material plane, and that dying is just a change of condition. According to his testimony, everyone is received by angels immediately after death, but what happens next is governed entirely by the habitual attitude and desires of the individual. On that plane, like attracts like, and the true personality cannot be hidden, so evil-doers find themselves in a hell made of frustration because there they are prevented from causing harm. That is their punishment from which they can only escape through their own enlightenment.

CASE STUDY: DREAM OF DESOLATION

Some of the characteristics of negative NDEs have been reported in the form of unusually vivid and meaningful dreams, as the experience of Lynn Hartup from London reveals:

"A few years ago I saw a television documentary about the Yorkshire Ripper [an infamous serial killer of women] and I wondered why his terrible murders didn't get to me as much as say, what Jack the Ripper [another infamous serial killer] did all those years before. I tried to be shocked, but somehow my imagination hadn't grasped the enormity of his crimes.

I went to bed puzzled and immediately had a dream ... unlike any I have ever had before or since. Dream? Really it was more like a vision, so vivid and immediate ... I will never forget it.

I was in a landscape of utter desolation. There was a low wind blowing – warm and cloying – and there were cinders underfoot. It was a place of no colour as if all the life had been drained out of it, and I felt alone ... So sad and afraid, I can hardly describe it. I looked around and saw a long shallow pit with people packed into it, just like sardines in a tin. At the end nearest to me was Peter Sutcliffe, the Yorkshire Ripper, his face absolutely white with horror, like someone beyond mere pain. A man dressed completely in black walked up to the pit with a long metal implement of some sort and prodded Sutcliffe and a few others. They all uttered ... it makes me go cold to remember it ... a sort of sighing groan ... it went right

through me ... it contained all their pain and loneliness ... then all the people in the pit turned over together, absolutely as one ... they had no choice, they were complete prisoners ... and in a few moments they were prodded again and turned over once more, all moaning together. It was a terrible spectacle.

I had the strong feeling that these were not people to be pitied, although in other circumstances it would have been a piteous sight. And there was something odd: there was only one 'torturer' prodding them with a rod – they weren't tied up or anything. I mean they could easily have got up and ran off. It was as if I was shown that they had somehow complied with this punishment, or couldn't imagine any way out of it ... Yes, there was a strong feeling that they could have escaped, but somehow didn't understand how to.

Suddenly a man with a kind face came into view and stood right in front of me, looking straight into my face. He said with deliberate emphasis: 'You see, there is evil and it is rewarded in hell.'

Shuddering, I woke up. Now I know what the phrase 'in a cold sweat' means ... Even though it was a dream, to this day I believe I had been shown the reality of evil and the horror of hell."

While denying the existence of hellish NDEs, Kenneth Ring has admitted that the NDEs of would-be suicides never included all the characteristic phases, always stopping short of the 'comforting white light ... or presence'. He notes that although there is the familiar sense of being out of the body, it often ends in 'a feeling of confused drifting in a dark or murky void – a sort of "twilight zone", which simply tends to fade out before the "transcendent elements" characteristic of the "core experience" make their appearance.' Their NDEs were, he suggests, comparatively 'aborted or truncated'.

Even Raymond Moody, who has also steadily refused to admit the existence of hellish NDEs, saying, 'In the mass of material I have collected no one has ever described to me a state like the archetypal hell,' has admitted that the experiences

of failed suicides are always described as being unpleasant. In every case they discovered that the problems and conflicts they had sought to escape by 'ending it all' were still there when they had left their bodies behind, often in a more raw, nightmarish and immediate form. And they were often shown the results of their actions – the horror and anguish of those who found them or who were left bereft – without being empowered to do anything about it.

Raymond Moody cites the example of a man who shot himself because his wife had died, and was himself clinically dead for a while. The man said: 'I didn't go where [my wife] was. I went to an awful place ... I immediately saw the mistake I had made ... I thought, "I wish I hadn't done it".' This man was not alone in his experience. As Dr Moody says:

"Others who experienced this unpleasant 'limbo' state have remarked that they had the feeling they would be there for a long time. This was their penalty for 'breaking the rules' by trying to release themselves prematurely from what was, in effect, an 'assignment' - to fulfil a certain purpose of life."

A particularly nightmarish experience resulted from the suicide bid of one young Englishwoman:

"I was eaten up with anger and hatred. I felt everyone had betrayed or let me down. I was broke, lonely and overwhelmed with problems so I sat down by the phone and took a lot of pills. Just before I lost consciousness I managed to phone every one of the people I wanted to get back at, to let them know what they'd 'made me

do'. I enjoyed hearing them saying worriedly, 'You're not serious', when I told them what I'd done. One even put the phone down, thinking I was winding him up. But to this day I don't think it was a cry for help, even though I'd let them all know. I really wanted to die, just to make them suffer.

I drifted into unconsciousness gloating at how they would ... feel when I was dead, knowing what I'd thought of them, and what they'd driven me to. I sort of drifted in a fine, greyish mist and began to feel frightened. Then suddenly I banged into, literally, a hideous man who leered at me from close up, his nose touching mine. He said, 'You're full of worms. You stink. They hate you. Is that what you want?' I was so terrified I was shaking violently. I said no, but he just ... laughed. Then I found myself in a room that was somehow familiar and there were two women and a man casually gossiping while they did something to a life-sized dummy on a bed. I realized it was a dead body, its features already changed by decomposition. These people were ... professional ... dreadfully

cold about what they were doing, roughly pushing and pulling the body about. Then they lifted it into a coffin and jammed on the lid. 'God, what a stinker!' The man said and the others said 'Whew! Stupid bitch'. And somehow I knew that the body was me, my corpse, and that they couldn't care less. Nobody could ... all my plans for revenge had fallen through. I was

just a disgusting piece of meat to them, but worse I was somehow condemned to witness all that. Who knows for how long? For ever, maybe. This vision ended when they broke the door down ... and eventually I was revived.

The whole thing was critical. It changed me, the way I saw my problems and my life, I suppose ... I saw clearly that you have to earn

respect, and that nobody is responsible for you except yourself. It was tough ... I had to be humble and honest, things totally foreign to my nature before that ... I had to accept responsibility for my own life. Nobody can 'make you' kill yourself like I kidded myself ... In the end I mended the fences between myself and those I had mistreated. **"**

Here the dominant theme is not so much guilt as self disgust, which is underlined by the emphasis on the grotesque physical aspects of death – the reaction of the man and two women (who appear to be undertakers) to the stench of her body, and the jibe about being 'full of worms'.

Although this case has elements of the typical negative NDE there is no lake of fire or sounds of despairing souls. Here the subject is confronted with a sort of morality play in which an alternative future is revealed. She is shown the likely outcome of her actions, rather like when Charles Dickens' Ghost of Christmas Yet To Come reveals to Scrooge his future, which will only come to fruition if he does not mend his ways.

Despite the traumatic elements of their NDEs, the 'returned' would-be suicides appear to be doubly lucky: not only are they given a new lease of life, but they come back with a new understanding of what happens if you 'break the rules'. It seems that suicide is the great offence against God, or some universal law. Perhaps humanity is even 'programmed' to avoid self-murder. If NDEs represent an objective reality, then perhaps the taking of life, whether someone else's or your own, is the mysterious 'sin against the Holy Ghost', and no matter how great your suffering or despair, the only thing to do is to

◀ **Photographic reconstruction of the emergence of the spirit from the body. This is believed to happen to both troubled and happy people every night during sleep, during NDEs and finally at death.**

AY DEMI QUE ARDIENDO QUEDO AY QUE

▲ The grim scenario from hell, according to artists all over the world, may owe its power to terrify to more than just imagination.

persevere until it is your allotted time to leave this life behind.

The battle for life

In some cases the negative, or even hellish, NDE is experienced as a battle for life, and patients may even feel they are being tricked into death, as this case from the files of researcher George Gallup Jnr illustrates:

"I had an operation - four and a half hours I was under, and I felt I was dying. I felt I was being tricked into death. In my mind I was fighting with faces unknown to me, and I felt that I had to have all my wits about me to keep from dying. I continued to fight for some time, but, as in a dream, which can seem hours, it might have only been seconds. I remember not breathing, and strange colours, lights and designs took shape in my brain. Later, I felt relieved and

woke up in the delivery room. I had stopped breathing on the operating table and was revived, I was told. I knew I had stopped breathing and I knew I was near death, even though I was under."

It would have been interesting to know this man's prior expectations. Did he have a particular fear or phobia about death before his NDE? Did he believe it was to be outwitted at all costs? Perhaps his beliefs and expectations helped to create the scenario in some way not yet understood. George Gallup does not address these questions, but makes the following comments:

One might immediately say that the unknown faces around him were merely vague perceptions of the medical personnel surrounding him during the operation. Similarly, the strange colours and designs might have been due to lack of oxygen getting to his brain when he stopped breathing. The problem with this explanation is that it presupposes a fuzzy, semi-conscious state, yet this man recalls being quite lucid as he battled with whatever was trying to trick him into death. With great clarity and concentration, he fought and used his wits to keep from dying. A more likely interpretation would seem to be that he found himself on the verge of extinction; there was some sort of volitional and personal quality in the evil that he was facing; and he realized instinctively that he had to marshal all his inner resources to fight back, to keep from going over the edge.

Gallup also cites the case of a man suffering from peritonitis and gangrene, who remembered this:

I felt like I was in a great black vacuum. All I could see was my arms hanging on to a set of parallel bars. I knew if I relaxed, my grip on life would cease. It was a complete sense of knowing that life had to be clung to. I knew without any question if I let go, I would die. The feeling of agony of hanging on only lasted a brief while.

And a Scotswoman who died during a road-traffic accident recalls:

I was standing on one side of an enormously deep abyss, with steam coming out of it, blowing up into my face. I knew there were people, maybe creatures of some kind, behind me, coming up fast to get me and drag me down into the pit. Was it hell, or was it death itself? I don't know, but I wasn't going to find out if I could help it! There was a crowd of people whose faces I couldn't see on the other side of the abyss, who kept shouting to me to jump over to them, but I was too scared. And while I was dithering there the demons or whatever they were, were getting closer all the time.

In everyday life I've never been very physical, always very scared of taking risks. I never climbed trees as a child, and so the thought of leaping across that gap utterly terrified me. But I shuddered at the idea of the demons getting hold of me. I could somehow feel their nasty hot little hands on me, and it was horrible. So I shut my eyes and leapt ... Oh I seemed to go up for ever, and then I started to fall. It was like ... my heart was in my mouth ... would I end up at the bottom of the abyss, fodder for the demons? I fell in slow motion, I prayed, oh how I prayed ... Then I landed with a thud on the other side - just. I was hanging on by my toes, but the others pulled me on properly. I knew then that I had cheated death. It was at that moment that the ambulance people brought me round.

In the 'battle for life' scenarios death is the great enemy, and life must be held on to at all costs. This is very much the ethos of the medical profession, although of course it is by no means exclusively theirs. However, the dying person may be unconsciously tuning in to the medics' thoughts as they desperately try to revive him, and somehow dramatizing it as a visionary battle for life. Perhaps it is significant that all the people in this section were hospitalized when they had their NDE. Certainly the would-be suicide described above admits:

I've always been terrified of death ever since my gran died 20 years ago. She had cancer and suffered terribly at the end, and afterwards she looked so different with all the life drained out of her like that. So waxy and putty coloured lying in her coffin. It was like some dreadful monster had stolen my gran and left an awful effigy to mock me. I couldn't love that thing in the box, because it wasn't my gran, because she wasn't anywhere any more. She'd just gone and wouldn't be coming back. I was only 14 at the time and it hit me hard. I think I suffered from deep depression for several months, and couldn't bear to think about it. I had nightmares about not being able to find her, and being chased by some evil menace that I knew was death. I knew I had to keep running. If I stopped it would get me and I would cease to exist.

While it does seem, at least in this case, that personal belief and prior expectations are factors in the tone of individual NDEs, there are problems with this hypothesis. As George Gallup commented on the man suffering from peritonitis who fought against death, one would not have expected such lucidity in someone suffering from lack of oxygen. On the contrary, his thought processes would have been confused and fuzzy. Even more inexplicable is the Scotswoman's battle for life – because she was clinically dead at the time. For about two minutes her heart was still and her brain showed no activity at all. Yet in some sense that was only too real to her, she was dithering on one side of an abyss with demons coming up behind her, willing herself to jump to safety – and a return to life. But how could she experience anything when her brain had ceased to function? How is it possible?

This conundrum applies to all true NDEs, in which the person actually dies in the clinical sense, but later

▲ Apocalyptic opening of the pit of hell – the archetypal image of a terrifying afterlife that is occasionally described by those who have had negative NDEs.

reports a vivid mental experience. Even when we are asleep and dreaming there is considerable brain activity, and some physical movement, including the rapid eye movement that gives its name to phases of dreaming. Yet during the true NDE the person is literally and measurably dead. How can this be?

More questions asked

One explanation might be that the NDE did not occur when the brain had ceased to function. Perhaps it is simply a particularly vivid dream that happens in a split second (despite its apparent duration, which might be very long) as the individual wakes up or is revived. However, there are several problems with this theory: many people report seeing and hearing things during an NDE that are later discovered to have really happened, which is not characteristic of a dream, whether long or short. Sometimes the person overhears conversations and repeats them verbatim afterwards – and the conversations must have taken place in real time.

So assuming that NDEs really do happen during periods of complete brain shutdown, what does this

mean? Although the implications of the NDE will be discussed in detail in the last chapter, suffice it to say that one conclusion, unpalatable though it may be to materialists, is that the mind is different from the brain, and that consciousness does not depend upon measurable mental activity. And, as we have seen in Chapter 3, there is abundant evidence for the existence of the invisible, astral self or soul.

However, even allowing for the reality of a consciousness that is autonomous and separate from the body/brain, there remains the question of whether or not the NDE is subjective or objective, and how far personal beliefs and expectations colour the experience. We have seen how the woman who had the miscarriage faced a barrage of hostility in her NDE, and was left in no doubt as to why she was in 'hell' ('You're no good … you lost your child …'). And would-be suicides frequently report hellish NDEs after which they realize that they had very nearly committed the gravest sin possible. But are such NDEs the result of personal guilt, or are they what they seem to be – actual encounters with demons and lakes of burning fire? Does the hellish NDE provide enough evidence to imply that hell is a reality?

Even the question is problematic, for hell was certainly what many people appeared to experience during their NDEs, so it was real for them. But if we mean did they really visit some hellish place or dimension, then we encounter another set of obstacles. For although many of these NDEs share certain similarities – for example, the clawing hands – they are never the same in all particulars, as one might reasonably expect from objective accounts. Although witnesses notoriously interpret and describe the same event differently, it is rare to find witnesses remembering entirely different events.

Perhaps, as certain researchers have suggested (see previous chapter), death itself is a kind of dream, however vivid or lucid, and that the contents of that final dream are dictated by a host of factors, including guilt and fear, and probably many others that will always remain outside our knowledge.

A tough lesson

All negative and hellish NDEs are disturbing, although some are clearly more instructive than others. The only lesson that some people, such as many of Rawlings's patients, seem to learn is to keep in good health and to put off the moment of permanent death as long as possible! They experience such terror that death comes to be synonymous with hell, without any of the comfort and hope of the more classic, positive NDEs.

Others are so shaken by their experience that they acquire a new lease of life, as do those who have positive NDEs, although for different reasons. They have seen what appears to await those whose attitude or actions are at odds with some universal law, and naturally this shapes their subsequent attitude to life.

Mediums have often passed on messages, purportedly coming from deceased people, that describe 'Winterland' (see page 102), a desolate place full of angry, obsessive and frustrated spirits. They are trapped in an ideoplastic world of their own making, and are so determined to be negative that they fail to notice, or to believe, the emissaries from 'Summerland' whose mission is to release them from their self-imposed bondage. Similarly we are told that when the 'judgment' comes to all newly dead spirits, it does not involve cowering before a vengeful God, or implacable angel, but takes the form of self-judgment, where every detail of one's life is finally seen for what it really was, and how it had an effect on others.

Perhaps in the world of the mind, where we all appear to go after death, there is only the unvarnished, inescapable truth that comes from our own consciences, whether or not

we had been aware of them previously. It is tempting to speculate that humankind is programmed to know right from wrong, but there is a problem with this (admittedly simplistic) hypothesis: although in general humankind agrees that murder and theft are wrong, many cultures differ markedly in their attitude to such matters as mercy, humility, and even the major issue of suicide. While it is wrong for modern Christians to commit suicide, for example, to Victorian aristocrats and soldiers of ancient Rome it was 'the honourable thing'. Do the rules, which those who experience negative NDEs discover they have broken, somehow change and evolve? How unfair otherwise to reserve the same unpleasant afterlife for a Roman soldier who had done the expected thing and 'fallen on his sword' as for a modern drug addict who took a fatal overdose!

The nature of the rules – if there are any – is unknown, and still less where they might come from and how they are applied. Perhaps as more people come forward with their NDE stories some clues may emerge, and the philosophical and spiritual implications of the experience can begin to be properly understood.

The Rawlings Factor

In his book *The Return From Silence*, D. Scott Rogo presents a statistical analysis of the negative NDEs reported in six studies, ranging from 1977 to 1985. Although the size of the samples varies greatly – from just 22 to 225 respondents – it is the disparity in the percentage of negative NDEs reported that is most remarkable. For example, Kenneth Ring's 1980 survey of 102 cases contained no negative experiences at all, while Margot Grey's 1985 sample of 31 people revealed that 12.5 per cent had had dark NDEs. And, most startling of all, Maurice Rawlings's 1978 study of just 33 cases included 27.5 negative NDEs! While a small margin can always be allowed for differences in reporting and collating, clearly there

is something drastically amiss in this particular league table.

Perhaps the dichotomy is due to Dr Rawlings's speciality: as a cardiologist with particular expertise in resuscitation he is often present at the moment the patient is revived. He is the first person the patient sees after the experience, when its full horror – or joy – is still fresh in their minds. It may be, as Margot Grey believes, that the event is so psychologically traumatic that it is almost immediately erased from memory.

As we have seen, many people fail to report negative NDEs because they see them as a punishment, or a comment on their moral status, and are often simply too ashamed to tell anyone about them, let alone a researcher intent on publishing the details. But Dr Rawlings suggests that there may be a more fundamental kind of fear involved here – being too frightened to remember the unpleasant or horrific NDE. We have seen how the postman reported both terrifying and uplifting NDEs, but as time went by he remembered only the pleasant one.

Perhaps, as some have suggested, every NDE begins as a hellish experience before transmuting into the classic heavenly encounter, but only the latter is acceptable to the psyche and is therefore the only one to be recalled. Why not hypothesize further? Perhaps everyone who is resuscitated actually undergoes an NDE of one sort or another, but the recovering consciousness blots it out, just as dreams dissolve in the light of day. Remember that Er, the ancient Greek, saw others being dipped in the River Lethe (the Waters of Forgetfulness) but for some reason he was not immersed and so remembered his experience.

But just as some believe that all dreams, whether recalled or not, still influence our lives, perhaps all NDEs cast their spell over those who have experienced them whether they are remembered or remain buried deep within the mind.

CHAPTER SEVEN

The Evidence

Few people argue that there is such a phenomenon as the NDE, that something very similar has been shared by thousands of people when they were either very close to death, or even clinically dead. This is largely due to the enthusiastic coverage of NDEs by the tabloid press, and by many television programmes.

These experiences, the black tunnel and the blinding light, have almost become clichés. But is the NDE real? Or is it somehow manufactured, perhaps chemically, by the dying brain? And how much does a person's belief system and religious background colour the experience?

By now the sheer mass of case histories from many different cultures suggests that it is not a matter of individual fabrication, nor is it created by cultural or religious expectation (although, as we have seen, NDEs are often coloured by such factors). But is the NDE simply what it appears to be – the most persuasive evidence humankind has ever had for the ultimate survival of the human soul and the reality of heaven (or hell)? Or is this 'survivalist' interpretation far too simplistic – is there another, more rational explanation for the NDE?

Of course the NDE is real enough to the individual who experiences it, in some cases more real than normal everyday life. As one man from Georgia put it:

◄ **Many people today have negative feelings towards stereotypical images, like this, of heaven. But NDEs reveal that there may be some truth in them after all.**

"I know it was real. I know that I was up there ... And I know that I seen me down there. I could swear on a Bible that I was there. I seen things just like I seen them now. I can't prove it to none of those people there because they didn't see me. There's no way you can prove it, but I was there."

And a British woman said:

"No one can tell me I imagined that place of light and bliss. I'd never known such ecstasy so how could I imagine it? I'd gone into unconsciousness deeply depressed with the pain and the weariness of my illness [cancer] and suddenly I was in a garden with my mother who died 29 years ago and whose face I can hardly remember if I'm honest. But there she was, radiant with happiness and looking ... well, not as she used to because there she was very healthy and sort of glowing. I couldn't have made that up. My mind couldn't have done it."

Of course these were not scientists, psychiatrists or parapsychologists who might offer alternative explanations for the phenomena associated with the NDE. To a layman it is inconceivable, for example, that he or she could imagine bliss which they have never experienced in waking life, but those familiar with the workings of the unconscious mind know that an altered state of consciousness such as dreaming or hypnosis will, more often than not, produce such uncharacteristic experiences.

Frequently it has been suggested that the NDE is no more than a kind of dream, although quite how brain-dead people can dream is never satisfactorily explained. Many have slipped in and out of comas, which in medical terms means they were totally without any cognitive processes. How can they dream when in effect they had no brain? Ironically, it is the sceptics who appear to be relying on a mysterious 'X factor' in order to allow clinically dead people to be able to dream or hallucinate, something that does not require the 'hardwiring' of the brain in order to function.

Wishful thinking?

Critics have suggested that the NDE is simply an elaborate exercise in wishful thinking, where the unconscious mind creates a heaven in order to remove the fear of death as the end. This is answered in much

▲ Relatively undeveloped societies also report NDEs, although research there is new, and respondents tend to believe their experiences are due to bad magic.

the same way as the theory that NDEs are the result of prior expectation due to religious or cultural imprinting. In fact, these are particularly weak arguments, for the mass of evidence suggests that many atheists and rationalists, whose own positions prior to their experiences were akin to those of such critics, had much the same NDEs as those who believed in heaven. And let us not forget that many respondents were would-be suicides whose sole wish was for total extinction to rid themselves of their problems. Yet still they found themselves in an inexplicable

world of light, with a heightened awareness of their surroundings and an increased ability to feel emotion.

More recent research has revealed that the 'stage management' and content of each NDE does appear to be partly dictated by cultural expectations, although the core experience is remarkably similar. The work of Dr Nsama Mumbwe of the University of Zambia reveals the extent of cultural influence on the interpretation of NDEs. Although her sample study was small – just 15 respondents – they were all simple people who had no prior knowledge of NDE research, but all of whom had an experience to describe. However, there are significant differences between their attitudes and those of Westerners to their NDEs. A 35-year-old clerk says:

"I had sustained a fractured femur and a head injury after an accident. I was unconscious for a day. I believed that I had died. I went to a place where I found a lot of people dressed in white robes – children and adults. I couldn't make out their races. These people seemed to be very happy. But when I appeared they stopped singing and someone said, 'we were not expecting you. Sorry!'. I hurried round and left. I could hear them start their singing after I had walked a good distance from them. [My belief is that] someone must have been trying to bewitch me but found me innocent."

Several of Dr Mumbwe's respondents said that they believed they had been bewitched, but escaped from the 'curse' of the NDE because of their innocence. Of course, this is a fundamental difference in interpretation that comes directly from a culture that sees magic and curses behind any unusual experience. But as Melvin Morse notes:

"These people in this remote Third World country have the same NDEs as people who were in my [Transformations] study. To me these case studies once again prove the validity of the NDE as an actual experience described as it happened and not made up later."

Significantly, the NDEs of the Japanese tend to involve beautiful gardens or rivers, and the Chinese often visit a great yellow river, beyond which they cannot go. This is reminiscent of the Lethe (River of Forgetfulness) described by Plato's Er. Malaysians and Indonesians describe a noisy, bustling afterlife in the form of a modern Western city, while Indians find it full of 'red tape'; they are sent back because their file cannot be found, or there is some mistake in their records! All of these differences obviously arise from the various beliefs, aspirations and fears

of the cultures concerned, but the core experience is the same.

NDEs happen to people who are devout believers in Christianity of every sort, to Jews, to Hindus, to those who believe in tribal gods, to Japanese Shintos, to Moslems, and to those who believe in nothing and expect even less to greet them after death. They happen to people who have died in car accidents, in childbirth, by attempted murder, drowning, heart attacks, during long illnesses such as cancer and a host of other 'ills that flesh is heir to'.

Sometimes the state of mind of a person who has an NDE is, if anything, less likely than usual to produce a vivid, positive 'hallucination'. Andrea, who was 24 years old at the time of her experience, tells the story of how she felt:

"I had a lot of physical problems and was in a great deal of pain. I'd given up really - more or less stopped eating and couldn't bear visitors. I just lay there miserable.

It was ironic because I was something of a New Ager, always looking for the positive and seeing the hand of the spiritual world behind every little thing ... But by the time the pain got to me I abandoned all that stuff and rapidly came round to the idea that death was the end, and that the physical side of life was all there was. And I started to long for death, for the end of everything that was me, this pain-wracked, thin little thing.

Then there was a loud buzzing sound close to my ears and a 'pop'! I was up on the ceiling looking at a grey-faced, shrivelled me lying open-mouthed on the sofa-bed. I was amazed, but not for long because it felt perfectly normal and it was pain free.

I moved around just by thinking about it, and discovered I could turn cartwheels in the air and not feel sick. Imagine! Two seconds before I'd been immobilized with pain, and here I was doing gymnastics by the ceiling!

▲ A classic Japanese image: NDEs from Japan mostly describe otherworldly encounters in beautiful gardens that evoke ineffable feelings of serenity.

A lot happened very fast then. I moved swiftly through a dark place, a very dark place but it wasn't frightening. I felt so good I was laughing, which was something I hadn't done for ages. In the middle of all this it struck me that I must be dead and that was the most hilarious thing of all. In fact you could say that I went to meet my maker absolutely doubled up - not with pain, but with mirth. And yes, I believe I really did meet God, who was a sort of bluey-white cloud of total ... what? Love, yes, but much more than that. Somehow he (or she) understood my laughter and joined in ... We had a long conversation, mind to mind, about my life and deeply personal matters, then I was told I had to go back to my body.

To tell the truth, it took me a

while to realize what he was talking about. A dim memory of that nasty grey thing on the sofa-bed came back to me and I shuddered. I begged over and over to be allowed to stay, but was told to go back because I had things to do, but that this experience was a gift. 'Don't you feel better now?' the God-cloud asked gently straight into my mind. 'Don't you know better now?' And suddenly I was back in my body, and there was a blanket of pain.

I was ill for a couple of weeks, but the pain completely disappeared without medication and I was on my feet in no time. One day I went for a long walk and looked up into the blue sky. 'Thank you,' I said, 'yes, I do feel better, and yes, I do know better now'. I'd wanted to die and for everything to stop. But it's this life that is 'nothing' compared to what awaits us. I know sceptics say it's all in the mind, but what had been in my mind was a true death wish. Now I just want life, either here or there. There is no death. ❞

The 'brain's last fling'

One of the most vociferous opponents of the NDE as a paranormal experience is British psychologist Dr Susan Blackmore, whose cannabis-induced OBE is discussed right. She argues that the components of the classic NDE are created by physiological changes in the 'dying brain': for example, travelling very fast up a black tunnel towards the light may be explained by the rapid degeneration of the eyes, which is then 'dramatized' by the brain.

Dr Blackmore suggests that NDEs are no more than 'the brain's last fling', with which we are 'programmed' to 'help us over the trauma of death'. She argues that death, being in her belief system total personal extinction, is so fearful that nature has provided us with this happy hallucination to cushion the blow of annihilation. However, as we

---

CASE STUDY: A CRITIC'S OBE

British sceptic Dr Susan Blackmore's own experience was induced through the effects of cannabis in the company of two Oxford friends, Vicky and Kevin:

❝*... the voices of my friends seemed a very long way off. If I thought about my own body it did not seem to be firmly on the hard floor but rather indistinct, as though surrounded by cotton wool. In my tiredness my mind seemed to follow the music into a scene of a tree-lined avenue ... The whole was like a tree-lined tunnel and I was hurtling through it ... simultaneously with this experience I was aware of Vicky asking if I would like some coffee. Kevin answered but I did not ... It is to Kevin's credit that he both initiated and helped me with the next stage. Quite out of the blue, and I have no idea why, he asked, 'Sue, where are you?'. I thought ... tried to see my own body, and then did see it. There it was below me. The words came out: 'I'm on the ceiling.' With some surprise I watched the mouth – my mouth – down below, opening and closing and I marvelled at its control.*

Kevin seemed quite calm at this pronouncement and proceeded to question me in detail. What was it like up there? What could I see? What was 'I'? ... Again, as I formulated answers, the mouth below spoke ... From the ceiling I could apparently see the room quite clearly. I saw the desk, chairs, window, my friends and myself all from above. Then I saw a string or cord, silvery, faintly glowing and moving gently, running

between the neck of my body below and the navel, or thereabouts, of a duplicate body above. With encouragement I moved out of the room, myself and my cord moving through the walls, another floor of rooms and the roof with ease. I clearly observed the red of the roofs and the row of chimneys before flying on to more distant places ... I visited Paris and New York and flew over South America.❞

However, unlike the OBEs reported as part of the NDE, Susan Blackmore's 'flight' did not check out. The roofs she described as being red were actually grey, and she apparently invented another floor of rooms. Moreover, she actually saw the 'silver cord' and a duplicate body, whereas during an NDE people feel the cord and are the 'other' body; they have no separate awareness of one.

---

have seen, there are serious arguments against this theory, not least being the fact that as a good Darwinist Dr Blackmore should believe that evolution only (allegedly) creates what is of practical use for every species. From her perspective

as a voice for the materialist/rationalist lobby, there should be no evolutionary value whatsoever in the NDE.

Why should evolution bestow the bliss of the NDE, and more particularly of deathbed visions, when there is nowhere and nothing to be 'helped over' to? Why are we programmed to have visions to help us into oblivion when we do not, as a species, have them to help us over bad patches in our lives, such as childbirth, bereavement, illness, even torture? We are left to get by as we can when there are years of our lives stretching ahead. But when, as Dr Blackmore believes, we are faced with total dissolution, we suddenly have 'help'. It does not make any sense, especially from her own perspective. On the other hand, a truly practical evolution would have removed all fear of death from us: then we could have lived and died like primitive animals, without any consciousness, creativity or spiritual awareness.

Just a drug 'trip'?

Several researchers, including Raymond Moody, have noticed that certain phenomena associated with NDEs have been reported as side-effects of anaesthesia. It is well known that drugs (prescription or 'recreational') can produce vivid hallucinations. Sometimes these take a heavenly form, presenting scenes of transcendental beauty that flood the experiencer with mystical awareness. But at other times the result of taking the drug is a 'bad trip', a hellish experience from which the individual emerges severely psychologically scarred. But are NDEs, as some have suggested, merely the result of drug taking?

Drug trips can take any weird and wonderful form, but as we have seen, NDEs are remarkably consistent in content and in the effects they have on the person afterwards. Besides, many NDEs happen spontaneously, without any drugs being involved at any stage, so this hypothesis is invalid as a blanket generalization.

The most often suggested physiological explanation for NDEs is that of lack of oxygen – cerebral anoxia. After all, the decreased blood pressure and heart and lung failure which precede death severely limit the amount of oxygen that gets through

> ## CHILDREN ARE MORE ATTUNED TO DEATH
> Dr Elisabeth Kubler-Ross believes that children accept their imminent death more easily than others. As she says in *Life, Death and Life after Death*:
>
> **"**When slowly preparing for death, as is often the case with children who have cancer, prior to death many of these children begin to be aware that they have the ability to leave their physical body and have what we call an OBE. All of us have these OBEs during certain stages of sleep. Very few of us are consciously aware of it. Dying children especially, who are much more tuned in, become more spiritual than healthy children of the same age. They become aware of these short trips out of their physical bodies which help them in the transition, which helps them familiarize themselves with the place they are going to. **"**

to the patient's brain. But is this the answer? Does cerebral anoxia cause the grand hallucination of the NDE? The answer must be no, for in many cases patients were suffering from hyperventilation (too much oxygen) when they had the NDE! And, as Margot Grey points out:

> **"***Finally, even if more proof were needed to cast doubt on the cerebral anoxia hypothesis, the fact remains that visionary aspects of the NDE were often found in conscious patients whose experience occurred well before the final descent into the coma that typically precedes death. It is therefore difficult to interpret the phenomenon from the standpoint of cerebral anoxia.* **"**

In fact, none of the physiological or pharmacological explanations offered for the NDE satisfactorily address the facts of the phenomenon: attempts to isolate certain features, as Susan Blackmore did by comparing her drug-induced OBE to spontaneous 'flights', are doomed to failure when the wider picture is examined.

Astonishing evidence

So far in this chapter we have discussed what the NDE is not. Now let us consider the evidence for its validity as an objective experience.

As we have seen, drug-induced OBEs may prove disappointing

afterwards when the things seen during the flight are found to be different, or even non-existent. But events witnessed and locations observed during NDEs are another matter, as the following stories reveal.

Joy, a 48-year-old British housewife, died during an operation. She says:

> **"***I found myself floating above the hospital bed, looking around. I wasn't much interested in the body lying there. So I drifted off up the ward and down a long corridor. It was the most incredible feeling of lightness and relief. I hadn't a care in the world. Nothing got in my way - I found I could slip through walls just like a ghost. Well, of course, I was a ghost - what a strange thought … I came to the reception area for casualty and saw my brother just coming in with a big bunch of flowers for me. Then I noticed a wild-looking man jump up from his seat and run towards the receptionist. I screamed at her to get help, because I knew he was going to attack her, but she couldn't hear me and just looked up. My brother glanced towards the noise, looking startled. The man stood there staring, then yelled an obscenity in the receptionist's face and punched her hard on the shoulder.*
> *Everything happened fast … afterwards [she visited a beautiful garden and met her mother] I told*

▲ How a person having an NDE sees cities: often he or she returns to consciousness with amazingly accurate stories of people seen and heard in far off places.

my brother about the incident, and he went white. I said he glanced over his shoulder when I yelled, even though no one could hear me. 'I don't know why,' he said. 'I just felt, you know, like someone had walked over my grave'. He also agreed with my description of the scene, which no one in our ward knew about until an hour after my brother's visit."

This story contains several common themes of NDEs such as separating from the body and floating free, invisibly travelling to other locations, and witnessing events that later turn out to be correct. 'Ted's' NDE took him to a part of the USA he had never visited before. He was electrocuted while greasing an overhead crane and was 'frozen solid' by the current. He describes to Melvin Morse what happened next:

"*I was sitting up there being shocked and the next thing I knew, I was in a strange place. I was in the air, going across a playing field. There was somebody with me but I couldn't see who they were because I couldn't turn my head. All of a sudden as we crossed this*

field, there was my girlfriend. She was walking along with her books to her bosom, arms clutched in front of her, heading toward this little house in a housing development outside of San Diego.

I had no idea where it was, but I could see two things: I could see a baseball diamond backstop and I could see a water tower with writing on it. I was with her as she walked. I could see the back of the houses she was headed for and knew which one was hers even though I had never been there."

Shortly afterwards, Ted resigned from his job and took a bus to visit his girlfriend. Abruptly, he felt he had

CASE STUDY: CHANGING SOULS

Meg's NDE is unique because of its novel 'boy on the bed' component. Very ill with measles as a four-year-old, she found herself up by the ceiling looking down:

"I saw a child lying on a bare mattress, where my lovely comfy bed should have been. And the walls were unpapered. The whole room was dark and drab – cold, too. I was curious and looked more closely at the child. It was a boy, about eight years old. He was wearing funny clothes. My memory of them is ... they were the sort of thing British boys would wear in the 1930s – long shorts and thick knitted socks up to the knee. His hair was badly cut and his shirt was a horrible thick grey material. I thought he was asleep, but looking back I realize he was dead, lying there unloved on a stripped mattress in that awful room.

Then the room disappeared in a blaze of wonderful light, which made me feel so happy. The boy was in the light ... he looked so much better and more normal, like a little boy should be ... not that drab waxwork, not a dead boy ...

There was a strange rusty sound and I was back in my bed, with mummy holding my hand. I got better quickly ... but everyone said how I'd changed. Before my illness I'd been timid and had hardly any appetite. But I'd become a tomboy who never stopped eating ... Sometimes – I know this sounds mad – I think I somehow became the little boy, as if he took my body while I was out of it. Strangely, though, I don't mind at all. I know we are destined to have a life together."

to get off the bus 'out in the boondocks'. It wasn't a rational decision, just a sudden strong instinct. He explains:

"This was a long time ago, and San Diego was just a puff of a town. I got off and started to walk in the direction of the bus stop. I looked up and saw the water tower I had seen when I left my body! I looked over and saw the baseball backstop in the playing field I had passed over! I saw the backs of a row of houses and walked up to the one I had seen in my experience. It was the right one ... I was shocked across the country. And to this day it gives me goosebumps to talk about it."

Another intriguing case with corroborative evidence is that of Yuri, a Soviet citizen, who told his story to Dr Morse's co-author, Paul Perry.

One night Yuri was hit by a car and left for dead. His inert body was taken to the morgue, although Yuri has stated that he 'had a strong sense of being dead' – a paradoxical remark that can only be understood completely by another who has had an NDE.

As a dissident, Yuri's body was put in cold storage until a doctor from Moscow could be brought to perform an autopsy (to prove he had not been assassinated). Consequently, Yuri was left in subzero temperatures for three days before he was discovered to show signs of life and was fully resuscitated. (This was miraculous given the length of time he had been near frozen.) But during that time Yuri had been out of his body.

He describes seeing a 'pinprick of light', towards which he crawled, managing to squeeze through it. He found himself surrounded by a light that was so strong that 'it burned my eyes like fire', but finally he found he grew accustomed to it. This light bestowed some extremely unusual abilities on him.

He discovered he could fly and went to visit his home, where he witnessed his wife and two children grieving for him. Unable to make them aware of his presence, he went next door, where they had a fractious new baby who would not stop crying no matter what they did. The parents had taken him to the doctor, who had no idea what was causing him to be so upset and sent him home.

But Yuri made an interesting discovery. As an invisible visitor, he found he could:

"... talk to the baby. It was amazing. I could not talk to the parents – my friends – but I could talk to their little boy who had just been born. I asked him what was wrong. No words were exchanged, but I

CASE STUDY: 'A HIGHWAY OPENED UP BEFORE ME'

A 60-year-old truck driver from Zambia describes his NDE after being badly mauled by a lioness:

"*I could see myself going into some kind of a trance. A highway suddenly opened up before me. It seemed to be going endlessly into the sky. Along it were a lot of stars, also spreading up to the sky. Each time I tried to get on the highway the stars would block my way. I just stood there not knowing what to do. After a while the highway and stars disappeared. I woke up and found myself in a hospital bed.*

*[I believe] it was a bad omen, because when my brother got home he found my mother very ill and she died the next day.***"**

▶ **Many Africans who experience NDEs see their visit to the stars as a bad omen.**

asked him maybe through telepathy what was wrong. He told me that his arm hurt. And when he told me that, I was able to see that the bone was twisted and broken. **"**

Later, after the revived Yuri was safely back at home he told the story of his OBE. No one believed him, until he told them about having talked to the baby, and the revelation about its arm. As a result of Yuri's story, his neighbours took the child to the doctor and had its arm X-rayed. They discovered it had a greenstick fracture, which had probably been caused at birth.

It is interesting that Yuri could telepathically communicate with a new-

◀ **The evidence suggests that tiny children respond to people who have NDEs, and may even pass on information that can result in crucial action being taken.**

born baby while out of the body, but could not do so with adults, including his own wife. This reinforces the idea, long known by psychics and mystics, that children are naturally open to what others call paranormal events because no one has told them they are impossible! As recent parapsychological research has shown, the younger the child the more naturally psychic they are, which implies that the state of innocence is synonymous with having psychic abilities. And it is in the experiences of children that much of the most persuasive evidence for NDEs is found.

Closer to God

The accusation of prior expectation may carry some weight in the case of adults who have NDEs: having heard about the phenomenon they may unconsciously create a false memory of having had a similar experience when seriously ill. But the same

charge cannot be levelled at tiny children. As we will see, some of these toddlers returned from their visit to the light with some very significant information.

Vivien, now in her early forties, remembers dying of an unspecified fever when she was three years old:

"*Mum was really worried about me, and called the doctor. She kept pressing face flannels soaked in cold water on my forehead and ... I have a vivid memory of her anxious face hovering close to mine. I shut my eyes and there was a red light, which I associated with the fever itself, under my eyelids. I seemed to be floating and burning up. It was not a nice sensation. Mum says I was muttering, 'I'm all swimmy'. By this I meant in a sort of heat haze.*

There was a sound like fabric tearing and I thought mum must

CASE STUDY: 'FAR AWAY TO THE STARS'

In the foothills of the Himalayas, in the autumn of 1968, Durdana Khan, aged two-and-a-half, died for about 15 minutes after becoming very ill from an unknown cause, perhaps viral encephalitis.

Her father, Dr A.G. Khan, worked on her lifeless body, all the while saying 'Come back, my child, come back.' Finally, after he administered a few drops of the respiratory stimulant nikethamide, she opened her eyes. Shortly afterwards, when her mother asked her where she had been during her illness, the tiny child replied: 'Far, far away to the stars.'

Asked what she saw there, Durdana replied:

"Gardens ... apples and grapes and pomegranates ... a white stream, a brown stream, a blue stream and a green stream ... My grandfather was there, and his mother, and another lady who looked like you ... Grandpa said he was glad to see me, and his mother took me in her lap and kissed me. Then I heard my daddy calling me, "Come back, my child, come back." I told grandpa that daddy was

calling me and I must go back. He said we should have to ask God. So we went to God, and grandpa told him that I wanted to go back. "Do you want to go back?" God asked me. "Yes," I said, "I must go back. My daddy is calling me." "All right," said God, "Go." And down, down, down I came from the stars on to daddy's bed."

Intrigued, her mother asked her what God was like. 'Blue,' came the startling reply. And try as they might to elicit more details ever afterwards, Durdana only ever said God was 'blue'.

A few months after her NDE, the little girl went with her parents for the first time to visit relatives in Karachi. Looking around, she suddenly called out excitedly, 'Mummy! Mummy!' She was pointing to an old photograph. 'This is my grandpa's mother. I met her in the stars. She took me in her lap and kissed me.' There was no

way the child could ever have seen a photograph of her great-grandmother, but she was right, this was Dr Khan's mother.

Later, when the family moved to England, Durdana's NDE was featured on a national television programme, complete with her recent paintings (she is a talented artist) of what she remembered of the garden she had visited while dead (see page 138).

---

have ripped her skirt (I don't know why). Then the horrible hot feeling completely disappeared and I was floating in a cool, balmy breeze under a bright blue sky. This time 'feeling swimmy' was utterly wonderful. I saw a butterfly go by and heard some birds singing. I seemed to float there for ages and felt quite happy to be on my own. This was very peculiar, because I was afraid of being left alone then. I discovered that I could turn over in the air and make little swimming movements that pushed me along, except it wasn't like air. It was indescribable ... as if it had a life of its own and somehow it tasted good, like perfect honey or maybe nectar ... Bliss ... very!

Then I heard a voice, female, in my mind. It had a sort of smile in it and I turned over in the air to face it. There was a woman on a

little cloud with her arms open wide. I rushed into them and she hugged me. It was the most perfect love ... and comfort. I hugged and hugged her and her warmth enveloped me. Somehow I knew that her name was Rita and that she was my auntie, although I'd never heard of her before.

She danced with me on the cloud and told me that she'd been bitten by a fly before she went to that place. 'I was very hot, just like you,' she said. 'But look at us now!' We laughed ... Then suddenly she moved away and said, 'Oh Vivvie, you've got to go back and finish it. Mummy's calling you.' I was horrified and started crying. I said, 'Oh Auntie Rita, please let me stay! I love dancing with you!' But she sort of moved backwards like she was on castors and soon I could hardly see her. But she smiled and

waved, then she was gone and I felt hot again. I was back in my body once more."

Vivien was given some medication by the doctor and began to drift off to a healing, dreamless sleep. But as she slipped into reverie, her mother told her she had murmured, 'Auntie Rita, Auntie Rita, can I play with you again?'

"To this day I don't know what the fever was, but mum said they thought they'd lost me. After what they called my 'crisis' I rapidly got well, and in about a week I was up and about again.

It was then that I started asking about Auntie Rita. At first mum said I'd imagined it, and there was no such person, but I kept on and finally ... she just said yes, I had an Auntie Rita once, but she'd died.

Mum died of cancer when I was in my late teens ... she wanted to get something off her chest ... although she could hardly speak ... she told me that she had an older sister, Rita, who was the black sheep of the family, and who'd run off with a married man to Singapore, where she'd died of blood poisoning when she was still a young woman, in her late twenties. Mum said the scandal had been too much to cope with in those days, mainly because the married man had been the deputy mayor of the town, and his wronged wife had been admitted to a mental hospital shortly afterwards suffering from ... something that sounded like severe depression. The whole family had moved to another town because of the gossip, and made a point of never mentioning Rita's name again.

Mum said she had been stunned – 'shocked to my core' was how she put it – when her tiny child had come back to her talking about 'Auntie Rita'. Well, you can imagine ... mum knew she didn't have long to go, and told me that it was a relief to talk about Rita after all that time. As a child she had adored her. 'She was like a goddess to me,' mum said. And she admitted she'd kept just one photograph of her sister, hidden away at the bottom of an old trunk in the attic. She gave me the key and I remember kneeling there among all the bric-a-brac, the accumulation of years, staring at a torn, discoloured photo of the black sheep of the family. It was a dreadful, out-of-focus picture, but it still captured the wild beauty of the young woman – her spirit shone through. My heart nearly stopped because it was the woman who had danced with me on the cloud when I'd died, although she was even more beautiful and radiant when I'd met her. I just knelt there and wept ... I'm not sure why, partly because, I think, it proved to me that I'd

really been to heaven, although I'd never doubted it, deep down.

I went for a long walk by the sea that evening and somehow felt Rita's presence. I can't explain it. It wasn't spooky or frightening, quite the reverse. She was with me. I could literally smell an exotic perfume and somehow feel her glamour. I looked out over the sea and strange images came into my head of being on a ship on New Year's Eve with crowds of people laughing and shouting, dancing the conga, kissing each other ... I had vivid images of women with harsh red lipstick and men in white tuxedos and an old-fashioned dance band. Maybe this was a scene from Rita's life ... anyway, that's the impression I got ... That's what I believe it was. Then I heard her say quite clearly, 'Go home now... Vivvie, darling, now!"

Vivien ran home to find her mother very distressed and in pain, and the home nurse arranging to have her taken into hospital. She says:

"*Everything in me reacted against this move. I just said no, leave her, she wants to be at home for the end. The nurse was shocked and tried to persuade me to let her go into hospital but I dug my heels in. I could see the woman was really surprised because I'd never been that forceful, never that assertive before.*

To my amazement, she caved in, which was very odd for a professional when you think about it, but I felt unstoppable. In the end the nurse called for the doctor and I sat holding mum's hand. She was fading fast, and grimacing with pain. I just squeezed her hand to let her know I was with her.

Then suddenly the strain lifted from her face and she really grinned. She beamed with pleasure directly at something she could see. 'Oh, Rita' she whispered. 'Look, Viv, it's Rita! Oh, this is wonder-

---

CASE STUDY: THE FACE

Recalling her NDE when she was five, Emily told Australian researcher Cherie Sutherland:

"*... I remember seeing Uncle Frank but I don't know how because what I remember most is just going up to heaven and seeing the man and the garden. Uncle Frank died before I was born. Afterwards I remember I told my Nana I'd seen his face in heaven ... [later] I told mum that when I was in heaven I'd seen the man in the photo at Nana's. I told her I remember seeing Uncle Frank. And mum was a bit shocked. And so was Nana when I told her later ... I'd never seen ... [his] photo before. I'd never heard anything about Uncle Frank. I just knew the name. And it really spooked my Nana. It really spooked me too.*"

---

ful.' Then mum sighed with happiness and ... very quietly, without fuss, she died. I found myself looking into the corner of the room where she'd been staring, but of course there was nothing to be seen, no one there. That night as I was staring out of the window, crying a little because I'd already started to miss mum, there was a sudden whiff of that glamorous perfume again. I'm sure it was Rita's way of comforting me, of telling me that mum was in good hands."

The black sheep's lesson

Clearly, this story possesses the characteristics of many associated paranormal phenomena, such as a childhood NDE containing checkable data unknown to the child at the time, subsequent psychic communication with her guardian, and the deathbed vision of her mother. If

▲ The death of a child is traumatic for relatives, but the evidence suggests that the body is nothing, whereas the spirit enters a wonderful world of love and light.

taken at face value, only the latter is open to the criticism of contamination by prior expectation: Vivien's discussion with her mother about Auntie Rita may have put the idea in her mind of being greeted on the other side by her sister. However,

Vivien herself is in no doubt about the message of the story:

"Why make things difficult? As far as I'm concerned, there is no way I could have invented Auntie Rita, nor did I ever hear about her before I died – her family made sure of that! She'd given me evidence by telling me she'd been bitten by a fly, because that's how she must have got the blood poisoning

that killed her. But how could a tiny child know a thing like that? I know I met her, and that she was extremely well and happy, and that she loved me so much she became my guardian – well, I was going to say 'angel' but given her history perhaps that's the wrong word. But then, think about it. When I met her there was never any suggestion that she'd died and been made to suffer for her sins by

124

a vengeful God. She was perfectly happy, blissfully so in fact. I have no doubt that this black sheep of the family was in heaven, and if she'd done wrong – don't we all in different ways – she'd been forgiven.

The whole story has impressed me with an idea of a totally forgiving, understanding God. You know, like the bit in the Bible about 'let him who is without sin cast the first stone'. I'm sure Rita had hurt a lot of people by her actions in life, and I'm sure she was remorseful about it. But she hadn't been thrown into a fiery pit. And now she was my guardian. I sometimes talk to her when things are tough, and the response is an overwhelming sense of love and understanding, which I know is not just my imagination. And once I was unhappily in love, with a married man! When it all fell through and he went back to his wife I sobbed for days. But suddenly I smelt that perfume again, and felt her love wash over me. I then pulled myself together, thanks to Rita's great spirit. **"**

It is impossible to reconcile the complex and lengthy unfolding of this story with the sceptics' theories of cerebral anoxia, the influence of drugs, prior expectation, religious belief, or downright fabrication. Remember that her family had taken care never to mention Rita, and she had never seen any photographs of her. Neither could she possibly have known that flies can cause fatal blood poisoning. There is no benefit in Vivien embellishing or inventing this tale. Like many whose stories are quoted in these pages, Vivien never sought publicity for her story. It is only as a favour to this author that she has allowed her story to be told.

Visions of the dead

Many professionals who work with dying children have noted that their NDE/deathbed visions never include encounters with people who are still alive, although they often describe those who were not known to be dead at the time, but whose deaths were subsequently discovered.

Elisabeth Kubler-Ross has devoted much of her medical career to dying children, and has written:

"*… I always ask my children, who would you like to have with you always, if you could choose one person? Ninety-nine per cent of the children, except for black children, name mommy and daddy. (With black children, it is very often aunties or grandmas, because auntie or grandma are the ones with them. But those are only cultural differences.) … But not one of these children who nearly died has ever seen mommy and daddy at this time unless their parents had preceded them in death.* **"**

To the sceptics who would say that this is nevertheless the result of wishful thinking in dying children, Dr Kubler-Ross is emphatic:

"*[Sceptics say that] somebody who dies is desperate, lonely, frightened, so they imagine somebody with them who they love. If this were true, 99 per cent of all my dying children, my five-, six-, and seven-year-olds, would see their mommies and their daddies. But not one of these children, in all these years that we have collected cases, saw their mommies and daddies because their mommies and their daddies were still alive. The factors determining who you see are that the person must have passed on before you, even if only by one minute, and that you must have genuinely loved them.* **"**

This last comment is interesting in the case of little Vivien and her Auntie Rita, because they did not know each other – in this life, anyway. Perhaps a bond had somehow formed during earlier periods of unconsciousness, such as dreaming, or maybe Rita had always been assigned to the child as her guardian angel.

Dr Kubler-Ross tells of how dying children are frequently aware of relatives whose deaths were very recent, and which had deliberately been kept from them to prevent added distress. She gives the example of a child on the brink of death who contentedly says, 'Everything's all right now. Mummy and Peter are already waiting for me.' Dr Kubler-Ross adds, 'Shortly afterwards I receive a call from the children's hospital that Peter died 10 minutes ago.'

Similarly, Dr Kubler-Ross tells the story of a Native American girl who was knocked down:

"*… by a hit-and-run driver on a highway when a stranger stopped his car in an attempt to help her. She very calmly told him that there was nothing else he could do for her except perhaps one day he might get near the Indian reservation where her mother lived about 700 miles from the scene of the accident. She had a message for her mother and maybe one day he would be able to convey this message to her. The message stated that she was okay, that she was not only okay, that she was very happy because she was already with her dad. She then died in the arms of the stranger.* **"**

Much moved by this incident, the stranger then drove the 700 miles (1127km) to call on the girl's mother with the message, only to discover that her father had died there just an hour before she had passed away.

Lost generation – found!

There are several very similar cases on record that further reveal the essential truth of the near-death vision. One of this group of cases is that of Melissa, whose NDE happened when she was 14 years old. She says:

"*I went to a beautiful place where the light was dazzling, only*

▲ The birth of stars is a massive and significant process. Yet the evidence of NDEs reveals that the life and death of each individual is just as important.

it didn't hurt my eyes - it couldn't because it could never hurt anything or anyone. My eyes sort of became accustomed to it and then I saw mummy [who died when Melissa was 10]. It was lovely seeing her again, looking so brilliant. She had a little girl with her, about eight or nine years old, who looked very much like her with lovely blonde hair and big blue eyes.

Mummy smiled at me and said, 'This is your little sister, Bunny'. And I was so happy to see her, but when I came back I was puzzled because I never had a little sister. I was very upset for ages - had I made it all up? But then I told daddy about it and his eyes just filled up with tears. Apparently I did have a sister who was about 18

months younger than me, but she was stillborn. They'd been planning to call her Eileen, but always used the nickname Bunny while they were expecting her. 'She's very much alive, daddy,' I said. 'She's grown up over there. You'd be very proud of her.'

The same strange knowledge also comes to those who are truly dying, as many deathbed visions reveal (see Chapter 1). A significant story was told to British writer Ian Wilson, who describes what happened in his book *The After Death Experience*:

"In 1968, Mrs Janet T ... gave birth to a baby daughter Jane, who sadly died of pneumonia two days later. Shortly after, some one hundred miles away in the village of Llangernyw near Abergele in North Wales, Janet's 96-year-old grandmother, Mrs Jane Charles, lay dying, attended by Janet's

father, Mr Geoffrey Charles, a newspaper reporter.

... Mr Charles had carefully avoided telling his mother that Janet had lost her baby, not least because the infant had quite specifically been given the Christian name Jane in honour of her great-grandmother. So he had no idea of the bombshell that was about to strike when ... Mrs Charles began to talk to apparent unseen visitors. Totally clear-headed, she first remarked on a woman who seemed to bother her. Then, just as in the cases observed by ... Kubler-Ross, she became 'calm and happy'. It was all right, she announced; she 'knew what it was all about now'. She very contentedly told her son that she had seen his father, her husband John, who had died in 1942. Then, with a puzzled expression, she remarked that the only thing she could not understand was that John had a baby with him. She said about this, very emphatically: 'It's one of our family. It's Janet's baby. Poor Janet. Never mind, she'll get over it.'"

Ian Wilson points out that although Janet was devastated by the death of her baby she did get over it, and went on to have two healthy children. He adds that the incident was not one that had been embellished over the years, 'for both she and her father wrote down what Mrs Charles said very shortly after Mrs Charles died', and that neither Janet nor her father were familiar with the literature on the NDE or deathbed visions.

Seeing is believing

Sceptics have suggested that the NDE might be more credible and less open to accusations of subjectivity if blind people described their heavenly experiences during an NDE in visual terms. Perhaps the critics believed they were on safe ground, for they made this suggestion when research into the subject was in its infancy and no such evidence was forthcoming. However, more recent cases have provided precisely that kind of evidence. As Dr Kubler-Ross writes:

"... in order to calm down the sceptics, we did a scientific project with blind people. Our condition was that we would involve only blind people who had not had any sight perception for at least the last 10 years. Those who had an OBE and came back can tell you in detail what colours and jewellery you were wearing if you were present. Furthermore, they can tell you the colour and pattern of your sweater, or of your tie, and so on. You understand that these statements refer to facts which one cannot invent."

She is most emphatic on this point:

"If [the NDE] was just wish fulfilment, these blind people would not be able to share with us the colour of a sweater, the design of a tie, or many details of shape, colours and designs of people's clothing. We have questioned several totally blind people and they were not only able to tell us who came into the room first and who worked on the resuscitation, but they were able to give minute details of the attire and the clothing of all the people present, something a totally blind person would never be able to do."

One woman who was blind from birth, and who naturally perceived the world with her other four senses, was hit by a car and collapsed, profoundly unconscious. She later sent her story to this author. Although anonymous, and therefore scientifically invalid, it carries the ring of truth. She says:

"It was a hot afternoon in August 1994. I was crossing the road, pat-patting with my stick, when a car took the corner too quickly and knocked me down. I felt a massive blow to my arm and side, then I heard a blaring sound - hard to describe, sorry - and I was up high in the air. It was very strange for several reasons. I was directly above my body, which was lying on the road. Now, that's odd enough, surely. But what was a million times odder was the fact that I could see it all! Me, who had never had the slightest bit of vision in my 40-odd years on this earth!

I swooped around, just looking. It was grand to see. I noticed how high the buildings were, because I thought of them as being rooted to the ground at the point where I could trace them with my stick. But they seemed to go up and up. I had my first understanding of a roof, and of the expanse of sky. I saw the back of people's heads, when normally I only get to feel a hand or a face, if I'm lucky. I saw cars, bikes, children, and could put images to the familiar sounds of everyday life. But most of all, I could see colours. I don't think any blind person has any concept of colours. How can they? It's what marks out the land of the sighted from the land of the blind. I saw, rather than talked about, the red of my jumper and the green of the grass in the nearby park, and the swirl of colours on the covers of magazines in the newsagent's. Then I saw them struggling to lift my head up. I felt as if someone was yanking on my soul, and I was back in my body - and blind again. It was awful, terrible. I cried for ages and couldn't explain. The one person I told said it must have been my imagination - how cruel, and how unrealistic!

But then I realized that I'd been very lucky and blessed. Because I'd seen what was in store for me when I died, that is, when I leave my body permanently. I realized then that being blind - like being in any kind of a body, sighted or blind - was just a temporary thing and that one day we would all be perfect in every way. Since I had that thought I've calmed down a lot and become happier. I feel almost as if I've been shown the face of God. How many people can say that?"

The weight of evidence

The cornerstone of modern rationalism is that the physical world is the limit of human existence, and that there is neither a separate spirit nor a life after death. To them we are mere machines, somehow thrown together by a 'blind watchmaker' – an impersonal evolution that causes us to live and have our being, then to cease to be. Somehow scientists have managed to persuade millions that they have 'proved' this materialist hypothesis, and that anyone who believes in the existence of a soul is at best wishfully thinking and at worst a deluded fool. Yet in fact, the weight of evidence is not on the side of the materialists/rationalists: it is stacked high on the side of the psychical researcher and the spiritual adventurer, the psychic and the mystic, and those who travel out of their bodies and return from death more alive than before.

As we have seen, suggestions that the phenomena of the NDE arise because of the side-effects of drugs, or the lack of oxygen, from wishful thinking, fantasy or prior expectation, are hopelessly inadequate to explain away the ever-increasing data. Of course this does not preclude the possibility of a rational explanation ever been found, but it does reduce that likelihood. Perhaps those who attempt to over-analyze and reduce the NDE to nothing more than a pretty dream are overlooking an opportunity to add to the sum of human knowledge.

Perhaps instead of trying to explain it away, they should devote their energies to eliciting its message, for arguably, the discovery of the NDE as a major human experience is the most exciting thing to happen to humankind in a very long time.

CHAPTER EIGHT

Working with the NDE

Research into the NDE is in its infancy, but already it has proved of enormous use in understanding the dying process, and in helping terminally ill patients and their families come to terms with death. Such knowledge also enables us to become better at coping with what is inevitable for us all one day – our own mortality.

In many cases, even knowing someone who has had an NDE can provide a life-changing inspiration. As one woman says:

"My sister Joan was very sick with cancer, going in and out of hospital for tests and operations. She was only 40, but she looked 60 – so grey and thin, not like her old self. I know it's a dreadful thing to say, but I didn't like seeing her like that. It was a real effort for me to pick her up and drive her to the hospital. We couldn't really talk any more either. It was a trial being with her, poor thing.

One evening I got a call from the ward sister (Joan was in hospital for a few days for tests), telling me to come quickly because she had collapsed and it was looking bad. I felt awful – if I'm honest it was because I really didn't want to see her dying like that ... I really had

◀ **The Virgin Mary: one of the religious figures who are reported to greet the newly dead. Sometimes an unknown 'lady', or goddess archetype, is described.**

to force myself to go, you see.

They'd saved her. She'd rallied. By the time I got there she was very weak but conscious, and, very strange ... she was different. Changed. She seemed to glow, even though of course she was still pin-thin. I kept staring at her and finally she managed a smile and beckoned for me to bend over closer to her. Then she told me an amazing story.

Joan said she'd tried to reach out of bed for a glass of water and the next thing she knew nurses were running around in a panic while ... she was looking down at the scene, unmoved by it. She described being in a 'shimmering, glorious light', just floating away. She thought, 'This must be death ... how lovely ...' Then she felt her old dog Prince lick her hand, and she knew it was going to be all right. Suddenly she stood upright and the hospital scene faded. Joan and the dog (he was young and frisky again) were in a beautiful forest glade, with wonderful music playing, and a waterfall (she always

loved water). A man and a woman came out of the trees and at first she didn't recognize them. They were dressed in white, glowing, like ... Then she realized that they were our parents, only young and healthy.

They went over to her and kissed her on the forehead. She said it was the most wonderful sensation, those kisses. Like complete love ... the end of pain and struggle ... coming home ... They seemed very excited about being with her, and took her to a little house ... a lovely place that seemed very familiar somehow ... and showed her a room that was hers. Our dad put his arm round her and said something like, 'Joanie sweetheart, you'll be living here with us for ever very soon. We'll come for you and it will be easy. But just for the minute you have to go back. Soon, I promise ...' Then it all faded and our Joan was in the hospital bed again, alive if only just.

But she'd changed. All the terrible strain had disappeared from her face. That haggard cancer look had gone. She was glowing. I hadn't seen her smile for months, come to think of it, but she was beaming ... so happy ... I knew then that the end was close. I'd been dreading it ... I know, it wasn't me who was dying, but I thought it was going to be unbearable ... but she died as I stood there, just breathing out one last time, with that amazing smile on her face. Her eyes were fixed on something just above and beyond me ... maybe it was mum and dad coming to collect her. I really believe that now.

Our Joanie's death changed me. I thought about what she'd said over and over, and I knew she hadn't made it up about meeting mum and dad and Prince, and the waterfall and everything. I felt it as she told me. I left the hospital in a daze, and I cried, but I wasn't unhappy really. I felt her spirit go and knew she was going to have a wonderful time. I hadn't believed in a life after death before ... frankly I thought it was religious codswallop ... but now I do. Yes, Joanie's death changed my life. **"**

Witnesses to someone else's NDEs are often shaken by their sincerity, and by the obvious power of the experience. This is striking in the case of childhood NDEs, when tiny children talk movingly of meeting Jesus, and being happy in the light, such as Cherie Sutherland's story of Daniel. His mother Bridget realized that she had to confront her own fears about his death, which she believed to be imminent, and had to learn to let go. She undertook an intensive course of counselling, and addressed the question of her possessiveness as a matter of urgency. It was clear to her that her son's confrontation with death highlighted her difficulties in confronting life that she had to overcome.

Daniel's NDEs came to change his mother's whole attitude to life and relationships. If his NDEs were a test for him, how much more of a test were they for his mother, who could do little to help him and who expected at any moment to lose him for ever? Yet once she had reached a point – unimaginable only months before – where she was ready to let him go, he did not die, but went on to live for years afterwards. It was as if her test was to confront her fear.

Fear is the key

The testimony of those who have NDEs can reach far beyond their own families. Their sincerity cuts right across space and time, to help many others. As we have seen with the story of Durdana Khan's NDE, it had a dramatic effect on Mrs Goldsmith, who recognized the heavenly place Durdana described (see page 122), and also provided the answer to a double prayer (see page 80). Her story continues to fascinate and inspire others.

In the course of my own occasional work as a dream interpreter I often answer phone-in questions for various radio stations in Britain, and I am amazed at how common are dreams about the fear of death. In my opinion, this lies behind many otherwise inexplicable nightmares, emotional confusion and even personality disorder. Death is the last great taboo of our society, to the extent that the majority of people simply refuse to acknowledge its existence, despite the fact that it is the one certainty we all share. When someone they know becomes gravely ill and dies their complacency is threatened, but their fear is too great to be seriously challenged. Instead, the denial goes deeper, soon even the *idea* of death becomes too traumatic to contemplate. We are a society of death phobics, and that is why so many people report horrific dreams that reflect this blind terror. Shirley, from Reading in Berkshire, describes a series of such dreams:

"*I've had some terrible dreams over the years, which began just after my next-door neighbour died.*

I've dreamt that every member of my family died (one per dream). Sometimes they were ill with something like AIDS or cancer - a slow horrible death - and I had to watch and do nothing. I couldn't do a thing to help ... not a thing ... oh, it was awful ... I dreamt my little boy, who was just 10, died in a fire as a baby and I couldn't save him. Then my husband had a car crash, then my mother had a tumour ... on and on. I wake up from them shaking and crying and they terrify me for days afterwards. It's as if I'm working through my entire family ... they just die.

Then the last thing was my own death. I fell into a deep black hole with wriggly things in it. I was screaming for help, but the earth filled my mouth and I was choking. I woke up in a dreadful state. **"**

Shirley was clearly in the grip of real denial about death at a conscious, everyday level, as further questioning revealed:

"*I don't think about death, no. I mean it comes to us all in the end, but it doesn't do to dwell on it, does it? I've never been one for horror films or anything morbid ... When Betty, my next-door neighbour, died it was like someone had taken the floor away from under my feet. I felt ... helpless and ... she'd gone, and didn't come back ... I'd never known anyone else close who'd died before that. I remember looking into her grave and shuddering. Poor Betty, going into that.* **"**

Clearly this woman was suffering from the great twentieth-century malaise, a death phobia, which, paradoxically, destroys the joy of life. She went through life with a terror so

▶ A view of hell from Thailand, showing the prevalence of the idea of an ongoing soul, and its accountability for sins and crimes committed in life.

secret that it was exiled to her deepest unconscious mind, where it festered like some ravening tumour, poisoning her psyche. This fear manifested in the series of death dreams, in which she was shown in no uncertain terms that, deny it as much as she liked, it was going to come to everyone she knew, including herself.

Another example of this modern blight is that of a 62-year-old man who lives alone and has no living family. His dreams worry him greatly. As he says:

"About twice a week I have this bad dream. Well, nightmare really. I'm in my flat and look in the mirror, but there's nothing there! I haven't got a reflection, I'm not there. Then it gets very dark and I can't find my way around. I keep stumbling over things ... there are creatures, demons I think, in the darkness and I'm getting very frightened ... I start to pray but it doesn't do any good, and I can feel the sides of the room closing in on me until I'm in a sort of trench, in the dark with the demons. I try to shout for help but I know no one can hear me. Then it dawns on me that I must be dead, that I've died ... gone, with no one to care ... I wake up screaming in terror.

I think it might have something to do with living next to a graveyard as a child. That was where everyone went when they died, no matter who they were or what they believed. When my mother died (I was too young to remember my father's death) I was only six, but I remember it as if it was yesterday. Seeing her in the coffin like a doll ... a stranger ... people in black ignoring me as if I was an embarrassment (I was an only child) or just patting me on the head as they went by. Then when they put her in that hole! Oh I can't tell you how horrified I was. I would lie awake at night thinking about my mother in the dark, wet ground and I'd sob my little heart out."

▲ Reminders of physical death, such as graveyards, often obscure the truth about death, where the true self – the spirit – begins a life of joy and adventure.

The poor child had been a victim of the spiritual emptiness of our outwardly Christian society. He says that he was taken to church every Sunday and 'never heard anything to cheer me up about my mother's fate'. Of course there are many enlightened ministers who understand the problems facing the bereaved, and whose own faith transcends the challenge of physical death, becoming a real inspiration to those left behind.

But on the other hand many ministers are disillusioned with what they see as superstitious belief – the Church of England has now demoted hell to a place of 'oblivion' on no better authority than a vote – and have nothing to offer those who are devastated by the death of a loved one. But there is hope to offer, as we have seen in the case of Cyril Picknett whose last days were immensely empowered by hearing the story of Durdana Khan's near-death experience (see page 122).

When asked for help with such nightmares as those described above, I always recommend the

kind of experience that is just as valid as any other in clinical life, and certainly of greater significance. They, and several like them have spoken out about the evidence of the NDE. When those who suffer from nightmares about death confront their fear, and take the first step to read about the meaning of death, their dreams begin to change. Shirley, whose nightmare is given above, said after reading Melvin Morse's *Transformed by the Light*:

"At first I put off even looking for the book, then I made myself ask for it. The first shop I tried didn't have it and they weren't very helpful, and I thought 'Well, I've tried, that's it then'. Afterwards I felt ashamed, so I kept trying and found it the next day. Even then I kept putting off actually opening it … why I don't know. Maybe something in me was so scared of death I didn't even want to see the word in print.

I don't know what I expected, but I got a pleasant surprise. This man [Melvin Morse] was sincere … I was impressed by his research, and by all the stories of people who had died and come back. I hadn't known about the NDE before, but now it puts things in perspective. All those people … said death isn't horrible. It isn't the end. You go to a beautiful place and feel blissfully happy. Reading about it … odd … I kept thinking 'I could do with some of that' - as if I was reading a holiday brochure!"

After finishing the book Shirley reported one more dream:

"I was in a doctor's waiting room. It was dark and I started to feel a bit scared, wondering … it's like, 'Is it supposed to be like this? Shouldn't they switch a light on?' Then I noticed the door to the street was open a bit and some light was coming in. It made me feel excited … I stopped being scared as soon

as I noticed it … I waited impatiently in the darkened waiting room, singing a little song … something like waiting for the boarding announcement for your holiday plane.

After what seemed like ages, the door opened a bit more and this huge … white light came out straight at me. I was knocked over by it, and lay on the floor shielding my eyes, but still trying to see into it. The light made me feel marvellous … I thought, 'If I have to, I'll crawl into that bloody light!'

I started to inch forwards on the floor, aiming to get through the door and into the light before 'They', whoever they might be, shut me out. Then a man's voice … American … said, 'Sorry, the doctor will see you when it's time. We're very busy. You'll have to come back.' I sat up and tried to focus on a dim shape I could see inside the light (by this time the crack in the door was bigger). I ached to get through the door into the light.

Then I was outside in the street. It was very early in the morning … the sun was just coming up and there was dew on the grass. Blossom on the trees. Springtime. I noticed a butterfly and laughed because it was so alive and so beautiful. Somehow I was happy to wait to get back through the door."

Here Shirley has symbolized her life before death as a doctor's waiting room. Perhaps this refers to Melvin Morse himself (reinforced by the American voice), or the idea that doctors are usually involved in the dying process. Access to the light and the afterlife was denied her because the time wasn't right, but she was allowed a tantalizing glimpse of it, which confirmed her new opinion that it was a wonderful and desirable experience. But the truly heartening aspect of her dream was her emergence into a spring dawn, a symbol of

books of Elisabeth Kubler-Ross and Melvin Morse. I explain that these are not some airy-fairy New Agers or religious missionaries with their own dogmatic axe to grind. Dr Ross went through the horror of picking up the pieces in the Polish concentration camps (she knows what 'nightmare' means) before becoming a psychiatrist and working for many years with the dying. That kind of background does not predispose one towards sentimentality. And Melvin Morse is a medical doctor who works in a busy hospital in Seattle.

What they both have in common is the courage to speak out about one

▲ One woman's dream of a butterfly fluttering its wings in the morning light expressed her coming to terms with her previous fear of death.

rebirth, renewal and hope. The butterfly is a classic representation of the soul.

Interestingly, this dramatic conversion from abject fear of death, which was so extreme that Shirley could hardly face seeing the word in print, to a longing to experience the afterlife took place simply because of a book containing the stories of those who have experienced NDEs. It would have been very easy for Shirley to have dismissed their claims, but once again, the peculiar power of their sincerity shone through. As Melvin Morse says:

"I have often been asked why I am so interested in near-death studies. Frankly, it is because I believe these stories ... [they] are told with such beauty and simplicity by children and adults alike who have nothing to gain by making them up. They demand to be investigated. "

In *Transformed by the Light*, Melvin Morse describes how he began as a sceptic of NDEs. He had dealt with resuscitated patients many times, and not one had ever reported an NDE. Now he says:

"Now I realize that many of my patients might have had NDEs. I just didn't spend enough time listening to them to find out. "

Dr Kubler-Ross also stresses the need to spend time with dying patients, and to take their insights and visions seriously. This not only helps the patient in their last hours on earth, it has an illuminating effect on their families – and on the doctor concerned. Too often medical staff respond like automatons in order to maintain their cool professionalism and prevent themselves from feeling the pain of emotion. But as Dr Morse says, 'I realize that there is room for emotion and spirituality in medicine.'

Death as an ally

Perhaps in an ideal world there would be special provision for the dying, instead of shunting them into side wards or trying to fool them that they are going to get better. The magic ingredient of spirituality might turn hospitals and hospices into places of beauty, where the act of dying is treated as a great rite of passage, at which families and friends are welcome and encouraged to play their part. There would be no denial and no embarrassment. No one would hurriedly dismiss the patient's NDEs; here they would be recorded as something important and instructive to the living. For when dying is no longer a monstrous enemy, but a natural ally, the otherwise unbearable grief of the bereaved will be alleviated. In the case of little Daisy, who died in the nineteenth century (see Chapter 1), her death was such a spiritual moment that her mother wrote: 'There was a solemn stillness in the room. We would not weep, and why should we?'

Dr Kubler-Ross regrets the practice of drugging terminally ill patients into death, noting that those who are only lightly medicated go into their passage with a conscious awareness of the beauty of the experience. As the moment of death draws closer, even those who had been in great pain and distress become more tranquil, and the pain vanishes. As we have seen, many people are aware of their coming death, even if it is not apparent to their doctors. The patient needs to communicate his or her feelings about the sensations that precede death. But only too often they receive more drugs – even the euphemistic 'injection', which effectively kills them off. As Dr Kubler-Ross says:

"No dying patient is going to ask for an overdose provided he is cared for with love, and is helped to finish his unfinished business."

However, she stresses that no one should be allowed to suffer, adding:

"Nowadays, medical science is so fantastic that anyone can be kept pain free. If your dying ones can be kept without pain, dry and nursed with care, and you have the courage to take them into your homes – I mean, all, if possible – then none of them will ask you for an overdose."

Perhaps there will come a time when doctors will actively work with the NDE, instead of fighting against it and everything it represents. And

---

CASE STUDY: LOOKING DOWN ON MY BODY

This OBE was reported to top NDE researcher Kenneth Ring by a young saleswoman from Florida who was knocked down by a car in 1964. She says:

"A man yelled at me ... apparently he was trying to warn me, and I was struck from behind ... That's the last thing I remember until I was above the whole scene viewing the accident. I was very detached. That was the amazing thing about it to me ... I don't remember hearing anything. I don't remember anybody saying anything. I was just viewing things ... It was just like I floated up there."

She reached the rooftops and beyond. She goes on:

"I was devoid of emotion. It was as though I was pure intellect. I wasn't frightened. You know, it was very pleasant ... [I remember] seeing my shoe, which was crushed under the car. I remember seeing the earring, which was smashed. I remember wearing a new dress and I was wearing it for the second time – at that time I made all my clothes – and I thought 'Oh, no. My new dress is ruined.' I wasn't even thinking about my body possibly being ruined too. I don't really think the seriousness of the situation dawned on me. I don't think I really had the realization at the time that, 'Oh, my God. I'm outside my body. What's happening to me?'"

Then she noticed the paramedics placing her body on a stretcher:

"I saw myself in profile. I was actually towards the front and side of the car, viewing all of this ... I was viewing my body as they picked it up from the ground and put it on to the stretcher. It was from a distance away, actually ... I remember them looking at my eyes. I guess they were checking my pupils."

---

when they do, many of the mysteries of curing the living will also become clear as a result.

Scientists and the NDE

Science is primarily, and in most cases exclusively, concerned with phenomena that are repeatable and verifiable. If a phenomenon is measured and monitored by a scientist in one part of the world and the results agree more or less with those from the same process repeated by another scientist elsewhere, then that is good science. But when a scientist takes seriously the visions of angels described by a dying patient, that is not considered good science, and that scientist stands every chance of being ridiculed, even hounded out of his job.

Over the past century, many highly respected scientists have attempted to persuade their colleagues of the validity of psychical research, only to discover that they became isolated and scoffed at. Of course there are great pitfalls for the unwary in investigating the paranormal. Unfortunately it is a field that attracts frauds and fakes, as we will see in Chapter 9. Nevertheless, an increasing number of courageous scientists all over the world are taking up the challenge of the paranormal. (And some of them, like Charles Tart of the Stanford Research Institute in California, have been actively encouraged in their work by the US Government.)

Into this muddled and highly controversial arena step the pioneers of NDE research: Kubler-Ross, Morse and Ring; in Britain, Dr Peter Fenwick and in Holland his colleague, Dr Pim van Lommel. And it is the last two scientists who may produce the most persuasive and scientifically acceptable evidence for the NDE.

Dr Fenwick is an eminently approachable member of the London Institute of Psychiatry, and a consultant neurophysiologist at two major London hospitals, besides being the President of the British branch of IANDS. Working with Dr van Lommel, a senior cardiologist at the Rynstate Hospital in the Dutch city of Arnhem, he set out to scientifically investigate NDEs. The pair aimed to interview all resuscitated cardiac patients at a pool of 10 hospitals in Britain and the Netherlands. (Cardiac patients were chosen because they are not heavily medicated, and the time of clinical death can be accurately monitored.)

Of the 345 patients in the study, 49 men and 13 women reported a classic NDE with most of the 'core experience' phases. But when, roughly a year after the initial interviews, the patients were interviewed for a

second time, 18 more admitted to having had an NDE, and had covered it up for personal reasons at the time. It is reasonable to assume that even more of the interviewees were hiding NDEs from the investigators.

The project went further: in each of the 10 hospitals an object was hidden near the ceiling of the cardiac arrest

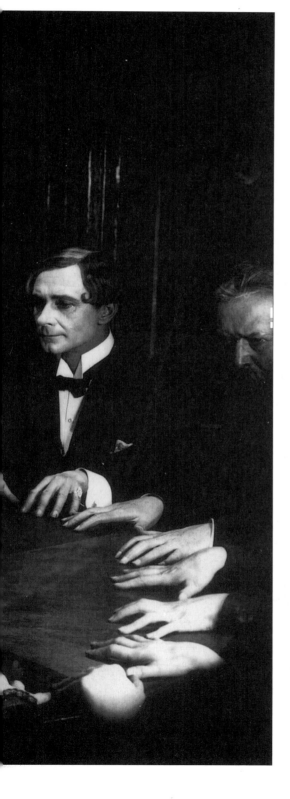

◄ A typical seance: although many psychics are genuinely gifted, many more are fake, and their contributions to knowledge of the afterlife are therefore dubious.

department, unknown to all but one of the team. The exact location of the target was frequently changed. The aim of this exercise was to discover if any of the subjects saw and described the object. So far Dr Fenwick and Dr van Lommel have not released the results of this experiment, although it will continue. But the difficulties involved in this should not be underestimated; remember that even those practised in OBEs experiences, such as Alex Tanous and Robert Monroe (see Chapter 3), found it hard to accurately describe the target in very similar experiments two decades ago. It may be that individuals have other things on their minds than examining the ceiling when they pop out of their bodies for the first time! Even so, the results of the Fenwick/van Lommel research is awaited with great interest.

Significant evidence?

In this context, one of Kenneth Ring's respondents told a significant tale. Undergoing surgery, she floated free of her body and described what happened next in these words:

"From where I was, I could look down on this enormous fluorescent light … and it was so dirty on top of the light … I was floating above the light fixture … it was filthy. And I remember thinking, 'Got to tell the nurses about that' … I don't know how long I was there [but] I could see what was going on in the cubicle next to mine. We were in a series of cubicles with curtains in between and I could see the woman in the cubicle next to me and she was asleep."

However, it may be that the NDE will never be provable in a scientifically acceptable way, unless science extends its boundaries to include consciousness research. The widespread reluctance among doctors even to discuss matters of the spirit is illustrated in an anecdote told by Melvin Morse when he asked what his colleagues thought of his talk on NDEs. One head of an intensive care unit dismissively said: 'Well, it conflicts with everything I believe to be true. The dying brain cannot have these kinds of images or activity.'

But a doctor of the older generation had this to say: 'Certainly what we don't know is far greater than what we do know. Science is like having a very bright flashlight in a gigantic cave.'

At that point the head of intensive care suddenly made a confession. He had once been treating an eight-year-old asthmatic boy, who appeared to be recovering enough to be sent home. But the boy said, 'I think I see my grandmother. She's coming for me and I'm going away with her.' His mother hastily said he was talking nonsense because his grandmother died years before.

However, the doctor had been so struck by the boy's story that, against his initial professional opinion, he kept him in intensive care. It was just as well that he did, for a short while afterwards the boy's condition suddenly worsened. If he had gone home as originally planned he would have died. But due to his vision, he had remained in hospital where he was resuscitated.

Remember that this story was told by a doctor who had begun by being scornful of Melvin Morse's talk of NDEs, perhaps only because such scepticism was expected of him. But his experience told a very different story. How many more doctors distort – or deny – their experience of spiritual matters in order to maintain their image as a scientist?

As science tentatively wrestles with the problems of investigating NDEs, other questions present themselves. Does the NDE provide real evidence for the existence of an afterlife? And how does it compare to the best evidence from other sources?

CHAPTER NINE

The Last Enemy

An NDE is almost always the single most profound and transformative experience an individual ever has, and its influence frequently extends well beyond his or her own life. These transcendental, regenerative visions of light are so intensely personal, that it often comes as a shock to discover that others have had very similar experiences.

An NDE is much more common than one might have guessed. Indeed, the NDE appears to be a fundamental human experience, a rite of passage akin to birth and second only to true, final death.

As we have seen, NDEs are experienced by people from all walks of life and religions, and although research into the subject is relatively new, it is a reasonable assumption that we only know of the tiniest tip of a very large iceberg of cases. The potential for furthering the sum of human knowledge through a greater understanding of the NDE is of course enormous, and we already possess a great deal of unique data, thanks to many courageous and enterprising researchers worldwide.

So what can we learn from the NDE? What is its message? What does it tell us about the nature of consciousness, and about the 'last enemy' – death itself? Many people are firmly convinced that the NDE is all the proof that is needed that consciousness does survive and thrive after death, but is this survivalist position vindicated by the facts?

◄ **Heaven in the memory of a child: this is how Durdana Khan remembered her visit as a toddler to 'the stars', where she met God.**

First, let us recapitulate on what the NDE is not. Except in a few rare cases the experience is not a deliberate fabrication for personal benefit or advantage, for example minor celebrity status in a tabloid newspaper. Most people who have had an NDE are extremely reticent about even discussing their experience anonymously with individual researchers, let alone going public in such a publicity-hungry fashion. Besides, true NDEs are transformative, bestowing noticeable change on the person who has one, almost always for the better.

Typical side-effects of the NDE include a change from a materialistic attitude to a much more spiritual, tolerant view of life and a rejection of values that fall short of their new high ideals. A person will be energized and purposeful ('zestaholics'), hungry for knowledge and keen to better themselves intellectually and spiritually after an NDE. They may exhibit psychic abilities, such as precognition or healing, and begin to have vivid dreams that come true (which are not always welcome). And they come to understand that their body is a gift that is not to be abused. They tend to look after their health more (Melvin Morse has noted that

they eat more fruit and vegetables and less meat and junk food than before their experience). Because it is difficult and largely pointless to fake those changes, any claims should be measured against the individual's 'transformation curve'.

Secondly, true NDEs are not the result of drugs or medical procedures. The visions are not some kind of hallucinogenic 'trip', as some sceptics frequently have asserted, although there may be certain apparent similarities, such as separating from the body and seeing the unfolding events from a different perspective, usually from above. Drug takers may also find themselves in a dark tunnel, or hurtling through a tube or corridor at great speed, and experience feelings of euphoria and mystical 'oneness' with the universe. But there is a qualitative and measurable difference between, for example, a cannabis-induced experience and a true NDE, which may be summed up in two words: the light. Although users of LSD and mescalin have reported seeing the world through very different eyes – ordinary objects such as chairs and tables may appear to glow, and their individual molecules can be seen in a sort of whirling dance – they report no

CASE STUDY: 'HEAVEN IS WAITING FOR ME'

Millie from Wales was 62 years old when she had a heart attack and died for 10 minutes.
Now 78, she recalls her experience:

"Funny, isn't it – there I was dead, and I think of it as the happiest time of my life! Of course it wasn't much fun having the heart attack and being rushed into hospital, and all the worry it caused my daughters and their families. I was in terrible pain and then lying there with all the hospital equipment everywhere. It seemed inhuman somehow. I remember thinking, 'I don't want to die here with tubes sticking out of me.'

But then I saw someone standing behind the doctor's shoulder. At first I couldn't place her, then I realized it was my sister-in-law Hilda, who'd died 20 years before in America. It had been very sudden – she was only 32 – and I couldn't afford to go all that way to the funeral. I was devastated. But there she was, happy and smiling. I sort of lost track of what the medics were doing and drifted up out of my body above their heads towards Hilda who had her arms out to me.

We hugged in mid-air. It wasn't like hugging ordinary flesh – we sort of merged. It felt odd but very, very nice, like all the love in the world. She looked wonderful and young – just as I remember her as a young woman in Cardiff before she and her husband emigrated to Cleveland, Ohio. Then she sort of lifted me up in her arms. The hospital scene disappeared below me and a tunnel opened up, with a low sound like wind whistling past. We flew, hand in hand. Oh, it was lovely, with a big white light coming straight at us. I wasn't afraid of it. I just wanted to fly into it and stay there. Then we were in a park full of little deer – you know, Bambis – and everything was peaceful. Hilda and me just walked around looking at the flowers with this light shining on us. It wasn't the sun, but something that had love in it, or maybe it was love.

Then suddenly Hilda said, 'Millie love, you've got to go back to look after the girls. But you will come again, won't you?' I just cried and cried and woke up crying, but I could never say anything to them in the hospital. They wouldn't have believed a word I said. But I know that heaven exists and that it's waiting for me. It's something I'm certainly looking forward to."

encounter with the brilliant and transformative light that characterizes the NDE and after which everything is different.

Neither is the NDE a dream, at least in the usual sense (although some researchers suggest that there are similarities). Normally, an observer can easily detect when any mammal has begun to dream: measurable physiological changes take place, the most obvious of which are rapid eye movements under closed lids, as the sleeper watches his dream take place in his mind's eye. But the eyes of a person having an NDE do not move either rapidly or slowly, neither do they exhibit any of the other well-known physiological changes associated with dreaming – this is because many of them have their experience when they are clinically dead.

Lack of oxygen or spasms in the optic nerves are sometimes cited by critics as causes of certain visions characteristic of the NDE, such as the opening up of the black tunnel.

These, they argue, are no more than reflexes, just as we tend to see stars after sustaining a blow to the head, or sometimes before fainting. However, nobody who has suffered from lack of oxygen or been hit on the head has returned to consciousness with stories of otherworldly journeys that include accurate information they could not otherwise have known.

But is the NDE, as one sceptic has called it, simply 'the brain's last fling' – an evolutionary programme whose sole function is to reduce the panic and trauma of facing oblivion? Are the euphoric visions of those who have gone before, or loving religious figures, only there to ease us over into the nothingness of death? The very semantics involved show the emptiness of this suggestion – why are we eased over when there is nothing to be eased over to? Why are we programmed to go out into oblivion in such a blaze of love and glory? If Darwin was right, evolution never bestows anything on a species that is

not of practical value where survival of the fittest is concerned. If nature wanted us to face death with equanimity, then why were we not all programmed just to lie down and die without a second thought? Where is the survival value in having a happy death? After all, whether our deaths are peaceful or traumatic, the species will still survive.

The fear-death experience

Many of the characteristic elements of the classic NDE have been experienced by people who only believed themselves to be at the point of death, but who, in fact, were not. For example, several mountaineers have reported seeing their life flash before them as they fell, apparently heading for certain death, only to find themselves saved by some unexpected twist of fate: perhaps their 'lifeline' rope held instead of breaking, or their fall was cushioned by a tree. These quasi-NDEs have been dubbed 'fear-death experiences', but what are their implications? What light do they shed on the true NDE?

Melvin Morse describes a case that Dr van Lommel, a respected Dutch cardiologist, shared with him about a man whose car crash encompassed both a fear-death and a near-death experience, so the two may be easily compared.

In the very last moments before the man crashed into the back of a truck, and he realized the inevitable was going to happen, everything seemed to go into slow motion. He slammed on his brakes, then the car went out of control, spinning wildly. At that point he left his body and his life flashed by as a series of short pictures. This Dr Morse believes was a fear-death experience – a true reflex when faced with a critical, apparently life-threatening situation. But after the car impacted with the truck, and the man was horrifically injured, something very different happened.

Critically ill and in a coma, he left his body once more and found himself in a dark tunnel, approaching a distant light. Then, without warning, a 'being of light' who was 'filled with love and light' appeared, ushering in another life review. But this time he understood his life in terms of all the moral choices he had made.

Dual system

Melvin Morse believes that this double experience perfectly illustrates his idea that we have a dual nervous system. One is the 'conventional, biochemical nervous system, which regulates motor and sensory abilities'. The seat of these operations is the left hemisphere of the brain, which is 'associated with our left temporal lobe'. The left side of the brain governs what we call 'thinking', the everyday logic in which one thought follows another in an associative chain, which sifts through facts and figures and makes sense of the world around us. (This left-brain perception is what links us with other people, because it enables us all to see things in much the same, objective way, helping to maintain a consensus

reality. If, as many religions have believed, the world is an illusion, then it is the left brain that keeps it stable, so we are all part of it and see it in the same way.)

According to Dr Morse's hypothesis, there is another, 'subtle, electromagnetic nervous system, which is responsible for healing bone breaks, regeneration of body tissue, and the psychosomatic linkages between the brain and body.' This, he believes, is governed by the all-important right temporal lobe (situated just above the right ear, deep inside the brain) in the right hemisphere of the brain. Melvin Morse suggests that 'this silent second brain – the circuit boards of mysticism – [enable us to] understand the nature of the near-death experience'. When the brain is dying, perhaps this area is suddenly activated, maybe for the first and last time. This 'allows us to receive a wonderful and loving light, which one patient called "the glow of God"'.

Melvin Morse does not see any contradiction in ascribing OBEs to an area of a dying brain, which is very

much part of a body, nor does he believe his right temporal lobe theory in any way invalidates or denigrates the mystical aspects of the NDE, although others may find it more difficult to reconcile the two. However, it is worth looking more closely at his idea of a physical medium – the brain – for an essentially spiritual experience. As he says, the quintessential point of an NDE is its power to transform – to change the personality of the individual and to completely change his or her subsequent life. And as Dr Morse adds, 'changes in personality – especially long-term changes – are almost always accompanied by changes in the actual makeup of the brain.'

Even so, this argument does seem, at first, as if Dr Morse is equating the brain with the soul, or 'mind' – an attitude that is essentially in keeping with that of the Newtonian materialists/rationalists: the physical universe is all there is. Those of a more spiritual turn of mind tend to view the body and brain as almost irrelevant to the experiences of the spirit.

CASE STUDY: A LITTLE BOY'S MESSAGE

One of the most famous – and controversial – mental mediums of recent years in Britain was Londoner Doris Stokes, who died in the mid 1980s. She had a huge following of devotees, including many prominent media people. One day in early 1981 she was invited to have lunch with the editor of a well-known publication, and afterwards he asked her if she would meet his staff, none of whom she had ever even heard of previously.

Immediately, Mrs Stokes homed in on one young woman, the magazine's secretary, and told rather than asked her about the recent death of her beloved gran. She even described the old lady's last preoccupation – whether they would let her keep her false teeth in heaven!

The medium also told the secretary that her real name was not the 'Janet' that everyone knew her as, but 'Jeanne-Mary' (hardly an easy guess) – but which was correct. Then she said to Jan, 'I've got a little boy here, love. He's about nine and says he's yours. He says he's fine and not to worry.' Everyone was embarrassed because Jan had no children and she and her husband would dearly have liked to have a family although it was proving difficult. The staff then became horrified when Jan burst into tears as Doris Stokes said gently, 'He says he forgives you ...'

After the medium had gone, Jan confessed that nine years before she had an abortion, and that the baby had been a boy.

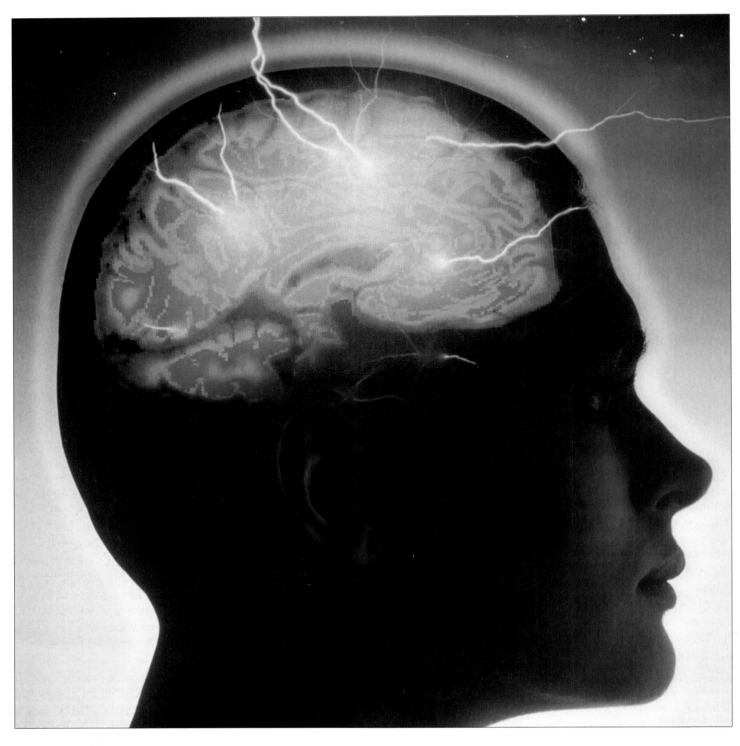

▲ Is the mind the same as the brain? Even some scientists believe that the brain is merely a receiver/transmitter for the far-reaching, but invisible, mind.

Yet perhaps neither attitude is either strictly correct or even theoretically useful.

Those great fearless seekers of knowledge in the Renaissance – the Hermeticists – had a saying that they shared with the alchemists: 'As above, so below'. This meant that everything on earth had its counterpart in heaven and vice versa. By extension the phrase also encompasses the idea that any spiritual manifestation has a material outlet or repercussion, so it is particularly relevant here. One scientist who is not afraid to consider this matter is the British 'heretical' scientist, the London-based plant physiologist Dr Rupert Sheldrake.

Dr Sheldrake considers that materialists (and therefore most scientists) perceive the human personality to be synonymous with and dependent on the brain. To them, once the brain is dead and has rotted away the personality cannot continue to exist. But what if it can be argued, plausibly and logically, that the personality

---

CASE STUDY: 'I HAD A CHANGE OF HEART'

William is an academic from Minnesota, whose NDE happened as a result of an accident while swimming off the coast at Honolulu in 1990. He is careful to point out that he had no belief in anything other than the material world before his experience:

"To my mind there were intelligent people who knew that what you see is what you get and that death is the end, and there were – quite frankly – uneducated and superstitious people who had an erroneous belief system that encompassed such idiocies as mind over matter and an afterlife. I was quite vociferous on this point, and even occasionally lectured on the subject. Then I drowned.

I was scuba diving and had a mishap with my mask. The next thing I knew was a horrible roaring sound in my ears. My lungs felt as though they were bursting and I blacked out. Everything fizzed at the edges and then I rose up through the water like a rocket. It was pure euphoria. I never stopped to think, 'Hey, this can't be happening. It's not in your world view, professor!' I just went with it.

Okay, I went to heaven and met an angel. It's not something I'm willing to stand up and admit just yet, although that may come. But I can say, hand on heart, that everything changed when I lost consciousness. What

happened was no dream or hallucination. Okay, so what was heaven like and what do I mean by an 'angel'?

Heaven is real, point one. Next point is that it speaks to the inner part of you so intensely and quintessentially that there is no question of it being misunderstood. Heaven exists and it is love. It makes me feel wonderful just recalling it. I'm sitting here with this big stupid smile on my face, just remembering being in a dazzling bluish light with a being speaking straight to my heart, telling me precious intimate things about my life. Sorry, but it's too … I need to keep it to myself for now. But the point is that when they dragged me to a boat and resuscitated me I was another man. I had changed completely. I went swimming as an arrogant sceptic-materialist and came back from death … as what or whom? It is very hard to describe, but the nearest I can say is that I came back as someone who had not only had a change of heart, but who had discovered he had a soul. I'm not ashamed to say that now."

---

is not dependent on the brain? Writing in the weekly publication *The Unexplained* in the early 1980s, Dr Sheldrake suggests a potentially useful analogy:

"Think of … a television set: the pictures on the screen can be affected by disturbing the wiring inside the set – or, for that matter, by pouring chemicals into it. But this does not mean that the pictures arise inside the set, or that the events shown on the screen are nothing but an aspect of what is happening within it. They do indeed depend upon the set, but they also depend on what the people are doing in the television studio, and on the electromagnetic waves by which the image of the events in the studio is transmitted."

Materialists who argue against the independent existence of a mind or soul often point to the fact that thought, behaviour and even personality can be dramatically changed

due to brain damage. But does this prove that the personality is synonymous with the brain? Sheldrake answers this objection by continuing his television set analogy:

"[Even] if the set is badly damaged and the pictures on the screen disappear, the activity in the studio continues; the people whose pictures appeared on the screen have not been destroyed just because the set has 'gone dead'."

He adds:

"There is … no evidence that every image or thought that we experience is paralleled in detail by specific physical or chemical changes inside the brain."

For example, it is possible to tell whether a sleeper is dreaming, but it is impossible to know what he is dreaming, even with the most sophisticated monitoring techniques. And, bizarrely perhaps, research has

shown that one does not even need (much of) a brain in order to be thought of as very intelligent!

Is a brain necessary?

It used to be thought that the level of intelligence was directly in proportion with the size of the brain, but there is evidence that the role of the brain has been vastly overestimated. In 1982, Professor John Lorber, of Sheffield University in the north of England, published a scientific paper with the provocative title: 'Is your brain really necessary?' He quoted the case of a university student who had been referred to him because he appeared to have a slightly larger head than usual. Lorber did a brain scan on the young man, and made an amazing discovery:

"… We saw that instead of the normal 4.5cm (2ins) thickness of brain tissue between the ventricles and the cortical surface, there was just a thin layer of mantle measuring a millimetre or so."

In other words, this young man had virtually no brain. This was all the more remarkable because he had an IQ of 126, and had gained a first-class honours degree in mathematics!

Sheldrake suggests that the mind is not merely an aspect of the functioning of the brain (as the materialists assert), but that the two interact. This would accord with, rather than oppose, the evidence of the existence of a soul gathered from a number of sources that are not usually accepted by scientists. These include:

- Spiritualist phenomena;
- Memories of past lives suggestive of reincarnation; and
- OBEs and remote viewing (discussed in Chapter 3).

Let us examine the first of those categories. What can spiritualist phenomena tell us about the nature of human consciousness, both in the here-and-now and in the hereafter?

Knock, knock

For most of the time that humankind has been on the earth, a belief in an afterlife has been, of necessity, a matter of faith. As Shakespeare has Hamlet say, no traveller returns from the 'undiscover'd country' that is death; there are no travellers' tales or guidebooks, no maps or ambassadors from the invisible land that is our destination. But many would argue that there have been two major breakthroughs in our understanding of that unknown world, each of course more historic in its way than even the first transatlantic telephone conversation. One is the NDE itself, and the other was the coming of the spiritualist movement.

It is hard today to begin to imagine the fervour with which this was greeted over 150 years ago. It seemed like an answer to a prayer. Life was

◀ Victorian table-tilting was a huge craze – almost anyone could get inanimate objects to move. But what does this tell us about the potential power of the human mind?

very hard and death was everywhere: childbirth and disease robbed the majority of families of many of their young children, and poor hygiene coupled with relatively primitive medical care meant that illness and accident carried off many more people in the prime of their lives than happens in the developed world today. Life expectancy was around 50 years. Custom also meant that almost everyone was familiar with the physical grimness of death – open coffins would be displayed in parlours for up to a week, the strongest scent of flowers hardly a match for the much sicklier stench of decomposition. Even the youngest children were familiar with the look and smell of death. So anything that could prove to them that, as the ministers said, there was a spirit, a something that survived and transcended the only too mortal body, was greeted with almost hysterical enthusiasm.

Although there have always been individuals who claim to have been able to converse with spirits, such as Emanuel Swedenborg (see page 104), it was only in the 1840s that such 'mediumship' became a mass movement. It began modestly enough in a log cabin in Hydesville, in the state of New York. Twelve-year-old Kate Fox and her 15-year-old sister Margaret claimed that they could communicate with the spirits of the dead through a code of raps. This had begun with what we would now call poltergeist (German for 'noisy spirit') activity. Terrifying and inexplicable rapping sounds emanated from walls, doors and ceilings. The previous inhabitants of the little log cabin had fled from the unwelcome visitations, but the girls proved to be a match for any otherworldly intruders. Soon they had evolved what is by now something of a joke – the two knocks for 'yes' and one for 'no' code with which to communicate with the discarnate (disembodied) spirits. That particular discarnate claimed to be a murder victim, and indeed some bones were later discovered walled up in

the house. But any truth that lay behind the story was soon obscured under a veritable landslide of notoriety that besmirched the name of the Fox sisters.

Even at its outset, spiritualism was to suffer the indignity of ridicule, accusations of fraud and the downright hostility of the Church, who saw the hand of the devil in all its phenomena. The girls themselves were by no means unsullied by such controversy, and it was to set the scene for an uneasy future for the movement as a whole. Within months of the Fox sisters taking their mediumship demonstration on tour, other similar acts sprang up like mushrooms. In most cases they were cynical – and often not very sophisticated – illusions created by conjurers and their accomplices. Within a short time, mediumship had gone a long way from simple demonstrations of rapping noises to fully fledged materializations of all sorts of objects (known as 'apports'), from flowers to pieces of jewellery, and finally to the 'full-form materializations' of the dead themselves.

Dark secrets

The Fox sisters eventually succumbed to a merciful obscurity. After being inundated with accusations of fraud, they confessed then retracted their confessions, and took to the bottle to forget their humiliations. By that time, spiritualism had become the rage on both sides of the Atlantic. Its appeal was immense, not only to the bereaved – genuine seekers after evidence of their loved ones' continued survival – but also among sensation seekers. The seance rooms (where the mediums plied their trade) provided a rich source of entertainment and even a certain erotic thrill, for the sittings took place in the dark, and all the 'sitters' had to hold hands to maintain 'vibrations' that would encourage the spirits to appear, as they sat silently, thigh to thigh. It is surely a mistake to underestimate the highly sexual

THE CONTROVERSIAL MEDIUM

Scotswoman Helen Duncan was one of the last of the famous physical mediums, who claimed to materialize the dead in (temporarily) material bodies. Her story reveals the difficulty in being objective about such a form of mediumship.

At the height of her fame in the 1930s and early 1940s, she would go into trance and, with the aid of her spirit guide 'Peggy' would allegedly produce the living likeness of the dead. Unfortunately, the only surviving pictures of 'Peggy' clearly reveal her to be made out of papier-mâché and coathangers.

In 1944, Mrs Duncan was arrested and became the last person to be charged under the eighteenth-century British Witchcraft Act. Accused of committing a felony, there were many witnesses in her defence, including two celebrated journalists of the day who claimed her mediumship was not only genuine, but impressive. Nevertheless, she spent nine months in jail in London. Shortly after her release she was seized while in a trance by a policewoman, and very nearly became the first person to be charged under the new Fraudulent Mediums' Act. But within weeks of this incident, she was dead – a true spiritualist martyr.

However, the story does not end there. Recently it was discovered that the reason she was arrested was that in 1943 she had passed on a communication from a dead sailor to his mother, which had included top-secret information! The British authorities had acted to prevent more classified information from leaking out.

And the discarnate Mrs Duncan herself is a regular visitor to the

▲ Medium Helen Duncan was the last person to be tried under the British Witchcraft Act.

seances of Rita Goold in Nottingham. There is even a tape of her singing along to one of her newly favourite songs – *I Did It My Way!*

---

undercurrent of the seance room in those frustrated, pre-Freudian days.

Yet it is difficult to sort the wheat from the chaff at this distance in time. For although many fake mediums were blatant in their exploitation of the bereaved – the American Davenport Brothers, for example, were well-known stage magicians who simply changed their act into a seance – there were a handful who defy accusations of fraud. The most notable of those in the early days was the Scots-American Daniel Dunglas ('D.D.') Home (pronounced 'Hume'), who took fashionable Europe by storm in the 1870s.

Mr Home's rise and rise

D.D. Home believed that the spirits of the dead caught hold of him and carried him ceiling high, returning him to the floor without harm, and that they enabled his body to mysteriously lengthen by several inches, rippling like a seal as it did so. He claimed they also allowed him to thrust his face and hands into a white-hot fire without either damage or pain, and caused objects such as musical instruments to materialize in mid-air, playing popular tunes (including, appropriately, *Home Sweet Home!*) as they flew about the seance room. Sometimes faces and parts of bodies, such as hands and arms, would appear around the entranced body of Mr Home.

These claims may appear outrageous, but Home seems to have had genuine paranormal powers. And while almost all other contemporary mediums operated in near-total darkness (light being deemed injurious to their health while in a trance) his demonstrations usually took place in daylight. While many mediums were discovered to work with accomplices who operated various gadgets to fake the phenomena, or who dressed up and masqueraded as the dead, D.D. Home worked alone, and often produced phenomena in private houses, which he had never even visited beforehand. It certainly seemed as if Daniel Dunglas Home was really, as he claimed, in touch with the dead.

Incredibly, D.D. Home was never even seriously accused of fraud, although he had his critics (one of them was the celebrated English poet Robert Browning, whose satirical verses entitled *Mr Sludge the Medium* were known to be aimed at Home). And if one eminent scientist was any judge, Home's powers were definitely genuine.

The scientist's seance

In the early 1870s, William (later to become Sir William) Crookes decided to investigate the claims of the spiritualists, despite the inevitable ridicule that would attend such a venture, both then and now. He began

▶ D.D. Home exhibited extraordinary powers: he routinely levitated in front of reliable witnesses, and despite attracting some criticism, he was never accused directly of fraudulent practice.

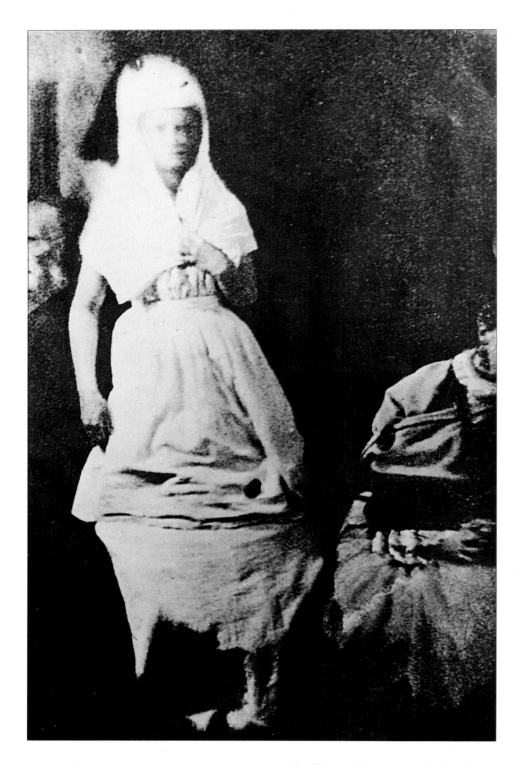

▲ This is just one of several photographs that fail to prove the separate existence of medium Florence Cook (allegedly on the right) and 'spirit' Kate King.

• Percussive noises – often raps, but sometimes faint scratchings, occasionally detonations.
• Alteration in the weight of objects.
• Movements of furniture with no contact.
• Levitation of furniture with no contact.
• Levitation of Home himself.
• Movement of articles at a distance.
• Tunes of musical instruments which nobody was playing.
• Luminescence.
• Materializations of human forms and faces.
• Materializations of hands (luminous or visible in light).
• Automatic writing (pens taken up by an invisible agency that wrote messages).
• Phantoms.
• Telepathy (or the production of information to which Home did not have direct access).
• Apports.

This is an impressive list. Crookes himself was certainly impressed, and was to remain so to the end of his long and very distinguished life. But first the scientist had another otherworldly encounter, the repercussions of which were to cast slurs on his good name to this very day.

Double trouble

Shortly after Home had left London to continue on his travels, a young woman called on Dr William Crookes and begged him to investigate her mediumship, which she suggested was considerably more impressive and far-reaching than that of any other medium. Just 17 years old, this remarkably pretty girl was Florence Cook from London's rough East End, and her gifts were already the talk of the spiritualist circuit. Perhaps this is not surprising, because her attending spirits had once had a habit of throwing her in the air and ripping all her clothes off! Now things may have become more decorous at her seances, but her claims – and those

with an exhaustive study of D.D. Home, then touring Europe, and was encouraged when the medium himself urged him to be particularly rigorous and watchful for cheating! At the end of months of experiments

with Home, Crookes published his findings, in which he confessed himself amazed by the medium's phenomena, among which he listed:

• The movement of heavy bodies with contact [of hands], but without physical pressure.
• [Inexplicable] currents of air.
• Changes of temperature [recorded on thermometers].

of her many admirers – were still astonishing. Florence Cook was said to produce the flesh-and-blood resurrection of a long-dead pirate's daughter, one Katie King, who walked and talked with the living. Miss Cook did not mind at all when it was claimed on her behalf that her phenomena constituted the final vindication of Jesus' own Resurrection.

The implications of this naturally caused a furore and not a little scepticism, which was neatly summed up by one contemporary, E.W. Dodds, who wrote:

"If genuine, their importance cannot be exaggerated; if frauds, their wickedness cannot be exceeded."

Crookes appeared to embrace the opportunity of investigating Miss Cook only too enthusiastically, even inviting her (and her mother) to stay at his marital home – although his wife was confined to her room with a troublesome tenth pregnancy. There followed a series of special demonstrations in the purpose-built seance room that Crookes had built in the laboratory in his home in Mornington Road, north London (since destroyed by a Nazi bomb).

Florence would obligingly go into the required trance in the medium's curtained-off recess (to avoid any light falling on her at this vulnerable time) and in a few minutes a young girl, dressed in white, would appear and walk and talk quite naturally with William and his hand-picked fellow 'sitters'. This was Katie King. However, there was one major obstacle in persuading a wider public of Florence's talents: Miss King, the long-dead pirate's daughter, was the living image of the medium herself. In order to counter the obvious accusation that Katie was no more than Florence dressed up, Crookes took over 40 photographs of the two young women together – one living and the other dead – but unfortunately destroyed most of them when his association with Florence ended, and

▲ Whoopi Goldberg's fake medium in the hit movie *Ghost* gets a shock when a real spirit (Patrick Swayze) contacts her. This unlikely partnership leads to his salvation.

in the remaining handful the features of one or the other women are always obscured in some way, perhaps by floating drapery, or through some uncharacteristic incompetence of the eminent photographer.

Crookes apparently ended his investigation of Miss Cook's mediumship abruptly when she confessed to having been secretly married for a few months, which coincided with Katie's announcement that she was returning to the spirit world. Later, Florence's new 'full-form materialization' – this time a girl called Marie who also looked amazingly like her medium – was exposed as none other than Florence herself attired only in her underwear. Florence Cook ended her days in Wales as a bored alcoholic housewife, seducing tradesmen, while William Crookes had a glittering career. For example, his inventions and discoveries made the cathode ray tube possible. Yet to the end of his days he remained a staunch champion of spiritualist phenomena, although he was never specifically to mention Florence Cook's mediumship, implying that it had been Home's he had admired.

Superficially, at least, this would seem to be merely a sad but predictable story of a sordid sexual scandal being covered up by a rather pathetic 'scientific investigation', if it

were not for an interesting postscript. Katie King appeared at least once more – 100 years later – at a seance in Rome, when yet again she looked suspiciously like her (very Italian) medium. However, this time the seance was recorded on infrared film, on which Katie appears and disappears between frames.

Crookes had somewhat defensively listed several distinct differences between Florence and Katie. For example, the dead girl was taller and heavier, and her ears were unpierced, whereas Florence had pierced ears. And on one occasion, when Florence had a large blister on her neck, Katie's remained unblemished. Katie had even said to the sitters at Mornington Road, 'I was prettier than this in life, but I can't help it.'

Could it possibly be that there was more to this than meets even the most cynical eye? Perhaps the matter was by no means so conclusive as it first appears. Perhaps, as some have suggested, the spirit Katie King was real enough but the medium was inadequate, or, ironically, like Whoopi Goldberg's character in the hit movie *Ghost*, Florence was a fake until she

---

CASE STUDY: 'I COULD HEAR THE DOCTORS...'

One coma victim was Antony, who spent several weeks in an intensive care unit in 1992 before
regaining consciousness and making a full recovery. He says:

"The worst of it was that I could hear everything to start with. Although I couldn't actually feel anything, I could hear the doctors and nurses discussing me and my reactions – or lack of them – to various tests. Some of them were very brisk and dismissive, as if I'd already been written off, or as if I was just a lump of meat.

One of them said, 'here we go again. How long before the family decide [to turn the life support machines off] so we can have the bed for someone else...' I was horrified and tried to sit up and show them that I was alright really, but I couldn't move, couldn't open my eyes, even to blink.

At some point things got a bit hazy and I blacked out. When I came to I was standing beside the doctor who was doing his rounds, I suppose. I thought, well, I'm better now, I'll just say goodbye to him. But when I tried to talk he took no notice, so I grabbed his arm but my hand was transparent and went right through him. Even I could hardly see it and it was obviously completely invisible to the doctor. I wondered if I was dead and tried to peer over his shoulder at whoever was in the bed. Then I found myself floating upwards, so I got a much better view anyway! I was up near the ceiling and could see everything in vivid detail.

I floated around and suddenly a white, cotton-wool sort of world opened up in front of me; it seemed like where I was supposed to be. I stepped into it and it was magical, exciting, happy. I seemed to stay there for a long time, occasionally overhearing bits of conversation that were, as it transpired, really happening around my poor old comatose body. And sometimes I popped back inside it, which was horrible, like waking up inside a thick wodge of wet flannel. It was then that I heard my mum talking to me, urging me to come back. I kept floating back to my cotton-wool world, but one day I just returned to my body and opened my eyes. She screamed and hugged me, and I knew I was really back. I still go cold at the thought that they might have pulled the plug on me. Yes, I would have loved being dead – it's brilliant! But no, it wouldn't have been good for my family. **"**

---

was taken up by Katie! Whatever the truth of the matter, because of the possible scandal attached to this case, it is no longer considered of any value as evidence for the afterlife.

Walking and talking again

D.D. Home and Florence Cook were examples of what is known as 'physical' mediumship, through which they claimed to produce an effect on the material world, even to produce objects or spirits from thin air.

Since their day there have been many other apparently talented physical mediums, with a wide variety of extraordinary phenomena, but on the whole modern mediumship is of the mental sort, with no attendant materializations.

Mental mediumship may be less dramatic, but many of its exponents have produced impressive information, which could only have been known by the dead, to relay to sitters. However, once again this is a ripe field for the unscrupulous, as the discomfiture of a certain famous

medium on the *Oprah Winfrey Show* recently revealed. A film of her earlier session with a small group of people showed some impressive results: she certainly seemed to know a great deal about the sitters and their loved ones. But once in the studio she seemed flustered when her 'cold' readings for members of the audience proved way off target.

Had she perhaps learnt before the show where certain people would be sitting and had done her homework about them, only to discover to her horror that on the day they were sitting somewhere else? It certainly seemed that way, and it would hardly have been the first time that mediums have resorted to this kind of trick.

There is a major problem with spiritualist phenomena, which the evidence of the NDE does nothing to dispel: are not the dead supposed to go on to another realm and leave the earth plane behind for ever? What are they doing flouncing around seance rooms like Katie King, or causing trumpets to float around, or

even whispering words of intimate information into the ears of today's mental mediums?

Even modern occultists, who might be expected to be familiar with spirits, are usually scathing about spiritualist communications. They claim that the dead who are contacted by mediums are merely 'low-level entities' who masquerade as spirits. These beings have no purpose other than to confuse and mislead, being more akin to the mischievous fairies of old rather than to demons or evil spirits. Nevertheless, their alleged communications will always prove to be unsatisfactory and a waste of time. According to this view, the 'spirit guides' of spiritualism do not provide any evidence for an afterlife: what they inhabit and therefore describe is a kind of twilight zone of subhuman, fairy-like entities. Or perhaps they were once living, breathing human beings but slipped through the net on death and remained close to the living as earthbound spirits. Some (like the Patrick Swayze character in the film *Ghost*) may fail to be absorbed by the light, due to an accident, but the majority become earthbound because their ties with the material plane are too strong. A large proportion of these are the obsessives – the misers, paedophiles, drug addicts and the like, who cannot conceive of a life without their particular fix. To them there is no kind of fulfilment possible beyond earth, so they remain here. Some may leech energy from pubescent children and enjoy causing havoc in the form of poltergeists, while others may haunt people or places without being consciously detected by the living.

Occasionally, ordinary people are believed to be trapped on the earth plane by meeting with their death without warning: it is said that many lost souls wander the world's highways trying to get help. They may have been killed in a car crash decades ago, but they believe the accident happened just hours or even minutes ago, and they are merely suffering from shock. Certain mediums specialize in rescuing these confused spirits, and drawing their attention to the welcoming light. Once they know it is there, they joyfully accept it and leave the earth plane behind.

The mission of spiritual rescue workers seems genuine and is often driven by the highest motives, and even the highly critical occultists praise them. But in general mediumship is, they say, at best tapping into the memory banks of dead people, or communicating with the mere etheric vestiges that are left behind when the soul goes on into the light. Or perhaps all mediums do is steal thoughts from the sitters' minds.

Certainly, as we have seen repeatedly from NDEs, once the spirit has encountered the light there is little or no temptation ever to come near the material world again. Those who have passed beyond death's door usually plead to be allowed to stay! It is hard to imagine them willingly giving up so much as a second of their afterlife in the light to chat to

mediums. But perhaps this is an oversimplification. Is there any genuine evidence for an afterlife in the annals of spiritualism?

The ultimate proof?

The Society for Psychical Research was founded by a group of Cambridge scholars in 1882, primarily to investigate telepathy. But soon they became interested in the question of the afterlife – does it exist, and if so, what would constitute the best evidence for its existence?

Ironically, the very men who founded the Society for Psychical Research (SPR) were themselves to provide some of the best, if curiously little-known, evidence for an afterlife. Shortly after the death in 1901 of

▲ Frederic Myers was a founder of the Society for Psychical Research, and his spirit may have provided the best evidence ever for the reality of an afterlife.

their leading light, the classical scholar Frederic Myers, several mediums in different parts of the world began to receive automatic writing that purported to come from him. All women, these 'automatists' were Mrs M. de G. Verrall, her daughter Helen, Mrs 'Willett' (Mrs Winifred Coombe-Tennant), Mrs 'Holland' (Mrs Fleming, sister of the poet Rudyard Kipling), and the American Mrs Leonora Piper, the only professional medium among them. Each script, the handwriting of which was very like Myers's own (some were even

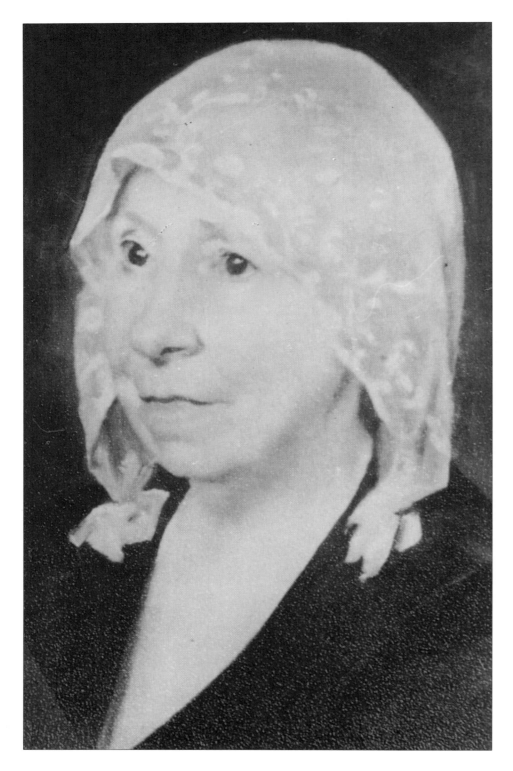

▲ 'Mrs Willett' (Mrs Coombe-Tennant): a medium of the early twentieth century whose integrity invites serious consideration of her communications with the dead.

apparently signed by him) gave the medium instructions about who to contact next. Each script was meant to lead to another, and eventually it was realized that the overall meaning became clear only when the fragments were put together. In other words, each scrap of automatic writings was a tiny part of a much greater whole, which was orchestrated as part of a definite plan. These interlinked scripts are now known as 'The Cross Correspondences'.

As other leading lights of the SPR died, so the content and range of these automatic scripts extended, revealing their distinctive styles. But there was something essentially confusing about these letters from the afterlife. They all contained fragments of what appeared to be Greek or Latin poetry (although not always instantly recognizable) – little-known classical allusions that were well beyond the understanding of the mediums concerned, and what appeared to be scholarly 'in jokes'. Taken on its own, each individual script made very little sense, but when all the fragments were put together an astonishing message emerged: the Cross Correspondences were organized in the afterlife by Myers and his colleagues, specifically to prove the survival of the personality.

But the most striking and evidential aspect of the Cross Correspondences is that they lasted over 30 years, from 1901 to 1932. As each SPR founding father had died, his signature appeared on the scripts, and new parts to the literary jigsaw were added. And as time passed, new mediums became involved, on three continents, all without any prior knowledge of the complex project of which they were part. And all that time, were dead men directing the proceedings?

The original scripts of the Cross Correspondences fill many folders that languish in the library of the SPR largely ignored. Considering that not even the most ingenious and vehement sceptic has ever been able to provide a persuasive alternative explanation for the Cross Correspondences, they do offer impressive evidence for the survival of at least Frederic Myers and his immediate circle. (And it seems unlikely that only the original gentlemen of the SPR get to survive death!) So why are the Cross Correspondences so obscure? Why have so few people heard of what is arguably the best evidence for an afterlife?

It is a great irony that the very

ingenuity involved in their making was to dissuade most modern researchers from making more of them. The Cross Correspondences may have been full of evidential in-jokes to their creators, but to most people today they are unbelievably tedious.

Even those with a classical education might well baulk at trying to piece together fragments of obscure Greek and Latin poems, but to those without such a background they are instantly off-putting. Yet the fact remains that they are, at least, exactly what Myers and his colleagues would have done if they could, and one is left with the feeling that they probably did.

First-class witnesses

Clearly, it would be a mistake to dismiss all the evidence of an afterlife ever offered by mediums. The most evidential has always been produced by psychics who never sought publicity, and certainly never appeared on a stage. As we have seen, some of the ladies (for once the term fits!) involved in the Cross Correspondences went as far as to hide behind aliases, and they were the ones whose work proved so persuasive.

Over the years a small group of mediums, who all kept well away from the limelight, produced information that purported to come from postmortem communicators about the afterlife. Much of this material paints a consistent and plausible picture and, more significantly where this investigation is concerned, one that matches the reports of people who have had NDEs. Unlike the publicity-seekers' alleged communications, this information is untainted by the need to impress, and may therefore be more valid.

The best digest of such communications is to be found in Paul Beard's book *Living On: a Study in Continuing Consciousness After Death* (1980), in which he discusses the work of such mediums as 'Mrs Willett' (real name Mrs Coombe-

Tennant), who was a Justice of the Peace and one of the mediums involved in the Cross Correspondences. When Mrs Willett herself died, she apparently communicated on many occasions with another medium of great integrity, Geraldine Cummins. Through her, the postmortem Mrs Willett explained the mystery of the human personality:

"A human being consists of a number of selves or aspects with a primary self, the total of a sum in arithmetic ... We only become unified in spirit on the higher level."

Paul Beard adds:

"Dying, it seems, is not the absolute event most people fear ... Evidence points to it being harder to get rid of the old earthly self than we had supposed."

In *Living On* he describes many communications purportedly from posthumous communicators that are in quite a different class from the messages relayed in packed theatre auditoriums through mediums with celebrity status. (And clearly they have nothing whatsoever in common with the flirtatious flouncings of Katie King, even if she was genuine!)

Not one of these communicators ever described going up a tunnel towards a bright light, or even the preliminary stage of separating from the body. In most cases death was a gradual withdrawal from life; even if they appeared to be in great pain or distress it hardly impinged upon their consciousness at the end. They slipped into their final sleep, and woke to find themselves surrounded by relatives who had died, and a being of light. The being is not a judge but a teacher, and, as one newly dead theologian reported:

"He evidently regarded my whole life on earth, which hitherto I have thought of as being so important, as mere preparation, a mere

preliminary to the real work I have to do here. That has been one of the greatest surprises."

Sometimes encounters with loved ones are not quite as hoped: Mrs Willett had long mourned the death of her beloved daughter Daphne, but discovered that they had considerably less in common in the afterlife than she had believed. And it seems the failings of our personalities survive until we confront them directly: T.E. Lawrence (the flamboyant Lawrence of Arabia) found his life-long inability to form close ties with women continued in the afterlife.

The evidence suggests that some spiritualist phenomena may be genuine, but the clarity and intelligibility of the communications are very much dependent on the competence and integrity of the medium involved. It seems that the dead have great difficulty in communicating with even the most accomplished medium, as the postmortem Frederic Myers complained through Mrs Willett:

"The nearest simile I can find to express the difficulty of sending a message is that I appear to be standing behind a sheet of frosted glass, which blurs sight and deadens sounds, dictating feebly to a reluctant and somewhat obtuse secretary. A feeling of terrible impotence burdens me. I am so powerless to tell what means so much. I cannot get into communication with those who would understand and believe me."

St Paul wrote: 'For now we see through a glass darkly, but then face to face.' It seems the view from the other side is not much clearer.

Never-ending dream

Rupert Sheldrake suggests that because we lose our bodies at death, what happens to our surviving consciousness may then take the form of a never-ending dream that is dependent upon our habitual beliefs and

A MAN-MADE GHOST

The annals of psychical research reveal that two things are needed to induce paranormal phenomena: belief and expectancy. And one might add a third: suspension of disbelief. With these conditions firmly in mind, it is almost incredible what can be achieved, as Dr A.R.G. Owen's psychical research group in Toronto, Canada, discovered in the 1970s.

They set out to create a ghost. Meeting at least once a week for many months, they ensured they shared an image of 'Philip', their imaginary phantom, by discussing his life in detail and memorizing his portrait that had been drawn by one of the group. Eventually they sat around a small card table and tried to contact Philip, using the old spiritualist code of raps. And Philip answered them.

The group discovered that a convivial atmosphere was most conducive to paranormal phenomena, so they would sit around the card table and sing. One evening the table, by now synonymous with Philip, began to jump up and down in time to the music. And on one occasion he chased Dr Owen across the room, moving like a cartoon table.

Philip's brilliant career culminated in his starring in a Toronto television show, in which he 'walked' around the studio and rapped out answers to questions.

It was an astonishing experiment, with far-reaching implications about the potential powers of the human mind. This is best exemplified by one incident in the Philip story. One evening the table was becoming very boisterous, so one of the group said, 'We only made you up, you know', and it immediately stopped moving and making rapping sounds. Perhaps objects are only inanimate until people invest them with life.

modes of thought. Just as in dreams we can find ourselves in all sorts of locations – either real or imagined – and in any kind of situation or adventure, the afterlife may be generated from a continuing process of imagination. And, perhaps worryingly, whether this is blissful or hellish would depend on many personal factors, including our sense of guilt and the limits of our imagination. In the afterlife, we are all mind.

Spiritualists claim that the afterlife is ideoplastic, a world where anything is possible as long as it can first be imagined, so this is largely in keeping with Dr Sheldrake's hypothesis. As soon as a place is thought of, the person can find himself there, in that reality, which is also characteristic of the preliminary out-of-the-body state of NDEs. But in the afterlife, the delights of creating a custom-made world for oneself may soon pall, and

the enlightened spirit quickly begins to seek more elevated outlets for his energy. Only then can he or she move on to the higher spiritual realms, leaving the world of desire and ambition behind. This is a dimension very removed from earthly concerns.

Heaven or hell

Rupert Sheldrake theorizes that 'the world we enter after death seems likely to depend on what we have done and believed while alive.' Some may have 'fantastic adventures', while others may be 'trapped in a hell created by their own minds.' He explains that others:

"... May experience a kind of paradise conjured up by their expectations; Muslims, for example, may tend to find themselves in green gardens ... attended by dancing girls ... enjoying the pleasures

vividly described in Islamic literature. Roman Catholics may encounter St Peter himself at the Pearly Gates. "

If NDEs possess the best clues we have as to what the afterlife is like (with the noble exception of the most scrupulous mediumship), then it raises certain objections to Dr Sheldrake's 'death-as-a-dream' hypothesis. First, many people go into the NDE without expecting to survive death in any form. But according to the theory that you get what you believe, they should enter a great nothingness. However, these people return converted to the survivalist belief through their own experience, which could not have been created by their thoughts or beliefs. And many with preconceptions about heaven or God are presented with completely different scenarios; those with rigidly dogmatic or strictly denominational beliefs tend to return with a much more tolerant and broader view of religion. Some no longer think in terms of religion at all, but rather in terms of spirituality. Once again, this change of heart was just as unpredictable as the version of the afterlife that they discovered during their NDE.

The NDE as evidence

And while it is true that some very special dreams have a strong, lingering flavour about them, most have no discernible or lasting influence on the dreamer's life or attitudes. On the other hand, NDEs often remain vivid for decades, completely turning the person's life around.

It seems likely, therefore, that neither the NDE, nor the after- or true-death experience are dreams in the normal sense, although they may bear a slight resemblance to them. What is important here is what Dr Moody calls the ineffability of the NDE, or the impossibility of doing the experience justice in mere words. Yes, it is somewhat like a dream, because that is the nearest analogy we can think of: in both we appear to

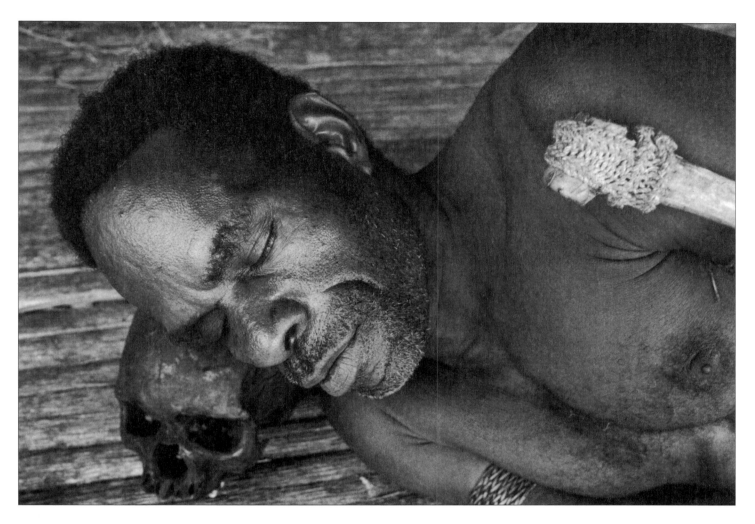

be disembodied and unusual scenarios present themselves. We are outside time and space, meeting people who are dead and travelling to the stars. But NDEs are not the same as dreams, any more than the events portrayed on the television screen are really happening in the corner of our living rooms. What we are watching may be science fiction, in which everything has been created out of the imagination, and impossible things take place. Or we may see old films or documentaries in which the people, although very much alive when they were made, have actually been dead for many years. For example, we may see President Kennedy waving from his motorcade in Dallas on that November day over 30 years ago, in the prime of his life: seconds later he was dead. We are watching these moments in time decades later, yet no one seriously claims that the real President is actually being

driven around in your living room. That is the difference between a dream and a NDE: the first is a shadow or at best a glimpse of the second. And even that may be a pale imitation of true death.

Because the NDE is new to us, it may be a mistake to attempt to make it fit any known category of human experience. It is now known that there are many different sorts of 'altered states of consciousness' (ASCs), such as dreaming, trance and hypnosis. The NDE, while bearing some similarity to certain aspects of those, appears to be another, quite distinct and separate ASC. Perhaps the time will come when death itself is seen as merely another altered state of consciousness!

Ironically, there may be some truth in Susan Blackmore's idea of the NDE as the 'brain's last fling', although not from a materialist point of view. As even the best mediums

▲ Tribal shamans routinely visit other realms in order to gain secret knowledge. Are NDEs also some kind of initiation, in which people discover spiritual truths?

have never passed on a description of death that matches the classic NDE in every detail, it seems likely that near-death and real-death are different experiences. Perhaps nearly dying (or, as we have seen, merely fearing that death is imminent) triggers a programme of visions in our minds that are intended to turn the trauma into something ineffable and positive.

The NDE is, in fact, very reminiscent of the traumatic initiations of the tribal shaman, and the members of the ancient Greek Mystery Schools. The older shamans or priests put the seeker of knowledge through extraordinary trials, usually involving extreme physical pain and terror. For example, Native American braves would be hung from tall trees

with spikes through their skin for many hours, or the would-be initiate would be left in a pitch-black cave where it was believed demons and wild animals lived. In this extremity of loneliness, agony, fear and doubt were the seeds of transformation born. These ordeals were not sadism for its own sake, but an essential preliminary to a great revelation, which was characterized by an ineffable light, by physical and spiritual illumination.

Perhaps it is no coincidence that such initiations mimic the NDE, especially the negative ones. It is known that many priests of the ancient world (of the mysteries of the Egyptian goddess Isis, for example) knew the secrets of consciousness that our culture is only beginning to discover for itself. They routinely used what we call RV, and induced OBEs as part of the healing process. Could it not be that the NDE was known and used as a model for the ordeals of initiation? Remember that the key to both of these processes is transformation.

Suppose that at some deep level we know that no matter how desperate our situation may appear to be we are not going to die this time. Suppose that as the evidence – from studies of dreaming and research into hypnosis – suggests our unconscious minds operate beyond space and time, so that they possess a complete knowledge of our past, present and future. So that when either the fear- or near-death experience kicks in, what we get is not a short visit to the afterlife, but to a realm of initiation and transformation. This is programmed into our minds (not our brains) and is intended as a rite of passage from one major part of our lives to the next. Essentially, people who have NDEs are initiates, but not of some elite group or secret society – but rather of humanity. They do not

◀ The mysteries of the Egyptian goddess Isis involved out-of-the-body adventures and mystical initiations. Does the NDE reflect such a seeking after enlightenment?

become gods themselves, but their experience takes them a little closer to the angels.

The problem with death

Many people continue to be aware of their surroundings even when in profound coma. They may try to communicate with those around them but discover they are incapable of making their bodies respond with the slightest twitch. Experienced nurses know that the last sense to go before death is that of hearing, and accordingly warn relatives to watch what they say, even though their loved one is, apparently, simply an inert body.

Many people who have recovered from a coma know how important the faculty of hearing was for them during that time. For example, the late Earl Spencer (father of Princess Diana) went into a coma as the result of a stroke. He owed his recovery to his wife Raine, who spent many hours sitting and talking to him as if he were awake and aware, even though he could give her no sign at all that he heard her. In the end her faith and persistence were rewarded, and although his mobility was to remain slightly impaired, he was able to escort his beautiful daughter to the altar on her historic wedding day.

Those in the medical profession are frequently amazed by such recoveries, for to them a certain depth of coma is labelled a 'persistent vegetative state', which although believed to be no more than the truth, actually reveals a profound lack of respect for their patients and also a deep ignorance about the nature of consciousness. Yet if they humbly turned to the mass of OBE and NDE literature that they scrupulously avoid, they might be able to do something constructive and compassionate for their patients. They might at least have greater insights into their condition, and therefore increased sensitivity.

As we enter a new millennium there can be no excuse for continuing to think of humans as mere machines. That we have a spirit that

operates separately from the body and which survives death should be indisputable: the evidence is in. Ideally, the next phase of enlightenment will be concerned with consciousness research, in which the transformative power of the spirit in healing, learning and creating a better world, is harnessed for the greater good.

The phenomenon of the NDE has opened up a vast and exciting field, which may represent nothing less than a new phase in history. At the very least, the discovery of the difference between the mind and the brain is a very significant step forward, and its capacity for creating or receiving ineffable visions may be very useful in future therapies for both mind and body.

And if, as many believe, the NDE proves the existence of a real otherworld peopled with angels and deceased loved ones, then that, too, is important for the development of humankind. Maybe the most useful research we can do in the immediate future is not genetic engineering, but an examination for the true nature of humankind. Judging by the evidence of the NDE, we are not intended to be unhappy or think of ourselves as worthless. Perhaps the Renaissance thinkers were right when they said, 'Know ye not that ye are gods?'

There may come a time when Elisabeth Kubler-Ross, Raymond Moody, Kenneth Ring, Margot Grey, Melvin Morse and their colleagues are ranked with the likes of Freud and Jung, and when children the world over learn about their research at school. For their pioneering work into the NDE goes beyond even revelations about dying. Their work has brought greater insights into the human condition from birth to death and beyond, and has helped remove the greatest shadow that hovers over most lives – the fear of death. They have shown that by dying we become more alive, more fulfilled and blissfully happy. As one little girl said to Dr Morse, 'Heaven's fun. You'll see.'

Index

PICTURE CREDITS

Corbis (Adam Woolfitt) 6; (Chris Rainier) 8-9, 155; (Richard T. Nowitz) 12; (Library of Congress) 14, 24, 41, 61, 114; (The National Gallery, London; Eustache Le Sueur) 17; (Sean Sexton Collection) 18; (Paul Almasy) 21, 124; (National Institutes of Health) 22, 53; (Jack Fields) 26; (The National Archives) 28, 50; (Earl Kowall) 31; (Chris Hellier) 32; (Patrick Bennett) 92-93; (Dave G. Houser) 37, 47, 49; (Gianni Dagli Orti) 39, 43, 44, 48, 96, 99, 156; (U.S. Department of Defense) 56; (Robert Holmes) 59; (Roger Ressmeyer) 62, 67; (Jonathan Blair) 74; (Bettmann/UPI) 76; (The Purcell Team) 78; (Hulton Deutsch Collection) 85, 90, 136-137; (Phil Schermeister) 86-87; (Bettmann) 94, 98, 104; (Roger Wood) 101; (Francesco Venturi; Kea Publishing Services Ltd) 108; (Christel Gerstenberg) 110; (Sakamoto Photo Research Laboratory) 115; (Kevin Fleming) 118-119; (Jenny Woodcock; Reflections Photolibrary) 120; (David Turnley) 121; (Space Telescope Science Institute) 126; (Arte Video Immagine Italia srl) 128; (Luca I. Tettoni) 131; (Darrell Gulin) 134; (Michael Freeman) 142.

Kobal Collection (The Archers/J. Arthur Rank) 10; (Columbia) 11; (Paramount) 149.

Fortean Picture Library 13, 70, 112; (Janet & Colin Bord) 72, 132-133; (Dr. Elmar R. Gruber) 82; (Dennis Stacy) 88; (Philip Panton) 106-107; (Lisa Anders) 116.

Ace Photo Agency (Phototake) 35.

Mary Evans Picture Library 51, 144, 146, 147; (Michael Buhler) 103; (Psychic News) 148; (Society For Psychical Research) 151; (The Cutten Collection) 152.

B & B Entertainment, Los Angeles 58.

Bridgeman Art Library/Palazzo Ducale, Venice 64.

Dickens House Museum, London 81.

Durdana Khan 122, 138.